THE NEW GAME
ON WALL STREET

THE NEW GAME
ON WALL STREET

ROBERT SOBEL

JOHN WILEY & SONS

New York • Chichester • Brisbane • Toronto • Singapore

ISBN 0-471-84527-2

Printed in the United States of America

10 9 8 7 6 5 4 3 2 1

For Michael and Lea Louis

PREFACE

In the summer of 1965, during the tail end of the longest-lived bull market in American history, I attended a seminar at which a mutual fund manager celebrated what he called "The New Game in Town." In his view, the investment climate had changed drastically from what it had been a generation earlier, during the last bull market. The differences derived from the influx of new investors, the rise of mutual funds, the dynamism of the American economy that would make bear markets a thing of the past, and most especially, the appearance of "The New Breed" of investment advisors, analysts, and brokers attuned to the current dispensation.

As I recall, the speaker was in his early twenties, an exemplar of the New Breed. Listening to him go on so enthusiastically I reflected on how most newcomers to the Street believe they have reinvented the wheel, have arrived to shake the markets to their very foundations, and how they assume the past was not prologue but, well, simply irrelevant.

The fact of the matter was that there *were* important differences between that period and the one that preceded it, the Great Bull Market of the 1920s. The most obvious of these had to do with reforms brought about by the New Deal and the Great Depression, especially the Securities Exchange and the Glass-Steagall Acts. The former put a police officer at the corner of Wall and Broad Streets, the latter separated investment and commercial banking. The depression of the 1930s all but wiped out the district, which for the better part of a decade was as close to being deserted as ever in its history.

Yet the similarities were even more striking. Stocks remained stocks and bonds were bonds, and there were few other financial instruments in both markets. We had a gold standard in the 1920s, and a gold bullion standard in the 1960s. While foreign bonds enjoyed a vogue in the 1920s, interest centered on stocks, and thus it was in the 1960s. True, there was that New Breed of the 1960s, but speculators came out in force in the 1920s, and they too had thought themselves unique. During both periods the Old Guard at the major investment banks ruled the Street. J. P. Morgan & Co. was district leader in 1925; Morgan Stanley occupied a similar niche 40 years later.

There were far fewer small investors in the 1920s than in the 1960s, and they used margin more easily than would their descendents, but they analyzed stocks in pretty much the same way. Cocktail party chatter about the virtues of glamour stocks such as RCA and Chrysler in the 1920s wasn't that much different from the same kind of talk and rumor regarding Syntex and Digital Equipment in the 1960s. Textbooks on investments written on the eve of the Great Crash might have been read and their maxims applied by small investors 40 years later. There were changes, to be sure, but the core remained.

Such no longer is the case. We now know that the market was close to its peak in 1965. Prices would climb above the Dow 1000 mark in early 1966, and then go into a free fall, winding up at 735 less than a year later. There would be rallies, declines, new rallies, and new sell offs for the next decade and a half. America experienced no new depression, but we did have the anti-Vietnam War movement, the closing of the Treasury gold window, Watergate, two oil crises, "stagflation," severe recessions, the move toward deregulation, and assorted other traumatic events. Say what you will about the period from 1966 through 1982, it certainly wasn't dull.

In the late 1960s a group of non-Establishment brokers mounted a challenge to the New York Stock Exchange and the entire securities market system. Organizing the "Third Market," they hoped to reshape the way stocks were traded in America. At the same time others were preparing to give the Establishment a run for it in the area of investment banking. The cutting of the gold cover and the inflationary bias of the economy were shaking the district to its very roots.

Small investors may have been vaguely aware of all of this, but it didn't alter the way they did business or perceived the investment process. The search for the next IBM continued, the rumor mills ground on, and we all wondered where the Dow Industrials would wind up at the end of the session. Not until 1975, when commissions were fully deregulated, did small investors find themselves in something of a new situation, but even then it hardly seemed so important a change.

We now know that the investment process was changing rapidly, importantly, and irretrievably. It came home to me in 1974, when conducting research for a book that was entitled *Inside Wall Street*, the goal of which was to inform readers of how the district operated. So it did—for a little while. Alas, it is as hopelessly outdated today as might be an atlas published prior to World War II. I discovered this when deciding to undertake a similar work for our time. Initially I thought the book might be updated, but soon realized that such a relic is beyond that. A completely new effort was needed, hence the writing of this book.

In 1975 I had hoped *Inside Wall Street* might become what in the trade is known as an "evergreen," an analysis that would last for generations. I harbor no such ambitions for *The New Game on Wall Street*. If the pace of change continues as it has it will serve for no more than two or three years. Why is this so? The answer can be found in Chapter 1.

Note that the masculine pronoun has been used in this book for ease in reading. The omission of the feminine pronoun is not intended as a slight.

ROBERT SOBEL

New College of Hofstra
January 1987

CONTENTS

1 DANCING IN THE DARK WITH ELEPHANTS

Pity the eponymous "little guy" who is trapped in an obsolete mind set established a generation ago. No matter that he may only be 25 years old, and may have even majored in finance, or at least had a few courses in the subject back in college. The investment terrain has shifted; shifted to the point where individuals who operate the way they did in the early 1970s or utilize expertise of that period are akin to those who might attempt to steer a steady course in San Francisco by means of a map of Los Angeles.

Start out by assuming that individuals who have accumulated sufficient funds to consider investing them will also possess the intelligence and diligence to undertake their care and nurture. This would imply a regular reading of such periodicals as *The Wall Street Journal, Forbes, Barron's,* perhaps a few investment newsletters and advisories sent out by their broker, and for good measure *Business Week* and *Fortune.* Such persons might refer to the Value Line publications and look up companies in which they expect to invest in the appropriate Moody's manual. The Standard &

Poor's "Stock Guide" would be bedtime reading, and "Wall Street Week" and like programs regular television fare.

Several times each business day there would be calls to brokers or a "hot line" to find out how the market was doing. Let the little guy come across a broker or analyst at a social gathering and in no time at all he would be asking about hot technology stocks and the peregrinations of T. Boone Pickens, Carl Icahn, or some other takeover artist. Visits to bookstores might end with the selection of a new work whose title seems to indicate the contents would turn out to be the key to investment success.

Like this one, you might be thinking.

Alas, no such book exists, for if one did, no other would ever be published, and the purveying of financial books is a long-lived cottage industry. While all that information gathered and processed can't do too much harm—assuming it isn't acted on without additional input—today's investor will find it an uncertain guide because as indicated, the old rules no longer apply, since the playing field has been altered drastically over the past decade or so. Even the vocabulary is different, as are the movers and shakers.

Any consideration of the investment process must begin here. So read on, even though at times you may wonder if it really is necessary to know this much about how the markets operate if all you want to do is find a resting place for a few thousand dollars.

THE DEREGULATION OF WALL STREET

The financial district and its methods are always changing, but never as much as they have since the early 1970s. Six of the more important alterations, roughly in order of their appearance, have been: (1) The breakdown of old relationships and the fading of the "Old Guard," (2) the maturing of institutional investing and the appearance of block trading, (3) the emergence of what for the American context was hyperinflation in 1973–1974 and again in 1979–1980, and its decline afterwards, (4) the rise of options creation and trading in its many manifestations, (5) the appearance of negotiated commissions, and finally, (6) the internationalization of markets and the steady crumbling of remaining political barriers to investment.

Much of this comes under the rubric of "deregulation." This is an unwinding of a process in American financial history which began in 1933 during the New Deal and was challenged in the late 1960s and early 1970s. The reaction against regulation became most visible during the Carter and Reagan Administrations. In the process the New York Stock Exchange (NYSE), symbol of the old order, has lost much of its cachet, as has "the white shoe crowd" which had dominated the district for generations. Everything is up for grabs today, from takeovers of multibillion dollar corporations to financial supermarkets to the de facto repeal of the Glass-Steagall Act which separated investment and commercial banking, to the regular creation of new financial and investment instruments.

Let's begin with the aforementioned unraveling of old ties. Time was when rank and position counted for almost everything in American business. As late as the 1950s a personable, attractive, male graduate of some Ivy League college, say Princeton or Yale, who nonetheless lacked ambition and wasn't necessarily an academic star, could find a niche on Wall Street, possibly at a hoary investment bank, where he would become one of a crew which tended to the financial needs of America's great corporations. This was a time when interest and currency rates were fairly secure and steady, when a Wall Street gentleman could keep "banker's hours," arriving in his office at 10:00 A.M. breaking for lunch, and leaving at 3:00 P.M. There would be long summer weekends at the Hamptons and some ski resort in winter, and the calendar would be dotted with two-week vacations.

Business was simple enough. Twice a year our dilettante would meet with the corporate treasurer of one of his bank's clients—a relationship that in all likelihood had begun many years before either was born—to discuss financing needs for the coming year. It was altogether pleasant and agreeable, with no competition or fussing about. Gentlemen didn't do such things, especially when they attended the same schools or belonged to the same fraternity. The big banks were Morgan Stanley, First Boston, Dillon Read, and Kuhn, Loeb, which together with others was known as "Club Seventeen," this referring to the number of institutions indicted on antitrust charges in the late 1940s. Such present-day big players like Salomon, Goldman Sachs, and even Merrill Lynch weren't deemed sufficiently important to be indicted, and for good reason: they weren't members of "the Club," or to put it another way, were not staffed by white shoe types.

Challenges to Club Seventeen gathered steam in the late 1950s and early 1960s, culminating in 1963 with the creation of what came to be known as "The Fearsome Foursome," comprised of Lehman, Merrill Lynch, Salomon, and Blyth, which bid for underwritings against the established firms. In effect, they were going after their clients, attempting to disrupt long-term relationships by offering better terms.

It worked, so much so that other non-Establishment houses such as Goldman Sachs, Bear Stearns, and Smith Barney entered in. Their positions threatened, the Establishment firms started to compete vigorously. Likewise, those somnolent bankers of the 1950s either started working longer hours—15 or 16 hours a day is not unusual nowadays—and weekends as well, or were shoved into new slots, to be replaced by aggressive hustlers with little social cachet but MBAs from top universities and an unquenchable desire to make money and win, and not necessarily in that order. "We look for bright people, of course," said the hiring partner at one of the large investment banks. "But we also look for people who participated in collegiate athletics, who can work well on teams in competitive situations and won't settle for second place."

Such individuals arrived at a time when the cake of custom was crumbling. "You are not *our* investment banker," one CEO told a shocked banker. "You are *an* investment banker." "More and more companies don't have bankers of record," observed Felix

Rohatyn of Lazard Freres, possibly the best known of the new breed. "On mergers the business is up for grabs."

All well and good, you might be thinking. Investment banking has changed considerably. But how does this affect me as an investor? After all, a person who is thinking of putting $10,000 or so into the market hardly is in the same position as a corporation hoping to raise $100 million. True enough, but there is a connection. In the old days the big question was whether that company should sell stocks or bonds to bring in additional capital. Nowadays the firm might call in several bankers, tell them of its needs, and ask each to come up with a financing plan. And that is where "creative investment banking" comes in. One underwriter might talk of selling Eurobonds, another of issuing zero coupon bonds, a third bonds which pay no interest for 10 years but then fetch a premium rate, a fourth could go for dollar denominated bonds paying interest in marks or yen, a fifth for an equity for debt or debt for equity swap combined with the sale of warrant-bearing stock or bonds, a sixth for securitizing assets, a seventh. . . .

But why go on? The fact of the matter is that competition let loose all sorts of creative juices on Wall Street, in the process creating a multitude of new investment media, some of which would be of interest to that small investor with $10,000 to put into the market—assuming of course he knew of them and their risks and rewards.

Institutional forces have always been important in the securities markets; trusts and estates, insurance companies, and various endowments have ever sought profitable outlets for reserves. So have pension funds, whose expansion has been nothing short of phenomenal, and in the growth of which might be perceived the enormity of changes in the institutional market.

One day last summer the investment manager of a large state teachers' pension fund called an investment banker to ask what looked good. She had $2 million to invest. "Things are pretty quiet right now," came the answer. "Why don't I get back to you tomorrow, after the Treasury auction, when the outlook will be clearer." "All right," said the manager, "but by then I'll have $4 million to place. That's the way it goes. $2 million a day." Into debt instruments, to be sure, but also into stocks.

The increasingly volatile nature of markets has impelled many institutional fund managers to structure their equities holdings in such a way as to reflect one or another of the popular averages, more often than not the Standard & Poor's 500. In other words, their accounts are close to mirror images of the S&P. If that index rose 2 percent, so would the value of the holdings. Perhaps this isn't all that thrilling, but at least the fund would never be accused of "underperforming the market." In addition, it does make some sense, since the S&P has achieved a compound annual return of close to 15 percent over the years, this being a shade better than the average of most money managers. How much money is geared to the S&P? In the summer of 1986 Seamon A. Lincoln, director of A. S. Hansen, Inc., which monitors this segment of the market, estimated it came to more than $110 billion. There were even mutual funds geared to the S&P, enabling the little guy to get in on the play.

This resulted in a new speculative opportunity for those willing to try to second-guess the fine folks at S&P. Suppose one or more stocks leave the list, due to mergers, leveraged buyouts, or some such development. Clearly the roster will not be renamed the S&P 494 or some such number. Substitutes will have to be found, and when these are announced, the fund managers will have to rush in and make purchases, so their holdings will continue to be a mirror of the index. If a speculator should develop some means of second-guessing S&P, he could make purchases ahead of the announcement, and clean up when the institutions enter the game. Major Wall Street houses assigned their top talent to the game.

Selecting the right entries can pay off nicely. On May 7, 1986, S&P announced that five stocks would be added to the list. Three of them—Bausch & Lomb, Rubbermaid, and Johnson Controls— responded by rising more than two points, while the other two went up a point. This was during a dismal session. Volume was high, and both prices and volume continued to rise during the next few sessions. Those who had placed bets on stocks not selected could look forward to a new round. RCA and Macy's were due to be removed from the list due to a merger and leveraged buyout respectively, while Chicago Pneumatic and MEI also looked as though they would depart. So additional stocks would have to be singled out by S&P.[1]

THE INSTITUTIONAL CHALLENGE

The move by pension funds and other institutions into equities changed the nature of that market. New York Stock Exchange specialists[2] accustomed in the 1960s to trading round lots (100 shares) of AT&T and IBM, were finding themselves with orders for 10,000 and more shares at a time. These orders, known as block trades, were only 3 percent of NYSE volume as late as 1965; by 1972, the figure came to almost 19 percent, worth more than $100 billion. Right now institutional trades account for more than half of NYSE volume, and the share is rising all the time.

If the development of block trading among institutions meant larger profits for traders (and a less orderly market, since specialists could hardly be expected to stand their ground when large scale buying and selling waves hit the floor), it also meant trouble for the smaller investors. A classic example of this occurred on January 7 and 8, 1985, when the market was hit by a double whammy. The first was news of a more than $10 billion judgment against Texaco in a suit brought by Pennzoil. The second was a prediction by Salomon Brothers' sage Henry Kaufman that the

[1] Vartanig G. Vartan, "Picking Stocks for S&P 500," *New York Times*, May 21, 1986.
[2] A specialist is an exchange member who "makes a market" in a stock, which is to say, stands ready to buy or sell it, and is expected to maintain a degree of stability. Terms like this will appear throughout the book. They will be explained fully if they aren't to be discussed later on, and in footnotes if a fuller explanation follows. As it happens, the specialist will be dissected in Chapter 2. But don't bother to flip ahead. Read on and all will be clarified. In fact there will be many more footnotes such as this, observing that all will be clarified in future chapters.

NYSE BLOCK TRANSACTIONS, 1965–1984

Year	Number of Transactions	Average per Session	Shares (000)	Percent of Volume
1965	2,171	9	48,262	3.1
1973	29,233	116	721,356	17.8
1974	23,300	92	549,387	15.6
1975	34,420	136	778,540	16.6
1976	47,632	188	1,001,254	18.7
1977	54,275	215	1,183,924	22.4
1978	75,036	298	1,646,905	22.9
1979	97,509	385	2,164,726	26.5
1980	133,597	528	3,311,132	29.2
1981	145,564	575	3,771,442	31.8
1982	254,707	1,007	6,742,481	41.0
1983	363,415	1,436	9,842,080	45.6
1984	433,427	1,713	11,492,091	49.8

Source: New York Stock Exchange Fact Book, 1984, ed., p. 71.

Fed would not cut its interest rate. The market had already declined by more than 15 Dow points, and thus was in a jittery mood. Kaufman spoke at 2:30 P.M. Between 3:00 and 4:00 the Index lost another 24 points, as specialists abandoned their stocks to preserve their own hides. Most understandable, but that's not the way it is supposed to happen.

That day Pennzoil opened lower, rose sharply, and then declined once again on a volume of 1.7 million shares. The high for the day was 91, the low 73½, the close 74½. During the session this stock traveled more than 35 points, an amazing journey. The NYSE and SEC announced there would be an investigation, which puts one in mind of the classic line delivered by Claude Raines portraying Inspector Renault in *Casablanca*: "Round up the usual suspects."

If for one reason or another several large institutions decide to sell even a highly capitalized and admired stock such as IBM, which has more than 600 million shares outstanding, they can batter down its price several points in a matter of an hour or less. Add to this the clout of the large investment banks. As recently as 1979 Merrill Lynch, capitalized at $794 million, was considered a behemoth. Six years later Merrill's capital came to over $2.6 billion. Ten investment banks had more than what the leader had reported in 1979, and there were rumors that several major insurance companies were considering mounting takeover bids for "the Thundering Herd." By the end of the decade there will be several $5 billion firms, and not all of them American.

The development of an institutional market in stocks and the emergence of investment colossi has meant larger volume and bigger trades, but now the little guy resembles a mouse trapped in a darkroom filled with prancing elephants. It might be fun, but one wrong step could spell disaster.

The reasons are clear enough. It used to be said that sophisticated investors, speculators, and traders might do well enough in over-the-counter (OTC) esoterica, but smaller investors who lack information and the time to study the markets, were best off in the solid blue chips. This changed with the arrival of institutional markets and heavy hitters. The former are more concerned with the large capitalization issues because of their liquidity, while the latter are on the prowl for big takeover candidates. In recent years there often has been as much volatility on the NYSE as on the OTC, and while it can be a heady experience on the way up, it can be dismal on the downside, especially if that small investor hoped for safety.

OPTIONS AND THE REVIVAL OF DEBTS

Most small investors probably have heard of options, though still wary of them and holding back from using them. This is understandable, since while options are easily explained, learning of their uses can cause headaches. Simply stated, an option gives the owner the right to purchase or sell a fixed amount of something or other at a fixed price on or before a certain date. As will be seen, they flourished as a trading vehicle in the 1980s.

If you haven't the foggiest idea of how all of this is done have no fear; all will be covered in Chapter 9. However, small investors should be aware that the options markets have become big time playgrounds for the pros, and their activities affect the prices of a round lot of Merck or the quotes for high grade bonds. The reason is that big players have entered the options market in recent years, playing them off against their underlying stocks. In addition, the creation of index options—options on popular market averages—has created market flurries on expiration days. This too will be discussed in some detail in Chapter 9, and it wouldn't do to repeat it here. Suffice it to say at this point that options have provided another headache for short-term traders, but as will be seen, have been great opportunities for long-term investors.

Paradoxically, while the equities market became increasingly dominated by large institutions and complicated by options, investors slowly became more interested in debts, and for good reason. That the nation experienced sharp inflationary pressures during the late 1960s and through the 1970s is so familiar that detailed analysis hardly is required. A quick scan of a tabular presentation of important interest rates would be instructive, however.

During the period from around 1949 through the 1960s the public concentrated on stocks while bonds were virtually ignored. In this span the Dow Jones Industrials soared from 161.6 to 968.9, while the Dow Bond Index declined from 98.22 to 68.07. Yields on Baa bonds were in the narrow bands of 3.24 percent to 5.19 percent.

Then came a remarkable change such as hadn't been seen in this century. As money market pressures intensified, bond prices collapsed and their yields rose from 4.87 to 16.04 percent from 1965 to 1981. These high returns attracted new investors, many of whom switched from other instruments. What we were exper-

BOND YIELDS AND INTEREST RATES, 1965–1981

Year	Corporate Bonds		High Grade Municipals	Federal Funds Rate
	AAA	Baa		
1965	4.49	4.87	3.27	4.07
1966	5.13	5.67	3.82	5.11
1967	5.51	6.23	3.98	4.22
1968	6.18	6.94	4.51	5.66
1969	7.03	7.81	5.81	8.20
1970	8.04	9.11	6.51	7.18
1971	7.39	8.56	5.70	4.66
1972	7.21	8.16	5.27	4.43
1973	7.44	8.24	5.18	8.73
1974	8.57	9.50	6.09	10.50
1975	8.83	10.61	6.89	5.83
1976	8.43	9.75	6.49	5.04
1977	8.02	8.97	5.56	5.54
1978	8.73	9.49	5.90	7.93
1979	9.63	10.69	6.39	11.19
1980	11.94	13.67	8.51	13.36
1981	14.17	16.04	11.23	16.38

Source: 1985 Economic Report to the President, p. 311.

iencing then was nothing less than the rebirth of the debt market. As late as 1974 a respected and deservedly popular book, entitled: *The New Science of Investing* could have a section entitled: "The Forgotten Instruments—Bonds," devoting only part of one chapter to the subject, while most of the other 30 dealt with stocks. That would no longer be the case in any such book offered today.

Of course the total debt market—government, foreign, and corporate—was always larger than that for equities. But with the increase in the national debt, the rise of mortgage backed securities, money funds, and debt hybrids, has become more important for small investors as well. This has been noticed by prescient individuals. Still, when those with most of their investments in money market funds, Ginnie Maes, and tax exempts hear the "market rose today," they immediately think of stocks.

Even so, they do care about money supply figures, the prime and discount rates, currency rates, the deficit, and the national debt—items hardly considered a decade and a half ago, and ones related more to bonds than stocks. Paul Volcker has become a celebrity, believed by many to be the second most powerful person in the United States, because of his post as chairman of the Federal Reserve Board. Do you know the name of the Chairman in 1965? It was William McChesney Martin, who in his time was every bit as influential as Volcker, but back then known only to a relatively small number of people. All of this is a sign of the growing awareness of forces which influence debts, and of course stocks as well. On March 20, 1986 the Street learned of the resignation of Volcker's chief antagonist at the Fed, vice chairman Preston Martin, named there by President Reagan and considered a spokesman for his point of view. This was taken to mean a victory for Volcker, who forced the President to back down, perhaps on threat of resignation. The news made the front pages of the business sections of newspapers throughout the country. Then followed a weakening of bond prices, so that while professional traders in stocks were talking about arbitrage activities the bond dealers pondered the meaning of Martin's resignation.

All the while money from individual retirement accounts poured into securities, the indication being that most of it—perhaps as much as 80 percent—was going into bond funds.

Despite this, because of the lag in perception, many investors who belong in debts remain wedded to stocks, usually through sheer inertia. Of course this is changing—how could it be otherwise when advertisements during the early 1980s trumpeted 15 percent yields on short-term funds at a time when stocks were declining? That this trend will continue seems likely; it has changed and will continue to alter the investment arena. It is also not an accident that the rising investment banks—Salomon Brothers, Goldman Sachs, and Drexel Burnham Lambert, among others—are more associated with debt instruments than with stocks.

If options altered the facade and influenced operations of the equities market, negotiation of commissions struck at its foundation, and arguably was even more important to small investors.

UNDER THE CARTEL

Those gentlemen bankers of the 1950s scorned competition as somehow degrading. Not only was the client base established and secure, but charges were fixed by custom and agreement. Everyone knew that commissions didn't vary an iota from financial house to financial house, something the NYSE had insisted on from the very start. It was in the original charter of May 17, 1792, which stated:

> We, the subscribers, brokers for the purchase and sale of public stocks, do hereby solemnly promise and pledge ourselves to each other that we will not buy or sell from this date, for any person whatsoever, any kind of public stock at a less rate than one-quarter of one per cent. commission on the specie value, and that we will give preference to each other in our negotiation.

Thus was born the cartel which became the exchange complex, erected upon a union against outsiders, meaning nonmembers, and also the customers. Listed stocks couldn't be traded on other exchanges. Commissions were fixed. Take it or leave it. So if you wanted to buy or sell the likes of GE, GM, IBM, or AT&T, it had to be done on the NYSE's terms. Moreover, it didn't matter if the customer purchased or sold 100 shares or 10,000; there were no discounts for volume, so the latter paid 100 times the commission as the former. What clearly was a combination in restraint of trade remained so 180 years later, though under strong attack. While defending the system as providing a stable atmosphere, NYSE members did compete for clients, especially those institutional clients wanting to place orders for large blocks.

In retrospect it can be seen that the institutional business was a major cause of the attack on fixed commissions. Even the old school ties amounted to little when set beside chances of obtaining those juicy fees. So the competition began, in the form of what was known as "soft dollars."

These came in many variations, some legitimate, others questionable, and toward the end, downright unethical. The most familiar was the "give up," by which the broker would return part of the commission to important clients. According to one study, between 1964 and 1968 NYSE-based firms gave up more than 38 percent of the $243 million they received in commissions from mutual funds in 1968, and of the 330 firms conducting a public business that year, the income of 95 consisted solely of give ups.

There were other ways of rewarding faithful clients. Did the investment manager at the large pension fund want extra research? The brokerages would offer whatever was needed. Did he want to hear it from the lips of the firm's famous guru? The great man would be pleased to journey to the fund and talk for as long as might be required—assuming of course, the commissions were sufficiently large. Did the client yearn to attend the Superbowl? The brokerage would get seats on the 50-yard line. How about a mid-winter investment seminar on a Caribbean cruise ship? It was his, without request. Cases of expensive liquor, gold plated humidors, and other trinkets were passed along at Christmas and other occasions when excuses could be provided for their transfer. And there were lavish parties to which the client would be invited, at which the food, booze, and women were available and plentiful, for all tastes and inclinations.

SMASHING THE CARTEL

All of this to preserve the fixed commission structure, which became even more attractive (and desirable) in a period when block trading was expanding. Wall Street leaders would bow to many changes, but they turned into tigers when reformers challenged their commissions. In 1969 NYSE Chairman and Goldman Sachs' CEO Gus Levy told a congressional subcommittee that fixed commissions were "at the very heart" of the financial system, and urged legislation to preserve the institution. To no avail. Pressures from NYSE's rival, the so-called Third Market, were such that the system's doom was inevitable. Levy bowed two years later. "We'll go along with negotiated rates," he said. "We're flexible." To which Merrill Lynch's CEO Donald Regan added, "Fixed commissions are one of the causes of trades leaving the NYSE and going to the Third Market," and he urged his fellows to abandon the practice. "There is no assurance that all else will fall into place if it (negotiated commissions) does come; but it is certain that nothing will fall into place without it."

In early 1971 the Securities and Exchange Commission ruled that negotiated commissions on trades of over $500,000 would begin in April, and that the figure would be lowered to $300,000 a year later. So the large blocks were the first to feel the impact of deregulation. Quoting President John F. Kennedy, Levy now said, "Let us never negotiate out of fear, but let us never fear to negotiate."

The final step came on what forever will be enshrined as "Mayday" in the Street's lexicon—May 1, 1975—when all commissions became fully negotiated, meaning the small investor got his chance to receive rate cuts. It was a strange time, and not only because of the new dispensation. The North Vietnamese-Viet Cong Army seized control of Saigon that day, bringing the Vietnam War to its effective conclusion, while on Wall Street talk was of a new commission war which might erupt.

From the start it was clear that block trading commissions would be slashed, but it was uncertain as to just how it would work with smaller trades. When asked about his new rates, Regan responded, "We're not saying. . . . If we reveal our minimum rate now, that's not negotiating, is it?" However, all knew that "unbundling" would be the path taken. The old full-line brokerages might offer some discounts, but since they still offered research and a friendly ear, along with advice, these would be minor.

Not so the new discount operations which sprang up all over the country. Clearing through member firms and operating with order takers rather than the more familiar brokers, discounters offered what amounted to "plain pipe rack services" with discounts ranging up to and beyond half the NYSE-posted rates. Some became large, and almost all advertised their rates, though some structures were so complex as to confuse customers as to just how they might obtain the lowest cost trades. Nor was it certain whether small investors would be best served by using discounters, especially when in the 1980s the investment universe became increasingly complex, and expert advice prior to committing funds seemed all the more necessary. Above all, negotiated commissions was a central part of the deregulation phenomenon, which while it brought benefits for small investors, complicated things considerably.

The sixth and final key change has been the internationalization of markets, which might be traced to events of 1971 to 1974. It began when President Nixon effectively took the United States off the gold bullion standard in August 1971, going on to Smithsonian Accord devaluing the dollar later that year, and then to the first "Oil Shock" in 1973–1974.

These events brought to an end the post-World War II era during which the entire Western world had essentially been on a U.S. dollar standard. Of course there were other factors, among them the European recovery and the rise of Japan, but it took the developments of the early 1970s to bring home the idea that Wall Street no longer was the sole center of the investment universe.

EXTERNAL SHOCKS

The tripling of oil prices and the Japanese trade surpluses meant that a shift in world wealth was taking place. Massive OPEC investments in western securities, the great international financial event of the decade, altered perspectives in New York, London,

Tokyo, and Zurich. Much of the money went into short-term deposits; in September 1985, the Bank of England estimated that of the $410 billion in OPEC money invested overseas, 41 percent was in deposits, and only 8 percent in bonds, with a minuscule amount in equities. Then came the Japanese, investing funds earned through trade surpluses in all parts of the western world, the United States in particular. In 1985 alone the Japanese purchased $60 billion in foreign securities, 98 percent of which went into bonds. This helped reinforce the renewed interest in debts, while at the same time troubling financial wise men in Europe and America, who wondered what might happen when and if the flow diminished greatly.

Yet there were still greater problems. Central banks which earlier had few foreign assets now found themselves having to live in a world of floating rates, in which hundreds of millions of dollars could shift from one currency to another at an uptick in the price of dollars, marks, or yen. A new dimension was thus added to the investment decision. Till then most investors were concerned with safety, yield, and growth, but gave little thought to the rise and fall of the dollar in relation to other currencies. Now this changed, and in some ways, tragically. Investors who have sent their money overseas may have realized profits when foreign currencies appreciated against the dollar, but suffered when the movement reversed itself.

Financial officers of large corporations invested part of their reserves in short-term European and Japanese paper, attempting to capitalize on anticipated currency moves or simply to hedge. The Chicago Board Options Exchange instituted trading in currency futures, which simplified the decision making. Time was when the post of foreign exchange officer at even a major bank could be held by the not-too-bright nephew of the CEO. This no longer was so. "I used to invest short-term based on interest rates," reminisced a veteran trader. "Now I am more concerned with currency rates."

This simple declaration was emblematic of the internationalization of the investment universe, the implications of which were soon to trickle down to the individual investor. Owners of stock-based pension funds might have noted that they were investing abroad, and not only in stocks, but bonds as well, the latter to hedge on currency movements as well as to obtain a better yield. Mutual funds specializing in Canadian investments appeared after World War II. They were followed by closed end trusts for other countries, such as the Japan Fund and ASA (American South Africa) Ltd., after which came the Mexico Fund and the Korea Fund. Then came funds concentrating on investing in Australia, Israel, France, and Italy, Scandinavia (there were two of these), and Germany.

What was behind all of this? Dreams of profit, to be sure, but did it make investment sense? The respected *Mutual Fund Forecaster* thought so, writing on June 5, 1986 that projected growth rates in these countries, combined with currency plays, might turn out well. On the other hand, the securities markets in some of these nations are notoriously thin. For example, the valuation for the entire Italian market is around half that for IBM alone, an indication of just how far such fads can go, prompting a suspicion that some of the national funds were counting on sales to ethnic investors. Several foreign markets are comparatively badly managed, and getting delivery on certificates can be difficult. Yet the move continued as Wall Streeters prowled the globe thinking up new product ideas to feed into the ravenous fund market.

Investment advisor and fund manager John Templeton, who for decades had purchased and sold foreign securities, now became a celebrity. Large mutual fund operations, such as Fidelity, T. Rowe Price, Vanguard, and the like organized international funds to permit their clients to participate in overseas markets. Then the big wire houses got into the game, with Merrill Lynch Pacific and Nomura Pacific Basin in the lead.[3] Individual investors, who used to limit their morning reading to looking up the prices of their holdings and scanning the news, now turned avidly to advisories on exchange and interest rates, and worried about the strength or weakness of the dollar.

---

[3]For more on this, see Chapter 10.

Note that one element is missing from the list of changes that have transformed Wall Street into a new game, and that is the presence of bankers using inside information to line their own pockets. In the spring 1986, news appeared that several had indeed done just that, and an ongoing SEC investigation promised more to come. The fact that several stocks took off prior to release of takeover news was attributed to such machinations.

True, these things do occur, and they are baffling. Put matters of simple honesty and ethics aside, and ask yourself, what could possibly impel a young investment banker making a six digit salary with the promise of much more to come to take such risks? It certainly wasn't the need for food, clothing, or shelter, or even to pay rent on a Park Avenue apartment—the accused had all of that already. Nor could it have been the yearning to get rich quick; they were doing that too. The supercharged atmosphere of the Street was part of the reason, and the feeling they would have no trouble getting away with it was also involved.

Rumor ever was food and drink to the denizens of the district, and that played a role. Consider that such operations were hardly novel; Wall Street ever had an element willing to transgress the rules in this fashion. What is new is electronic surveillance; the chances of being caught are probably greater today than they were at any other time in this century.

It remains to be said that the ethical standards and behavior of big time members of the new Establishment are as high as ever, and those who violate conventions though remaining within the law risk the loss of confidence and respect. For every individual who appeared on page one as an inside trader there are dozens, perhaps scores, who were eased out of jobs for violating trusts and confidences. Wall Street is a place where written contracts play a relatively small role. Deals at the major houses are made orally, and those who make them know that without trust they can't play the game. Self interest dictates honesty, and the vast majority indeed are honest.

By now you may be a trifle confused, attempting to separate and then connect all of these diverse strands and discover their

unifying theme. To state the matter starkly, since 1970 or therea-
bouts the Wall Street scene has altered dramatically. The way
bankers and others operated in the 1960s has been revolutionized
to an extent never before seen in American financial history, and
the process continues. Just as the Newtonian billiard ball universe
where laws regulating events seemed to work flawlessly was replaced by Einsteinian one of uncertainty and relativity, so the apparently straightforward investment universe of the earlier period
has been succeeded by a far more complicated and dangerous
one.

We have seen how the old school tie now counts for far less today than it once did, how large institutional forces have altered
the markets, and how the development of new methods of raising funds resulted in the creation of new investment and trading
vehicles. Add to this the manifold impact of deregulation and the
traumas attending inflation and deflation, and cap it off with the
end of the post-World War II dollar domination, and you have the
elements which went into creating this new environment.

All well and good, you might be thinking, but how does it affect
me? I still own shares in IBM and General Motors, and if Houston
Power and Light is now Houston Industries, it remains in my
portfolio. Part of my holdings are in mutual funds, and though
they now are individual retirement accounts and a Keogh they
still are mutual funds. I learned a few things about some new investments, such as Ginnie Maes and zero coupon bonds, and
may even dabble in them occasionally, as I do with bank certificates of deposit. My old checking account is now a supersaver, on
which I earn interest, and my big bills are paid out of a money
market account. So I have adjusted pretty well to the new dispensation.

If this more or less approximates your thoughts, you are akin to
a passenger on the top deck of the Titanic who, aware of fog and a
sudden bump, may conclude that as a well-informed individual it
might be well to get a nightcap and turn in. Which is to say that
you may have an imprecise idea of factors that have become a key
element on any investment decision—including the one to re-

main out of the markets entirely. Namely risk. Risk always ex-isted, but today is different from what it used to be, as has been hinted at already. A clear idea of just what these are is a prerequi-site to any buy or sell decision, and is next on the agenda.

2 THE NEW FACE OF RISK

In 1909 Roger W. Babson, one of the earliest and most perspicacious market analysts, prefaced his book, *Business Barometers for Anticipating Conditions*, with two quotations, neither from an individual ordinarily associated with securities. The first was from the controversial mid-nineteenth century preacher Henry Ward Beecher.

> If one man, or twenty men, looking at the state of the nation here, at the crops, at the possible contingencies and risks of climate, at the conditions in Europe; in other words, taking all the elements that belong to the world into consideration are sagacious enough to prophesy the best of action, I don't know why it is not legitimate.

The second was from Associate Supreme Court Justice Oliver Wendell Holmes, who said:

> People will endeavor to forecast the future and make agreements according to their prophecy. Speculation of this kind by competent men is self-adjustment of society to the probability.

Babson himself opened with this:

> Neither this book nor any other can aid a banker, merchant, or investor to become rich *within a short time*. Nobody knows nor *can know* what conditions or prices are to exist within a few weeks, or even months, and 96 percent of the men who endeavor to take advantage of these monthly movements—or even who worry about them—never make much headway.

Babson founded and led an institute bearing his name, wrote a half dozen other books, and gained fame by predicting the 1929 stock market crash—in 1924, 1925, 1926, 1927, 1928, and again in the summer 1929. He was responsible for the training of hundreds of stock brokers, and the Babson Institute in Babson Park remains one of the better schools of its kind.

Just about everything taught there and in the many courses of study dealing with investments was and is a commentary on the Beecher and Holmes quotations. Beecher suggested that *sagacious* individuals, knowing the present and past, might on that knowledge attempt to forecast the future, while Holmes recognized that such projections are a necessary part of life.

Unless one is a complete determinalist, it would appear evident that given the complexities of individuals and societies, except in its broadest outlines the future is unknowable, and that all we can do is act on the best information we have in making decisions. This goes from figuring out the best route to get to work on any given day to making career choices. In this we recognize that in so acting we are at risk, and by utilizing a subconscious calculus we attempt to obtain the greatest possible rewards with the least possible risks, or at the very least make certain the rewards are commensurate with the dangers inherent in the exercise.

Risk is at the heart of the investment process, and if we have learned anything in the past decade it is that this is one element that can and should never be underestimated. We live in dangerous times, on Wall Street as everywhere else.

Yet far too many investors appear only vaguely aware of this, while too few of those who have the knowledge appear willing to draw logical conclusions and act on them. Rather, most yearn for the impossible.

THE IMPOSSIBLE DREAM

Picture the scene. It is a fashionable cocktail party at a beach front bungalow in Southampton on a balmy early evening in late August. Some barefoot lovers are walking in the sand, martinis in hand, while on the raised porch, in one corner, is a knot of equally martinized bankers talking about art, while in the other is a gaggle of artists swapping investment information.

One of the artists approaches a banker, and after a few pleasantries he turns the talk to stocks. They continue on to other subjects, but always return to home base. Finally the artist confides that he just made a big sale, and was looking for an investment vehicle. "What is it you are after?" asks the banker, to which the artist replies, "Well, I would want a decent return." Then after a few elaborations, he adds that he heard the high tech segment was turning around, and muses on the possibilities of making a killing on a start-up situation. Finally in an aside about the chanciness of being an artist in today's America, our artist confides that given this situation, he would require "something safe."

The banker doesn't blink. He has heard this before. All the artist wants is a safe investment that will grow rapidly paying a large dividend or interest.

In the vernacular, "There ain't no such animal." But an analysis of why this is so is a good enough place to open a discussion of the investment decision and the role played by risk.

Consider this diagram, a triangle whose points are growth, income, and safety, all of which the artist wants. Now reflect that the closer to get to one point, the further you will be from the others.

Do you want the closest to absolute safety known on the planet? How about Treasury bills, which are short-term U.S. fed-

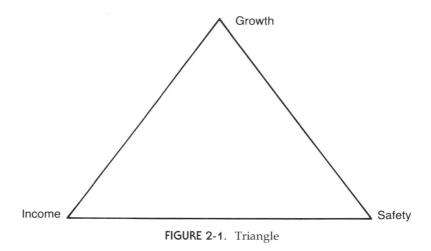

FIGURE 2-1. Triangle

eral government obligations. All you are doing is lending money to Washington for a few months. You wouldn't be running much of a risk regarding interest rates or currency rate changes, since the time span is so short. What could be safer? Barring atomic war, you would get the money back, plus interest. But there is no growth of principle, and the yield will be lower than funds loaned to your cousin Frank, and under even that commanded by the paper of such blue chip firms as IBM, Exxon, or GM.

But is it truly *completely* safe? As safe, perhaps, as Federal Reserve notes in your wallet? Not really, because they are not as liquid. You can purchase pretty much whatever you want for cash, but not for that Treasury bill, which wouldn't be accepted as partial payment for a new car. It still is extraordinarily liquid and marketable, which is to say that it can be sold readily and usually at pretty close to its last transaction price. There is the matter of making that telephone call to the broker, paying the commission, and waiting a short period until the funds come to you by mail, or are deposited to your account. There are transaction fees and charges, which you accept in order to obtain that interest. And you can't do any of this when the markets are closed.

Generally speaking, interest and dividends are payments for

risk, inconvenience, and the use of money over time. Eliminate all of these three, and you would have an investment which was not what most would call an investment—cash—which pays no yield, and for ordinary purposes, barring catastrophes, is safe and offers no growth.

Extraordinary growth might be obtained through an investment in a company with a radical new technology for which demand seems bound to be strong. We saw this a while back with stocks of genetic engineering companies and microcomputers. Let the scientists and engineers at one of those firms come up with a new product or technique, give it to astute packagers and savvy marketers, and growth could be exponential.

Of course, while growing the firm would need all of its earnings for expansion, so stockholders would receive no dividends. And the promise of growth would be such as to attract other firms, many of them well-established, other new ones equally hungry, to the field. So risks would be high. But the payoff *could* be worth it.

Live long enough in the investment universe and you will have ample occasion to kick yourself figuratively for having missed a splendid opportunity. Indeed, one of the words that marks the amateur from the pro is "shudda," as in "I shudda bought Xerox in 1959." Really? When it was a struggling young concern bringing its first commercial copier to the market? At that time most thought the field would be dominated by the "giants"— Minnesota Mining & Manufacturing and American Photocopy— and that in any case it hardly was a major industry segment. Then consider talk of new competition once copying took hold. Could Xerox make it once IBM, Eastman Kodak, and others entered the field, and 3M came up with new models? So the business was risky, though the rewards were potentially great.

Go down the line. Buy Polaroid? When Eastman Kodak was around, rumored to be preparing an instant camera of its own? Buy Digital Equipment? When IBM could swat it without so much as a glance? Buy Apple? Ditto, and besides, how many of those small machines could be sold? Go through your own short list of "shuddas," and consider the risks involved at the inception. Now think about all of those competitors of Xerox, Polaroid, DEC, and Apple that are no longer with us.

Or think about a new company about to come to market, which your broker tells you is developing a perpetual motion machine. Or a method of extracting petroleum from garbage. Or a cure for acne. Or word processing software anyone this side of an 80 IQ can learn in a twinkling. But you get the idea by now. The greater the chance for growth, the more risk and the absence of income.

High income isn't too difficult to come by, assuming you have few scruples and a cadre of toughs to back you up. Loan sharking is one such occupation in which interest rates are high—1 percent per day and 10 percent weekly aren't unknown, and given compounding that really adds up. (This is income, not growth of principle, which is different.) Of course there are risks we needn't go into here, since they are familiar to all who follow the doings of organized crime. So let's turn back to securities.

In early autumn 1985, when IBM's 9⅜ percent bonds maturing in 2004 were selling to yield 10.4 percent, Beker's 15⅞s of 2003 offered 23.3 percent. Now there were a variety of reasons for this, but one of the more important is quality. There is no need to mention that IBM has the highest quality rating around. Not so Beker, whose common was rated C by Standard & Poor's. A smallish factor in the fertilizer field, Beker had posted losses and was in arrears on the preferred dividends. So with that 23.3 percent yield went high risk.

Wait. What if Beker turned around, became profitable, cleaned up those arrears, and in other ways gave evidence of improvement? The bond, selling for 66, would rise and with this the yield would decline. For example, if the bond went to par (100) from its then price of 68 it would have shown a rise of more than 50 percent, while the yield would have declined to 15.87 percent. Individuals knowledgeable about this situation and optimistic about the company's prospects might believe the bond should be placed halfway between yield and growth on that diagram, though far from safety. At that time the market was telling you that it should be squarely at the yield apex.

Not for long, however, within weeks Beker fell into Chapter 11 bankruptcy, and stopped paying interest. Where should the Beker bonds be placed now? Certainly not anywhere near yield or safety. The bond could be considered a risky growth situation, for if and when the firm emerged from bankruptcy and cleared up arrearages on its bonds, its paper could soar.

Risk is a more complicated factor than often is imagined. Tell an investor that due to the nature of the company behind the shares there is a high degree of risk in them, and he or she probably will think this means it can advance or decline fairly quickly. There is far more to it than that. Indeed, risk is one of the most difficult concepts for investors to grasp, and for that reason has always occupied an important place in college financial textbooks. Freshmen students in such courses could count on one sure final examination question: "Enumerate the risks involved in investing," to which they would intone the litany—market, interest rate, business, inflation, liquidity and marketability, and some would throw in the unexpected. These are all still there, but others have to be added, while the relative importance of each of the above has shifted.

SHOULD I BUY SONY?

For example, take the stock of Sony Corp., the Japanese consumer electronics firm, whose American Depository Receipts (ADR) are listed on the NYSE.[1] A generation ago Americans limited their purchase of foreign stocks to Royal Dutch and Shell Transport & Trading, considered Unilever and Volkswagen a

---

[1]An ADR is an instrument issued by an American bank backed by shares in a foreign company on deposit at a correspondent bank, usually in the home country of the company.

trifle esoteric and knew next to nothing about foreign markets. Those same American investors have now been drawn to the likes of Sony, Mitsubishi, and other Japanese stocks, know about some Australian, Hong Kong, and Korean firms, and are spread across the map in continental Europe. Part of this has to do with the fact that many of our consumer goods bear foreign labels, and we hear stories in the press and on television about trade problems. The financial pages carry reports of foreign markets, and readers know that at times it pays to be there rather than in the United States. Indeed, during the first half of 1986 mutual funds specializing in overseas investments outperformed all others. Just as American stocks are traded on many foreign markets, so the European and Pacific basin companies are appearing in greater numbers at the New York Stock Exchange, the American Stock Exchange, or the National Association of Securities Dealers Automatic Quotation System (NASDAQ). The London exchange and NASDAQ have formed a link which is bound to grow, and in time include the other markets. Round the clock trading is just around the corner.

Return to Sony. Highly profitable, well regarded, with a balance sheet in very good shape by Japanese standards, the company has paid dividends since 1957 and is generally thought of as the class of its field. The marketer of consumer electronics *par excellence*, a recent poll showed that a majority of Americans thought it was a domestic company, and considered its television sets superior to those turned out by Panasonic (just the opposite conclusion than that indicated by polls taken in Japan). In the spring 1986 the stock was selling to yield less than 1 percent, a sure sign of a growth situation, which indeed it was. You might think the message of the market here was that while Sony was a distance from the yield apex, it rated high on safety and growth.

Think again. While far safer than, say, Beker, Sony does carry risks, which can be subdivided into several categories.

First and most obvious nowadays, there is the currency risk, and the related interest rate risk. While Sony's earnings are converted into dollars for the ADRs, they are translated from yen.

The dollar-yen exchange ratio is determined by a variety of factors, all of which come down to the matter of supply and demand, which can be natural or manipulated. In 1985 and for several years before that Americans had argued that the Japanese had kept the yen artificially low, so as to encourage Americans to purchase Japanese goods and make American products higher in price to Japanese than they should have been.

Pressure on the Japanese to do something to alter the situation, and thus rectify the balance of trade between the two countries, was finally paying off. The yen, which had been over 300 to the dollar a few years earlier, declined to almost half that amount. This meant that Americans wanting to purchase, say, a Sony television set, selling for the equivalent of 150,000 yen, would have paid around $500 for it at 300 yen to the dollar, but $750 at 200 yen to the dollar and $1000 at 150, which might prove disadvantageous to the company. So prices of Japanese goods sold in the United States were bound to rise over time. Now most of GE's television receivers come from the Orient, and that company's earnings would be affected by currency risks. But not to the extent as those of Sony.

Interest rate risk is much more visible, especially to a generation that went through the roller-coaster situation of the 1970s and early 1980s. We are light years away from the kind of market in which blue chip corporations (usually railroads) issued 3 percent gold bonds maturing in a hundred years, or when bond salespeople would leave Wall Street in early May to take to the road, selling bonds to banks in their territories, armed with little but an offering list, and make deals from it in late June, confident the prices hadn't moved a whit. From 1900 to 1920 long-term bond yields inched upward, going from 4 percent to slightly under 6 percent in the 20-year span, before gently drifting downward, to just under 2½ percent 25 years later.

Contrast this to the situation in the second half of the 1960s, when due to the growth of inflationary pressures yields rose from 6 to 9 percent in two years, or that of the first half of the 1980s, when yields went from under 9 to over 13 percent in three years.

Bonds move fairly rapidly nowadays, though usually not as fast or dramatically as can stock prices. Indeed, while stocks rose sharply in 1985 and the first half of 1986, bonds did even better, as interest rates collapsed.

Given the leverage available from some financial instruments, going with bonds can be a roller-coast ride. Once an arcane, barely interesting matter, interest rate changes have made bonds one of the more fascinating investment areas.

MARKET RISK

Market risk was at one time considered of paramount importance by most investors, and for good reason: why care whether a company is doing well if the stock is declining? Some might argue that market risk embraces all the others, since the paramount question for all investors involves how the stock is performing in terms of price. So what if record earnings were just posted if the stock's quote has been halved due to market conditions?

Methods of minimizing market risk while maximizing market opportunities are the paramount concern of hoards of analysts peering at charts, graphs, statistics, cycles, waves, and anything else from imprecise statistics to their very bowels to come up with forecasts, and will be discussed in some detail later on. Suffice it to say there is no such thing as a foolproof method of safeguarding against market risk when it comes to equities. One may only devise techniques and formulas to iron out short- and long-term flutters. There used to be some rules one might follow; at one time investors would flee from bonds when inflation came and go to stocks, and reverse direction when deflation began. In the late 1970s, however, investors dumped both stocks and bonds, and went to money market instruments of various kinds.

Stock prices can be affected by a multitude of market factors, but bonds by four basic ones: the reliability of the issuer, the coupon, the maturity date, and the availability of attractive alternate investments. Assuming the absence of an economic disaster and

CHANGES IN THE CONSUMER PRICE INDEX AND STOCK PRICES, 1967–1980

Year	Change in CPI	Closing Dow Jones Industrials	Closing Dow Jones Bonds
1967	2.3	905.11	74.64
1968	4.2	943.75	73.98
1969	5.4	800.36	68.11
1970	5.6	838.92	68.77
1971	4.3	890.20	73.29
1972	3.3	1020.02	75.01
1973	6.2	850.86	72.75
1974	11.0	616.24	66.14
1975	9.1	852.41	69.02
1976	5.7	1004.65	93.20
1977	6.4	831.17	90.95
1978	7.6	805.01	84.54
1979	11.3	838.74	73.35
1980	13.5	963.99	63.68

Source: Council of Economic Advisors, *Economic Report of the President, 1985;* Phyllis Pierce, ed. *The Dow-Jones Averages, 1985–1980.*

stability of the Dow Jones Bond Index in regard to maturities, the key factor is the market's perception of where interest rates are headed. Presumption of a rise would lead to a decline in bond price, while a general sentiment that rates are declining result in a bond market rally.

You can see that bonds were relatively stable from 1967 to 1972, when it appeared inflation was increasing at a steady rate ranging from 4 to 5 percent. Then when the Consumer Price Index rose by only 3.3 percent in 1972, bonds rallied, as expected. But then inflation heated up and bonds sank, and this too might have been anticipated. The 1975 rally was due largely to a respite from the then-torrid pace of 11 percent the previous year. The advance continued spectacularly in 1976, resulting from an even sharper decline in inflation. Investors who were in bonds rather than stocks throughout the entire period from 1967 to 1977 not only slept sounder, but did much better. Then, as inflationary pressures intensified, bonds fell once again.

Note, however, that the bond index at the end of 1979 was above where it had been on December 31, 1973. Yet in 1973 the CPI had increased by 6.2 percent, and in 1979, almost twice that, 11.3 percent. The message of the bond market in 1973, after a period of calm, was that more of the same was expected in the future. On the other hand, in 1979, bond prices, heading downward as they were, seemed to be telling us that rates would head higher, and that the toboggan from the 1976 peak was to continue, as it did.

The message from stocks is different. The relatively gentle inflation from 1969–1972 helped the stock market, as it was supposed to, but then, as inflationary pressures became intense, stocks collapsed. Of course there were many other factors at work in this period, but at that point investors were beginning to lose faith in the old axiom that stocks were a safeguard against inflation. Accelerating inflation from 1976 to 1979, accompanied by declining stock prices, provided the coup de grace. Textbooks which in the early 1970s had said little about inflation as part of market risk now had to be revised, and at the same time the old belief that the stock and bond markets tended to go in different directions was altered too, as both declined in the late 1970s.

Where was the money going? To the aforementioned money market instruments, most of which weren't around in the 1960s, and which form an important part of the investment arena today, and to exotic debt instruments that either didn't exist in the mid-1970s or were relatively unknown. Or to overseas markets, or into real estate syndications. The investment terrain has changed. The old rules no longer apply as once they did. And this is one of the most important risks individual investors face in today's markets.

Investments in stocks may be hedged in several ways to protect against market risk. Some methods require the use of options, and will be discussed in Chapter 9. Others involve the use of automatic formulas that enabled the investor to spread risk but limit reward (there is no free lunch in any of this). It is the difference between shooting at a target with a rifle or a shotgun. You may hit the target with the former, but unless you are a marksman, expect many misses, in which case you'll have nothing. A hit is more probable with a shotgun shell, but there are a lot of wasted pellets as well.

FORMULA INVESTING

One of the most familiar formulas—it goes back to at least the pre-World War I period—is dollar cost averaging. Assume that stock prices are fluctuating day to day in ways that are difficult to predict, and that you have conflicting ideas regarding where they will be years, even months or weeks from now. This is not unrealistic, because only geniuses have anything near consistent success in the market, and these are few and far between, and generally don't give away their secrets in magazine articles, books, or seminars. In other words, start out with the supposition that you are uncertain about prices and willing to hedge your bets, by accepting the chance of lower profits as a tradeoff for lower risks. Next select a stock you are *reasonably* convinced will be higher a number of years from now. In addition, the stock should swing up and down with more velocity than the market as a whole, which is to say has a high "beta."

You probably sense what beta is even though the term may be unfamiliar. The beta coefficient of stocks, which became a popular concept in the late 1970s, is nothing more than the ratio of that stock's volatility to that of the market as a whole. This means that if the stock tends to rise and fall along with the general market, its beta would be 1. If it rises 20 percent more than the market, the beta would be 1.2; should it fluctuate 50 percent less than the market, the beta would be .5. You will soon see that dollar-cost averaging makes no sense at all unless the stock fluctuates, and would be an unprofitable exercise if it declined and stayed there. What you want is a stock that moves around, but over the long term, does reasonably well. Your broker can tell you what the beta is for most stocks, and you can find out on your own by referring to Value Line publications. Some candidates and recent betas are: Apple Computer (1.60), Beverly Enterprises (1.50), Boeing (1.20), Digital Equipment (1.25), Federal Express (1.05), Hewlett Packard (1.30), International Business Machines (1.05), McDonald's (1.10), and Upjohn (1.00).

Begin with a promise to yourself that you will place a specified fixed dollar amount into that security at regular intervals, say, $1000 the first business day of every year. If the security is rising in price you may be tempted to buy more, and if it falls, less. Or your reactions could be the other way. No matter; fight it, and invest that $1000, no more or less.

This creates an immediate problem. Suppose you select the stock of International Business Machines, a worthy choice for dollar cost averaging. But at the time of your initial purchase the stock is selling for $160 ½ per share, which means you should buy 6.2305 shares (not counting commissions), and you know that such a fractional purchase is not possible. In addition, when you purchase less than 100 shares you must pay an odd lot differential, which adds to the price. Clearly dollar cost averaging doesn't work as well as it might with individual stocks. The best alternative is a mutual fund, in this case one specializing in established growth stocks, since that is the category into which IBM falls.

So you choose a good no-load fund, the nature of which and method of selection to be covered in Chapter 10, and start out with that first $1000. Let's assume the fund's shares that day are at $12.55. Your $1000 would purchase 79.68 shares. A year later the fund is at $11.66, as the market has fallen, which means you get 85.76 shares, the rule being that the lower the price, the more shares you get. You now have a total of 165.44 shares for your total investment of $2000, which comes to an average cost of $12.09 per share, lower than the first price of $12.55, but higher than the second of $11.66. A year passes, the market has rallied, and the price has gone to $12.03, so the $1000 buys 83.12 shares, giving you 248.56, for an average cost of $12.06.

Rather than going through each year's investment, let's look at what might have happened in tabular form:

DOLLAR COST AVERAGING

Year	Investment	Price	Shares Purchased
1	$1000	$12.55	79.68
2	1000	11.66	85.76
3	1000	12.03	83.12
4	1000	11.51	86.88
5	1000	11.65	85.83
6	1000	12.12	82.50
7	1000	11.98	83.47
8	1000	12.03	83.12
	$8000		670.36

After eight years you have invested $8000 and have 670.36 shares, at an average cost of $11.93. Shares were purchased for prices as high as $12.55 and as low as $11.51. Three of your purchases were made for under $11.99, one at that price, and four above it. The total value of your holdings are $8064.43, so you have a slight profit. Looking backward you would have wished you had purchased more shares at $11.51, but aren't you glad you didn't put the entire $8000 in at $12.55?

You have made the same financial commitment each year, but in fact have really purchased more shares when the price was low than you did when it was high, and so the average price of the shares has a bias toward the low side. Note too that you made money even though the fund ended up below where it had been when you began.

How does this work out in the "real world?" Consider a worst case real life situation, that of RCA, a stock that paced the great bull market of the 1920s. Assume the investor purchased $1000 of the stock on the last trading day of the year from 1928, when the stock sold for 75⅛, and continued doing so through 1945, when the price was 16½, and look at what happened:

RADIO CORPORATION OF AMERICA
DOLLAR COST AVERAGING, 1928–1950

Year	Amount Invested	Price	Shares Purchased	Total	Total Cost	Market Value
1928	$1000	75⅛	13.31	13.31	$1000	$1000.00
1929	1000	43¼	23.12	36.43	2000	1575.66
1930	1000	12⅛	82.47	118.90	3000	1441.71
1931	1000	5⅝	177.78	296.68	4000	1668.81
1932	1000	5¼	190.48	487.16	5000	2557.57
1933	1000	6¾	148.15	635.31	6000	4228.44
1934	1000	5½	181.81	817.12	7000	4494.16
1935	1000	12⅜	80.89	898.01	8000	11112.87
1936	1000	11½	86.96	984.97	9000	11327.16
1937	1000	6	166.67	1151.64	10000	6909.84
1938	1000	7⅞	127.02	1278.66	11000	10069.53
1939	1000	5½	181.81	1460.47	12000	8032.64
1940	1000	4⅝	214.05	1647.52	13000	7744.70
1941	1000	2½	400.00	2074.52	14000	5186.32
1942	1000	5	200.00	2274.52	15000	11372.65
1943	1000	9½	105.26	2378.78	16000	22608.00
1944	1000	10½	95.24	2475.02	17000	25987.81
1945	1000	17⅜	57.55	2532.57	18000	44003.57
1946	1000	9¼	108.11	2640.68	19000	24426.38
1947	1000	9⅜	106.45	2747.13	20000	25754.43

Year	Amount Invested	Price	Shares Purchased	Total	Total Cost	Market Value
1948	1000	13⅝	73.79	2820.52	21000	38429.72
1949	1000	12½	80.00	2900.52	22000	36256.63
1950	1000	16½	60.61	2961.13	23000	48858.81

Think of how you might have felt at the end of each year along the way, how often you might have considered cashing in and abandoning the program, and how you might have been tempted to increase your purchases in the mid-1930s when RCA returned to a double digit price, only to collapse to new lows in the early 1940s.

The 1928 date was selected because at that point RCA was at its peak, and 1950 because that was the approximate start of the next bull market. Had you continued the program into that major upward sweep your results would have been most pleasing. At the end of 1959 RCA closed at 69½, and your $1000 investment on that occasion would have purchased 14.34 shares, bringing the total to $222,796.79, on an investment of $32,000.

But there is one caveat. Suppose that instead of buying stocks you had put the money into a savings account that paid 3 percent on net balances? By 1937 you would have had $11,807.94 instead of the $6,909.84 obtained through dollar cost averaging, and doubtless sleeping a lot better. By the end of 1950 your total would have come to $32,143.49, less than would have been obtained through dollar cost averaging RCA, but obtained through much less anguish. That money would have been insured after 1933, while there was no guarantee RCA would ever recover.

Dollar cost averaging in stocks works well over the market cycle where there is no important *opportunity cost* in the form of lost chances to invest in higher yielding money market instruments. Many studies have shown convincingly over long periods of time, say 10 years or so, that investors would have been better off in stocks than bonds or bank deposits. And through dollar cost averaging one can minimize these risks. But the risks cannot be eliminated. In addition to the matter of opportunity costs, one can lose if the fund selected drops and never recovers. Such issues as Xerox, Polaroid, Texas Instruments, ITT, and Avon were prime candidates for dollar cost averaging in the late 1960s, when they looked virtually impregnable. All fell, perhaps never again will reach their bull market heights. But one might have said that about RCA, which even in 1959 hadn't recovered entirely from the 1929 crash.

Dollar cost averaging would have moderated the pain, but individuals who began dollar cost averaging in these stocks in that period had regrets for much of the rest of their lives.

So the method can lessen risk, but not remove it. Individual investors should know this, and consider dollar-cost averaging a method of winning moderately when faced with a market dominated by those savvy institutional managers, who spend most waking hours thinking about placing their big chips on securities, and then go home at night to dream about it. They should also know that one of the dirty secrets of several major pension funds is that they have been dollar-cost averaging for years, and don't talk much about it, because if it were recognized the fund's participants might want to have those big management fees slashed.

RISKS IN BONDS

For bondholders, market risk holds a different kind of challenge than it does for owners of equities. Take the situation of an individual in the process of constructing a bond portfolio in early 1987. Maturities are staggered, there is a proper blend of municipals and corporates, of qualities ranging from AAA to as low as Baa, and of maturities running from 1990 through 2010. (If some of these terms are confusing, see Chapter 7 for a quick survey. All that is meant here, however, is that the portfolio is comprised of bonds maturing at specified times with differing degrees of risk and reward and tax status.)

Suppose such a person, in the process of accumulation, learns that interest rates are sinking. This means that bonds with the same maturity and quality as ones he purchased a few months back for $10,000 carrying an 8 percent interest rate, now has one of only, say, 7 percent. This might mean that the bonds in the investor's portfolio could now be sold for around $11,500, at which price the yield would approximate 7 percent. As noted, the general rule is that a decline in interest rates leads to a rally in bonds. Conversely, an increase in rates would cause bond prices to fall.

How might our bondholder feel about this situation? On the one hand he has an unrealized capital gain, but for what purpose? Suppose he purchased that bond, maturing in five years, with the intention of holding on to maturity? The bond price increase may make him feel good, but it will not enrich him if he carries through on his original intention. In fact he might welcome an increase in bond yields, which would enable him to make the next purchase at a lower price than might otherwise be the case.

The reason is the same in both cases: at maturity he will turn in the bond and receive $10,000. It will be that amount if interest rates rise or fall between now and then. This is in sharp contrast to the owner of stocks, who sells at what he considers the best price available. On the one hand, the stockholder knows that his holding can soar to the stratosphere. The bond buyer, realizing that maturity comes closer every day, won't pay much of a premium for a higher yield for the next five years. Which is to say, as previously noted, the greater the risk, the greater the possibilities of reward or failure.

What concerns our bondholder in this case is not market risk, but inflation risk. The owner of a $10,000 face value bond maturing in 2000 knows that $10,000 will purchase a car today; in an inflationary environment that amount might fetch him a set of tires. On the other hand, inflation tends to stimulate the stock market. Or at least this was the general view until the highly inflationary environment of the 1970s, when all bets were off.

Constant ratio investing, which is based on maintaining a balanced portfolio of stocks and bonds, was very much in vogue during the 1950s, but fell into disfavor when stocks started to rise sharply, and bonds became less desirable. "Balanced" mutual funds, some of which were advertised as following this general formula, started to lose ground to equity funds, and by the late 1960s were deemed stodgy and old fashioned, and lost thousands of accounts. The balanced funds still haven't done well, even as bonds rose in popularity, because today's investors seem much more interested in bond and/or stock funds, deciding on their own how much to have in each. Those who do so are interested in lessening the risks, and so they do—but as might be expected, the potential rewards are diminished as well.

In its simplest form, the investor decides to maintain half the portfolio in debt securities, the other half in stocks. The selected vehicle is a family of no-load mutual funds that permits switches at no cost (more on this in Chapter 10), and the switches will be made at selected intervals, say every six months. We start out with an investment of $20,000 in bonds, and another $20,000 in stocks. Unlike the dollar cost averaging, more funds will be placed in at the same ratio whenever desired.

There remains that aforementioned tendency for bonds to fall when stocks rise, though as noted this isn't carved in stone and hasn't worked well in recent years. The reason is rather complicated, but two factors should be considered. In the first place, a strong economy contains inflationary pressures, since the factors of production are being utilized almost fully and more capital is demanded for expansion purposes. This causes an upward pressure on interest rates, which start to rise. And this leads to lower bond prices. For example, that 8 percent bond you purchased at par, or $10,000, doesn't look so appealing if new bonds of the same quality and maturity are coming to market at 10 percent. In this case the bond price will fall, probably to around $8000, while stocks, buoyed by the higher earnings that come with an economic boom, will rise. There is another way of looking at it, which is closer to the mark insofar as market action is concerned. A strong economy, accompanied by higher earnings, is translated into an atmosphere in which stocks look appealing, and so institutional and individual investors sell bonds and purchase stocks.

This works in reverse as well. Declining interest rates, caused by sluggish demand and a generally poor economy, cause bonds to rise and stocks to fall. But even if this were not so, it still might be prudent to make the split, if only to obtain the benefits of diversification into different instruments.

Assume we have a recession, with lower corporate profits and interest rates, and that the value of the stock portfolio after a fixed interval is $18,000, and bonds have gone to $22,000. The investor would take steps to equalize the amounts, this being possible by putting another $4000 into stocks or selling $2000 worth of bonds and investing that amount in stocks. Now assume that we have a stock market rally, and at the next interval the stock portfolio is $30,000 and bonds remain at $22,000. This would call for the sale of $4000 in stocks and that amount being committed to bonds, or in some other way bring the two into balance.

As can be seen, the investor is always selling the better performing investment and putting the money into the lesser one. The supposition here is that bonds and stocks move in cycles, and constant ratio investing has a tendency to get out toward the top of the cycle and in toward the bottom, as well as permitting a diversity of investments.

POLITICAL RISK

Next think about risks of the political kind. Political risk can always be a problem, one that every investor who ventures abroad has to consider. Of course, the risk can bring the familiar rewards was well. John Templeton is ever shifting assets from one country to another. In the 1950s and 1960s Templeton invested in Japan and then Singapore and Hong Kong, before others knew of the opportunities there, and then he went into Korea.

Get into a foreign market when capitalism there is budding and you could reap a fortune, as Templeton did on several occasions. But it can turn out disastrously for those who are unacquainted with the details of the country's politics and economics. For example, after World War II astute investors deposited their funds in

Mexican *financerias*, somewhat akin to savings and loan associations, which paid upward of twice the interest rate of their American counterparts. It was simple enough: dollars were sent south of the border, where they were exchanged for pesos, and then deposited. When withdrawals were desired, the pesos would be exchanged back into dollars. All went smoothly for a while, and since the dollar-peso exchange rate was stable, many didn't give the matter much thought. Then, in the early 1980s, Mexico devalued the peso sharply, and individuals who thought they had $10,000 in the *financeria* discovered to their horror that it had melted to around $3000.

Of course it could go in the opposite direction; Americans who had deposits in most European countries or Japan in 1985–1986 reaped windfall profits as the dollar weakened.

Let's return to that investment in Sony common. Japan is as secure a country politically as might be imagined, but nothing is certain in this world. Might the country elect a socialistically minded government? It doesn't seem likely right now, but during the post-war period the Socialists did rule for a brief period, though this was when American tutelage was being exercised. The developments that might lead to a rise in that party's popularity are the same that would make Sony appear a less attractive investment—weakening of ties with the United States, a perceived military advantage of the Soviets in the area, the growth of neutralism, and/or a major economic collapse could do it. Any or a combination of these should lead one to dump Sony and other Japanese stocks, and is a problem that owners of foreign securities continually face.

What might happen if a trade war develops between the United States and Japan? Sony's American sales, which account for a substantial portion of its revenues and profits, could decline considerably, preceded by the price of its common. On the other hand, the growing tendency for Japanese firms to establish factories in countries for which they have large markets, would mitigate effects.

Around 10 years ago, investment banks had few qualms about

making "sovereign loans," which are debts owed by governments. Of course there was the aforementioned currency risk, but that could be reflected in the coupon rate. The thought that governments would renege on financial obligations appeared remote. After all, went the reasoning, the United States and the World Bank had a major interest in making certain friendly governments remained on their feet, and some form of bail-out could be arranged. The commercial banks also had a stake in assuring their loans didn't go bad, and would arrange for refinancings. If all else failed, the governments could turn to the printing press—in moderation, it was hoped—and pay off the debt by issuing new paper this way.

However, it should be noted that sovereigns have always looked on refusal to pay as an acceptable alternative. Scores of countries and municipalities defaulted in the early stages of the Great Depression. The country that resorted to default most frequently in the nineteenth century was the United States, with states and municipalities notorious for the practice. In the aftermath of the great canal mania of the 1830s many of the state-sponsored projects went bankrupt and foreigners, assuming that the governments would meet the obligations, found this wasn't so. When one of President Martin Van Buren's envoys attempted to obtain a loan in Paris he was informed by the Rothschilds in icy language that "you may tell your government that you have seen the man who is at the head of the finances of Europe, and that he has told you that they cannot borrow a dollar, not a dollar," while the London *Times* editorialized, "The people of the United States may be fully persuaded that there is a certain class of securities to which no abundance of money, however great, can give value, and that in this class their own securities stand pre-eminent," and a banker of that city said he wouldn't purchase American state paper "even if countersigned by an angel."

The situation is different today, of course; thus far the foreign debts have been refinanced. But due to recurrent crises the bonds of such countries as Mexico, Brazil, and Argentina fell sharply, always when the front pages featured stories of their inability to meet current obligations. Do you think that no matter what happens these countries will continue to pay their obligations? Then by all means buy their bonds now, concentrating on the shorter maturities to minimize the impact of inflation. Avoid them, however, if you believe otherwise. But while you're peering through the newspapers looking up prices of Mexican obligations, take a gander at Cuban bonds, or call your broker for quotes. As these words are being written Cuba's 4¼ percents that were to have matured in 1977 are selling for around 10. What might happen if Cuban-American relations took a turn for the better? Those bonds would rise, and should relations between the two countries return to "normal," they could be paid off in full, with back interest and penalties. In such a situation the bond could rise to over 120.

Is this probable or even possible? Occasionally an East European municipality or country will make a settlement with bondowners for pre-World War II obligations, though not at face value. Rumblings out of China indicate that some of the old Nationalist bonds might be redeemed as part of a deal to encourage American investment there. And there are still some dreamers around who believe that one of these days the U.S.S.R. will make a settlement on Czarist debts. Would you like to take a flyer on Russia's 2s of 1920? There are dealers who will oblige you, but it will take some time, and in any case most buyers do so for pictorial and collecting purposes, and not in the hope of redemption (in both senses of the term).

One interesting play might be in Puerto Rico agency bonds, some of which carry Baa ratings. Based on purely economic and financial factors, these ratings are probably merited. But there is a political aspect to consider. Suppose the situation in the Commonwealth becomes such that the water or electricity resources authority could not pay interest or make redemption? Theoretically the bondholders could step in and seize the utility, denying service unless and until payments are made. Practically speaking, however, this would not happen. Given the nature of Caribbean politics, and with Fidel Castro only a handful of miles away, Uncle Sam can be relied on to do all in his power to keep Puerto Rico on an even keel. If Washington can save New York City and Chrysler, it certainly would do the same for Puerto Rico.

Political risks also directly and indirectly affect American stocks, though in a different way. The last government antitrust suit against IBM not only cast doubts on that company's future but also caused management to tread cautiously in the marketplace, fearful of providing Justice Department attorneys with ammunition to substantiate charges of unfair practices. It is no accident that IBM became far more aggressive after the suit was dropped than it had been earlier. Would Big Blue have purchased Rolm and enter into close arrangements with MCI if the case was still being heard? Hardly.

Likewise, deregulation of airlines, a political decision, made a difference for the stocks and bonds of New York Air, Eastern, Delta, and Northeast, to name just a few. Deregulatory forces in broadcasting helped cause the takeover activity in that industry, and absent the politics of oil, T. Boone Pickens and others would not have raided the oil companies. A partial deregulation of the drug industry, not likely but nonetheless possible, would cause investors to reassess their views toward that business.

WHAT ABOUT THE COMPANY?

The business risk is far more familiar and common, a matter that takes up most of management's time and should be pondered seriously by investors. Generally speaking the greater the business risk, the likelier the chance for major moves in the stock in either direction. The reason should be obvious. There is far more competition and rapid change in an industry in which opportunities abound than one which is settled. What are the chances for a new domestic car maker to make a splash? The answer is "nil." Or another large integrated steel company? The same. What about a new producer of microcomputers? Possibly, but at this stage of the game not likely. How about another firm in genetic engineering or electronics? Not only possible, but probable. General Motors and Bethlehem Steel follow the business cycle, Compaq and Apple hold out the promise of long-term growth—or sharp decline as IBM uses its considerable muscle in the marketplace. What about Genentech and Cetus in genetic engineering? Either could be a multibillion dollar company a decade from now, high up on the *Fortune 100*—or go out of business.

Business creation is running at near-record levels, as are business failures. More than two companies fold every hour of every business day, most never to reappear. Of course, only a small percentage of these are publicly owned, but there are enough of these to give one pause when considering placing a few thousand dollars on the nose of a company your Uncle Charlie swears is the next IBM or another Syntex. We celebrate successes in this country, but tend to forget failures. Remember Clint Hartung? Thirty years ago the New York Giants touted him as the next Babe Ruth, but he proved to be a flop. Or Joe Tepsic? The Brooklyn Dodgers thought he was the next Joe DiMaggio. (Remember the New York Giants and the Brooklyn Dodgers?) Wall Street is littered with the detritus of their investment counterparts—Transitron was to have been the next Texas Instruments, U.S. Industries the next ITT, and Zoecon the next Merck.

And yet . . .

Think back to that triangle at the beginning of the chapter. Without risk little reward can be expected. The trick is to minimize the former and maximize the chances of the latter. The trouble is, none of this can be quantified, and has to be calculated by utilizing the familiar seat of the pants.

Occasionally one comes across such situations, but it takes more than a trifle of daring to recognize them. For example, in retrospect it appears the federal government had no alternative but to help bail out New York during its 1975 fiscal crisis, but the atmosphere was such that many investors had their doubts, and dumped New York City bonds. The city had reneged on its notes, but through it all paid interest on bonds, and it apparently had no intention of doing otherwise at least as long as there was a chance of a government bail-out. Perspicacious investors might have picked up those bonds and reaped large profits when the clouds passed.

Similarly, at a time when Chrysler's future was in doubt the bonds of Chrysler Financial had collapsed to the point where they were yielding over 20 percent. Now, these bonds were backed by time purchase contracts on cars, not earnings of the parent. Had Chrysler gone under, owners of those cars would continue making their payments. Yet Chrysler Financial was selling to yield almost twice as much as General Motors Acceptance, to which it might justifiably be compared. Was it a buy? Yes, but most of us can see this only in retrospect.

One of the more enduring Wall Street cliches is that the two motivating drives in the district are fear and greed, and that one buys when the former is at its peak and sells when the latter is prevalent. This is a good enough rule to follow when it comes to business risks. Are rumors of a bad quarter at General Electric causing that stock to lag? Buy, because even if true, GE has a way of bouncing back. Is General Dynamics undergoing a Department of Defense probe on excess profits, causing the stock to tumble? Buy, because the federal government will do nothing to cripple the company, since a strong General Dynamics is important to the defense effort. Did it seem Coca-Cola or Procter & Gamble have blundered on the new Coke and Pringles, and this is reflected in the price of their stocks? Buy, because these firms have records of recovering from adversity.

All of these are short-term problems for essentially strong and sound enterprises. The business risks to be on the alert for are of a long-term variety. Secular problems in steel were surfacing in the early 1960s, and while some of the groups's stocks had their innings during the next 20 years it should have been obvious that performance would be mediocre at best over the long term. Problems in most textile issues are of a like kind. But there is this to consider; if individual companies are doing something significant to alter their circumstances it might be wise to buy their stocks and bonds while the entire group is dumped on by the investment community. For example, in its 1982 takeover of Marathon

Oil and subsequent activities it became evident that U.S. Steel was on its way to lessening its dependence on metals, and is well on the way to becoming USX,—a company weaned from its dependence on steel.

The situation to watch out for is one like Central Leather, a now forgotten company which in 1917 was the nation's 23rd largest industrial, a blue chip if ever there was one. As the name indicates, Central dominated the leather business, and its stock was a growth issue in the age of horse and buggy and steam powered factories, when bridles and belting were vitally important. Two years later, when its revenues came to $118 million and earnings were $16 million, Central paid an $8 dividend and the stock peaked at 118.

Central Leather owned large forests and glue works, and at a time when the nation was turning to the automobile and electrification of factories might have switched to chemicals and lumber. It didn't, and while the stock had its moments during the Great Bull Market of the 1920s it was evident that the company was an increasing business risk. Central went belly up in 1926, was taken over by United States Leather, another staunch horse-related firm, which declared bankruptcy in 1932. American Ice, American Locomotive, and American Woolen, all giants in their day, also succumbed to business risks and are no longer with us.

The key to any corporation's long-term prospects is a willingness to engage in what economist Joseph Schumpeter once called "creative destruction," ridding itself of declining operations so as to enter those with better prospects. IBM did it when switching from its highly profitable business in giant calculators to enter the computer field, then dominated by Univac, and there are scores of other examples. Minnesota Mining & Manufacturing prides itself on doing half or more of its business in products that didn't even exist 10 years earlier. Of course there will be failures along the way, but astute investors will ask if the risk made sense and note how the company recovers—a good example here is the way IBM handled its multiple problems with the PCjr. Beware the firm that rarely makes mistakes, has large cash balances and virtually no debt, and a product line that hardly varies year to year. This is as much a business risk as that new drug company seeking a cure for cancer.

Companies always run the risk of some unexpected event clouding its future, and while there is little investors can do about this, they should ever be prepared to act quickly when the news breaks. It could be an especially severe hurricane season that shatters the profits of the casualty companies, the Bhopal tragedy in India which could lead to the diminution of Union Carbide, adverse rulings in asbestos cases that pushed Johns-Manville into a Chapter 11 bankruptcy, or nowadays, the problems the tobacco companies face in suits charging them with having knowingly marketed products causing lung cancer.

There is nothing wrong with taking risks. Indeed, unless you are willing to do so, you don't belong in the market. The trick is to know just how much of it you are willing to assume, and then make certain the potential rewards from any investment are commensurate with the dangers incurred. This sounds simple, but of course it isn't.

3 AN INTRODUCTION TO STOCKS

Anyone sufficiently interested in the investment scene and process to have read this far—or indeed, to have picked up this book in the first place—surely doesn't have to be offered a definition of stocks. But a quick once over about their history wouldn't hurt or occupy much time or space, and it might provide a perspective on securities to help explain why they are viewed as they are today. Also, such understanding may stimulate thought as to whether you belong in stocks and if so, what kinds of brokers should be employed.

To begin with the obvious, both common and preferred stock represents ownership of a corporation. At one time, as late as the mid-nineteenth century, common stock was taken by backers of a new enterprise in exchange for seed capital. The certificate would be issued at par, usually $100, with the owner liable for "calls" up to that amount. Thus the enterprise might require $20 of that sum initially, and payment would be marked on the certificate, the owner knowing that up to $80 more might be demanded. Nowadays par is a meaningless concept, of interest to accountants but few others.

In that period the stockholders expected to retain ownership indefinitely, and in addition manage the firm. Common stockholders might be paid dividends if the board was so inclined, and since the boards of industrial concerns were comprised of majority stockholders, they really were slicing the pie for themselves. Dividends tended to be irregular, draining the surplus. When companies became larger and required regular financings, they drifted toward payouts smaller than the surplus, but declared regularly (usually quarterly) and at an established rate, the understanding that in bad times payments might be cut or eliminated entirely. In essence, the stockholders owned and managed the company, and were the first to place money into the enterprise and the last to be rewarded. The desire to control and manage an ongoing operation, and not the dream of capital gains, motivated ante-bellum stockholders.

Management would borrow money when needed, usually in the form of bonds, sometimes as preferred stock. Owners of the former became the company's creditors, while holders of preferred occupied a sort of middle ground, in that while they were still considered owners they usually couldn't vote for company directors.[1]

REMEMBER PREFERRED STOCK?

A brief discussion of preferred stock should be made at this point —brief, because the subject doesn't call for more than that. As the name indicates, preferred stock enjoys a dividend preference over the common. Holders of preferred stock receive their payment only after all the bondholders are paid their interest. Unlike common shares, these dividends are fixed in the sense that while they can be lowered they cannot *ordinarily* be increased. Several new, unusual kinds of preferred hybrids have appeared in recent

---

[1]Since the post-World War II period there has been a tendency to grant voting rights to preferred stock.

years that have changed the rules somewhat. This should cause little problem for most individual investors, who in all probability will never purchase a share of preferred stock unless it is convertible into common.

At one time it was said that preferred had a nice blend of the qualities of stocks and bonds, and indeed they do—in profitable companies they offer a payout somewhat higher than that of the company's bonds since they are riskier, and they offer a safety of return not available from common issued by the same firm. Nowadays, however, preferred stock is often seen as having the liabilities of both. Unlike bonds, preferred stock is perpetual, in the sense that they have no fixed redemption date (though many issues can be called in at a specific price at the option of the company). And given the many different kinds of bonds outstanding today, with more to come, individual investors who at one time might have found preferred stock to their liking probably would be better off in straight debts. For the most part preferred is appealing only to corporations, which get a special tax deal on dividends.

That is about all most individual investors have to know about preferred stock.

EVOLUTION OF MARKETS

As the small local companies of the early nineteenth century evolved into larger ones, the functions of management and ownership started to separate. It began first with the railroads and then spilled over into the industrials. The individual who organized a company would purchase stock in order to get the enterprise off the ground, and also played a role in its management. These individuals were often succeeded by those who wanted the stock so as to take over the company (Jay Cooke, Jim Fisk, and others of their ilk were every bit as astute as T. Boone Pickens and Carl Icahn when it came to this). Speculators also bought stock in the hope it would advance in price, perhaps through manipulation by the "high rollers," who in those days were sometimes called "Young Napoleons of Wall Street." Wall Street was a place for gamblers and plungers, not investors who merely purchased bonds, placed them in vaults, clipped coupons, and then wagged their heads and clucked their tongues in disapproval when they heard of wheeling and dealing in the district.

At the same time the market system itself changed. Once there were scores of securities markets; virtually every sizable city had one or more. The reason was communications: a resident of Springfield, Massachusetts might use the facilities of the Boston market, while one who lived in Springfield, Illinois looked to Chicago. The coming of the telegraph, combined with express mail services, enabled New York to become the paramount market, and this success was annealed with the arrival of the telephone. By the late nineteenth century the New York Stock Exchange—"The Big Board"—was *the* central market, a place dominated by speculators, rogues, and scoundrels.

A large majority of individuals who owned and traded stocks in the first three decades of the twentieth century continued to be speculators rather than those who today would be considered investors. Wall Street was led by manipulators who organized large pools, among the more notorious of these being Jesse Livermore and Arthur Cutten, who engaged in deals that would land them in jail if attempted today. The others followed in the van, wondering which stocks they would take up or down, and hoping to get in and out so as to go with the "big fellows." These were the ones who lost out during the crash of 1929, a period when bonds—the preferred choice for investors—rose. For example, the Dow Industrials was at 343.45 and the Railroads at 173.78 at the end of September 1929, and wound up at 164.58 and 96.59 at the close of trading on December 31, 1930. In the same period the Dow Bonds advanced from 92.11 to 95.20

Stocks remained vehicles for speculation in the 1930s, which helps explain why volume was so low. In all of 1941 a grand total of 125 million shares was traded, an amount that exchanges handle today in a fairly quiet Big Board session. That year a NYSE seat changed owners at $19,000. During the 1930s even such blue chips as General Motors, Standard Oil of New Jersey, and Pennsylvania Railroad—the last having paid dividends every year since 1848—were deemed chancy when compared to the bonds of these same companies.

In this period there began a change in attitude regarding what those certificates entailed and offered. By then the thought that holding shares somehow meant ownership of a portion of the issuing company had almost completely faded.

Investors (as distinct from speculators) purchased stocks and bonds for two basic reasons: yield and the hope for capital gains. The person who owned a round lot of General Motors and bought a Chevy rather than a Ford because he felt the profits were going back into his pocket was deluding himself. Likewise, the ones who attended annual meetings in order to hear "their" chairman report on what was going on as their company was engaging in a quaint exercise, interesting perhaps and on occasion even informative, but hardly like the shareholders meetings of the 1840s and 1850s, which were more like a gathering of management plus a few locals.[2] This severance of the linkage between ownership and management, observed in a classic study of the time, Adolph Berle and Gardner Means, *The Modern Corporation and Private Property* (New York: Macmillan, 1934), provided a rationale for investors of the post-war period, who would come to replace the gamblers of the 1920s as the bulwark of the stock market. The closer relationship in attitudes regarding stocks and bonds would be picked up by investors in the 1970s, and is one of the key elements of today's markets.

The debt-based mentality continued on during World War II, when in spite of a new prosperity individuals concentrated on liquidating their debts, fattening their savings accounts, and of course purchasing defense and then war bonds.

Stocks continued as speculative vehicles in the early post-World War II period. But when it became increasingly clear that

---

[2]The CEO of one large firm once told me that so long as he was in office there would be no dividend. His rationale? "Why give money to strangers?" The honesty—and accuracy— of the thought was refreshing.

the nation was entering into a new period of prosperity, some interest in them developed, though there were only nibbles at first. In 1950, for example, the average price/earnings ratio for the Dow Industrials was 7.0, the lowest to that time except for 1931–1933, when due to a lack of earnings there was no meaningful figure.[3] The average daily volume that year was less than 2 million shares (it had been close to 3 million in 1930), and the busiest session for 1950 saw 4.8 million shares change hands.

THE REBIRTH OF EQUITIES

There were voices on the Street calling for greater public participation, and the loudest of these belonged to Charles Merrill, CEO of what then was Merrill Lynch, Pierce, Fenner and Beane, who said, "We must draw the new capital required for industrial might and growth *not* from among a few large investors but from the savings of thousands of people of moderate incomes." In 1950 Merrill Lynch, which catered to the needs of such people, had a mere 150,000 accounts, many of which were inactive, but at the time was the largest wire house in the nation. Others echoed the call. Keith Funston, president of NYSE became spokesman for what he called "People's Capitalism" urging individuals to "Buy a Share of America."

Finally, and most importantly, there was the team of General Motors Chairman Charles Wilson and United Auto Workers President Walter Reuther. The 1950 contract signed by these two provided for a pension plan, which in itself hardly was unusual, but did have a novel twist. In place of the accepted notion that funds

---

[3]A definition is in order here. Price/earnings ratio (P/E), is one of the more common measurements utilized in securities analysis. It refers to the ratio of earnings to price. Thus a stock selling for 10 with earnings of $1.00 has a P/E of 10. Let the stock rise to 20 with earnings remaining at $1, and the P/E will rise to 20. The same effect would be had should the earnings fall to $0.50 while the price stays at 20. A rising P/E signifies one of the two. Generally speaking, the higher the P/E, the more richly priced is the stock—or in this case, the Dow Industrials.

be invested in bonds and other safe paper, Wilson proposed and Reuther accepted the principle that a substantial portion of the holdings be in corporate common shares. Wilson wasn't especially prescient and Reuther hadn't any views on stocks worth mentioning; neither realized a major bull market was brewing, and indeed had already gotten underway. Rather, Wilson had been influenced by the writings of management guru Peter Drucker, who had told him this kind of arrangement would "make the employees, within 25 years, the owners of American business." At the time Wilson responded that this was "exactly what they should be, and what they must be. For the income distribution in this country surely means that no one else can own American industry unless it be the government."

In time other plans followed GM's lead. Pension fund assets rose from under $15 billion in 1951 to more than $150 billion two decades later. Initially the bulk of these funds were placed in bonds, since these alone were deemed sufficiently safe for so important a reserve. This attitude changed during the 1950s, and the move toward equities accelerated in the next decade. The proportion of stocks in state and local pension funds went from 3 percent in 1962 to 20 percent in 1987, while in the same period the amounts for noninsured pensions rose from 46 percent to 73 percent and for life insurance reserves, 5 to 12 percent.

The work of individuals like Wilson, Reuther, Funston, and Merrill came at a time when the nation was ripe for investments in equities. A further nudge was provided by a growing army of mutual funds salespeople, who, banging on doors and through the use of blind telephone calls, wheedled thousands of middle class individuals into purchasing shares of high front load funds. The vast majority of the salespeople were more concerned with their commissions, extracted from the first purchases of the planned investment program, than with the well being of clients. As it turned out, however, most of those who had been inveigled into entering the plans did well due to the rising stock market of the period. In 1950 there were fewer than 100 mutual funds in existence, with a total of 939,000 accounts and assets of $2.5 billion;

10 years later there were 161 funds, almost 5 million accounts, whose assets stood at over $17 billion. The individual who was pressured into buying mutual fund shares around 1950 and made a profit, was a candidate for a Merrill Lynch account a few years, even months later. In this way was laid the foundation for individual and institutional participation in the equities markets of the post-war world.

A NYSE-sponsored poll in 1952 indicated that there were some 6.5 million shareholders. A similar poll conducted in 1956 indicated the stockholder population had increased to 8.6 million. One out of every sixteen adults owned shares in 1952; the amount had expanded to one out of twelve in just four years.

Thus began the massive switch from an individual and institutional investor mentality based on savings accounts and bonds to one founded on stocks. The greatest, longest-lived bull market in American history was underway. The price-earnings ratio on the Dow Industrials, which as noted was mired at 7.0 in 1950, peaked at 21.7 in 1961, and in the same period the index rose from a low of 196.81 to a high of 734.91, and would crest at 1051.70 in early 1973 before going into decline. The long-term bull market lasted a generation, and even though stocks entered into a secular decline and debts regained some of their old luster, when someone asks, "How did the market do today?" we know the question refers to stocks, and usually wants to know what the action had been at the NYSE, not the Amex or the OTC market.

The NYSE is located at the southwest corner of Wall and Broad streets just across from the offices of J. P. Morgan & Co. Part of the folklore of the district is that Morgan wanted it there so as to keep an eye on business, but this wasn't the case. Indeed, there is no record that the Great Man ever set foot on the Exchange floor. During his period the NYSE was a place for the second echelon and the second raters, which is to say it was run by those partners at the heavy hitting investment banks who were not deemed sufficiently astute to organize and manage underwritings, help direct corporations, or in some other way function effectively in the business world. The commission brokers were deemed servants of speculators and raiders. They worked through specialists, who "made markets" in stocks and in this period were relatively uninfluential.

The eclipse of the bankers in the 1930s enabled the specialists to become the dominant force at the Big Board. Today specialists are a vestigial remain from the time the NYSE was a true auction market. These are individuals (really consortia) who theoretically stand prepared to buy and sell any amount of stock at any time during trading hours (currently 9:30 A.M. to 4:00 P.M.), and strive to keep it stable, which is to say the next sale will be at or around the price of the previous one. The NYSE monitors the "stabilization ratio" of each specialist with great care, investigating those that are very low, supposedly standing prepared to take away stocks from errant specialists. In practice this is not the case. Even so, should there be some nonmarket reason for violent fluctuations—extremely favorable or unfavorable news regarding the company—the specialist can ask to have trading suspended while he strives to match buy and sell orders and hopes things cool down. Then, after a while, he will resume trading. It isn't unusual for a stock to be suspended at, say, 50, and reopen at 55 or 45. Some might say the specialist did the best as might be expected under the circumstances, others would observe that in calm markets you don't really need the specialists, while in choppy ones they abandon their functions.

Every listed stock has its own specialist, and some have more than one. The specialist system came under attack in the 1970s as being outmoded and inefficient, and there is much to this. In recent years the NYSE has been pushed and pulled into the new investment atmosphere discussed in Chapter 1, and alterations have made it more efficient. Still, the rise of institutions and block trading have made it more a place where deals are made elsewhere and brought ot the floor afterwards than the central market it once was.

The small investor may still entertain the notion of how a trade is executed the NYSE likes to promulgate. A person in one part of the country wants to buy 100 shares of AT&T, and a person at the other end would like to sell his holding. The NYSE is the instrument that brings them together. In point of fact, the seller would call his broker and the stock would be purchased from the specialist—electronically, for that is the way such small trades are handled at the NYSE. And the buyer would do the same. Such would be the case with *any* broker, be he at a full scale house like Merrill Lynch or Prudential-Bache, or the smallest discount operation, charging a fraction of their commissions.

This is about all the average investor needs to know about the market structure. One can function very well on the investment scene with even less knowledge. After all, you don't have to know very much about the whys and wherefores of electronics to punch out a letter on a word processor, or the workings of the internal combustion engine to drive a car.

If you can get to it without too much difficulty, you might want to spend an hour or so in the NYSE Visitor's Gallery. Walking past displays and a small theater, you can go to the platform that overlooks the trading floor, pick up a device and listen to a recorded voice explain just what is happening there. It isn't very exciting; you'll see clusters of grubby-looking individuals milling around, chatting, or simply standing alone, perhaps staring at you. Individuals who arrive at the NYSE believing they are there to view the mighty engine of American finance chugging away invariably come away disappointed. So do go if this kind of thing interests you. Otherwise you can confine your contacts to the telephone.

WHAT ABOUT BROKERS?

The care and feeding of a stock broker is another matter. The stress here is on the word *stock*. While several major wire houses pride themselves on being "full service brokers," and in the past most investors got by well with the use of a single person, it might be wiser today to have several brokers, specifically two for stocks, one for bonds, and a fourth or fifth for other kinds of investments. There are some who do well by having only one, However, most serious investors should have at least two.

To place this in perspective, consider the situation in the early 1970s. At that time the three most important attributes large houses looked for in trainee applicants were the ability to generate a customer base, a sense of humor and glibness, the knack for using a telephone smoothly, and the ability to read and digest reports put out by the research department and translate them for clients. If they had the first, the others might be ignored. The broker had to have an instinct for customer psychology and a way with people—not necessarily the market. The conventional wisdom of the period was that the best background for a stock broker wasn't a Harvard MBA but rather two or three years in door-to-door sales.

Most full-service brokers then were amiable enough individuals who had gone through poorly thought out training programs and afterwards operated in a sheltered environment. They were prepared to talk about stocks, and some of the more energetic and imaginative ones relied not only on their research staffs but made a conscientious effort to obtain additional information when needed. The best of the lot possessed a feel for the market and the movement of the tape they would share with customers. A brokerage resembled a factory, where the researchers churned out product that was sold by the brokers. To a large degree, it remains so to this day.

Competition was keen; everyone knew all brokerages charged the same commissions, and so customers might be lured from one house to another by what was felt to be superior research and executions. As previously noted, this has changed, and those brokers who survived changed along with the times.

Today a good broker should know a great deal about alternate investments and be prepared to steer clients into them when the markets dictate. He should be able to function as a guide through the investment thicket. Which is to suggest that a broker who is knowledgeable in stocks but knows next to nothing of the consequences regarding debt instruments, options, and real estate syndications, and has few insights regarding precious metals and commodities, really doesn't belong at his desk in a full-service operation.

This may be rejected by investors who have little or no use for full-service brokers. It is easy to be negative about them, to conclude that they aren't worth their commissions. This attitude results from their low level of preparation in past years, a case of perception lagging reality. The profession is still trying to upgrade its image, with some success. In 1973, when embarrassed by a broker's exam only slightly more difficult to pass than the written test to receive a driver's license, the industry toughened standards and wrote a new qualifying exam. This test— conceived prior to the massive changes that took place after 1975— was still being administered to new brokers in 1986. The entire panoply of new products was not covered. When it was learned that a new exam embodying the latest changes would be administered starting June 1, hundreds of trainees lined up to take the old, presumably simpler test. But anyone able to get through the rigorous training programs at the major houses would have had little difficulty with either exam.

Those entering the brokerage business this year will have much better credentials than their predecessors, if only because they have to know more to get by. Few of today's newcomers are there because of familial pull or winning ways on the telephone. What this means is that the older brokers tend to be survivors; those who managed to hold on during the whipsaw, rapidly changing markets of the 1970s have really gone through the fire. The younger ones are no longer the mixed bag they used to be. So the good news is that simply by walking through the door of any reputable house and asking to open an account more than likely will put clients into contact with a reasonably competent individual.

Assume you are interested in locating a proper broker, and lack recommendations from friends or a nephew in the business. Then go to several brokerages, ask to be assigned one, then make an appointment to talk things over. You shouldn't expect it to be that day, or during a time when the markets are open, but a half hour or so before or after trading hours should suit fine. Before arriving you might compile a list of assets and liabilities and family income. It would be sensible to consider investment objectives, the priorities assigned to safety and income, and just how much risk can be afforded. Then you should lay it all out before the broker and ask for recommendations.

Here are a few hints for those who feel they are in this category. Be wary if the broker is not on load mutual funds or packaged tax shelters, since there is no earthly reason to buy almost any load fund and brokers get whopping commissions for selling many of their company's products. Watch out for individuals who cannot explain themselves without resorting to jargon. Look for signs of professionalism.

Ask yourself if you are comfortable with him, all the while making the distinction between trusting and liking the individual. Brokers may be compared to doctors in this regard. Just because a doctor has a soothing bedside manner doesn't mean you would use him for brain surgery. The best in that field may be a lout, but he's the person you would want to employ. Likewise, some brokers who are excellent at their work are miserable characters. If you come across one of these, use him. Likewise, should you find yourself stuck with a delightful loser, get rid of him. The broker is supposed to earn his commissions by making you more money than you might on your own. This is the only gauge of worth.

Having said this, there are brokers who are both good pickers and timers and decent enough individuals; perhaps you can find one. There used to be a litmus test used by successful investors: if you can imagine the broker working as a hot-shot on a used car lot, head for the door.

Take notes on suggestions, and when you have sufficient information, offer thanks and leave. Return home and think about it. Did the advice make sense? Expect telephone calls and possibly entreaties, but don't act on them for a while—don't let yourself be rushed. Instead, visit several other brokers, and in the end, open an account at the one with whom you feel most comfortable and whose outlook reflects both your own inclinations and common sense.

If this seems like a lot of trouble, compare it with the agonies of purchasing an automobile. Reflect that if you have a good relationship with the broker, who outperforms the market, you may be buying and selling a far greater volume of business there than the price of that car.

Suppose you called your broker and discuss the merits of purchasing 400 shares of General Electric, and all you got was generalities and a few items from *The Wall Street Journal*, or a mention of what his "gut feeling" was regarding the stock? Was that worth the commission? Probably not.

There aren't many of these around today; the pre-Mayday brokers either shaped up or shipped out. Go to an astute full-service broker today with the thought of purchasing 400 shares of GE and you may hear some thoughts regarding alternate investments and far better information than you managed to garner from an astute research staff. Through the broker's hookup with data bases (unavailable in 1975) you will get all sorts of updates and pertinent information.

Look for brokers who will go out of their way to get reports on stocks that interest you, will keep an eye on your portfolio and warn you if any bad news comes over the wire about one of your holdings. Don't expect daily calls, but you should get some of these services for giving the broker your business. As for research advice, in the wake of Mayday most of the big houses have boosted their publications staffs and send clients regular mailings. Merrill Lynch, Prudential-Bache, and a few others have put together what have to be considered investment magazines, and these alone could be sufficient reason to have an active account with a full-service house. On top of all this, a regular customer can expect a modest discount, say 10 to 20 percent, from posted commissions.

Such brokers are worth the extra money. Take it a step further: novice investors and those who don't follow markets with any regularity, or simply don't trust their knowledge or instincts, would be well advised to use a full-service broker.

Many customers nowadays are willing to accept inferior research or forgo it entirely in exchange for a 50 percent or better discount on commissions. Employing discounters to the exclusion of other brokers may make sense for those primarily concerned with stocks—a group comprised of novices on the one extreme and highly sophisticated investors on the other.

The former have little awareness of the many alterations of the investment scene resulting from the appearance of a bewildering variety of products, and can't be helped unless and until they recognize the need to obtain information. The latter know just what they want, and don't need the services of individuals who may be less qualified than they are to make investment decisions. For both of them the order takers at the discount houses provide all that is needed. Do you want to buy 100 shares of IBM and think you possess all the information necessary about the market and stock? The discounter is for you. Do you want to write a straddle on GE? Get thee to a discounter. Are you interested in finding a way to invest $15,000? Perhaps a talk with a full-service broker would be best.

Should *you* use the services of a discount broker? It made sense for many in the second half of the 1970s, and may even be the way to go today, depending on what you expect from such a person. If you do, use the least expensive one that can be found, realizing that this changes constantly. The best way to locate one would be to scan *The Wall Street Journal, Barron's,* and other financial papers for their advertisements, call the 800 numbers provided, or if there are none, place a collect call, and ask to be mailed their commission schedules. Compare them and pick out the one charging the least. This may be trickier than it sounds, for most use formulas, have minimum charges, and alterations in fees are fairly common. One discounter may have the best rates for stocks over $40, another for blocks, a third for options, and so on. So you should go to the one with the lowest rates for the kind of trading you do most of the time.

In your application indicate a desire to take delivery of the certificates, this because if you do leave for a less expensive house later on, there won't be any complications or time lost. In fact investors may want to open accounts at several discounters to ease such switches.

Suppose you receive a really hot tip from a reputable source—this happens two or three times in the life of many investors, assuming they live to a ripe old age. There may be no reason to go to a full-service broker on this one; a discounter will do fine. So have two accounts, one at the discounter, the other at the full service house, and use them appropriately.

One final thought, this regarding investing ethics. There are some investors who solicit recommendations or try out ideas on full-service brokers, obtain information, and then give the trade to the discounter. But of course there also are shoplifters and other cheats, and I suppose there's nothing to be done about it.

4 STOCK MARKET PERSPECTIVES: THE GRAND STRATEGIES

The curtain opens for Act II of *Iolanthe* with the sentry, Private Gilbert, musing aloud about the nature of things. W.S. Gilbert has him observe that:

I often think it's comical -Fal, lal, la!
How Nature always does contrive —Fal, lal, la!
That every boy and every gal
That's born into the world alive
Is either a little Liberal
Or else a little Conservative!
Fal, lal, la!

Each of us has an essential character, Gilbert was saying, which puts him or her into one or the other category, always allowing for subtleties and complexities, variations on the theme.

In the same vein, almost all analysts and investors are essentially either fundamentalists or technicians, as are even novices

69

who don't know the meaning of the terms when applied to securities analysis. To complicate matters there is a third group as well, known as the random walkers, who deny the efficacy of all forms of analysis, and are the investment equivalents of agnostics. However, when pressed random walkers reveal themselves to lean in one direction or another, with most of them closet fundamentalists.

First a word or two about security analysts in general, those individuals whose reports are gobbled by institutions and individual investors alike. Who are they? According to a study done by the Financial Analysts Federation, approximately a third of all analysts are between the ages of 40 and 49, 7 out of 8 are male, more than half have graduate degrees (usually the MBA), and a quarter of them earn more than $100,000 a year.

In the aftermath of Mayday they have become far more active than had previously been the case. Time was when the typical analyst was squirreled away in the back office, content with his charts and telephone, venturing into the world only to visit companies he followed, where he spoke only with managements, and then returned to his desk to write advisories to be sent to clients.

All of this has changed, especially for the superstars. Now he (and increasingly, she) is available to shareholders (not the small ones, to be sure, but the institutions), and has taken on some of the aspects of brokers. Some have become spokespersons for their brokerages, quoted regularly in the financial press and appearing on talk shows. "Analysts who couldn't sell were driven out of the business," observed Robert Errigo, who heads Merrill Lynch's team of more than 100 analysts, and knows whereof he speaks. This implies that analysts have to devote more time to currying favor than picking stocks. "Try to be right," said one of them, "but if you can't be right, be *there*." Meaning that accessibility is the key to a career on Wall Street, be one a fundamentalist or technically oriented. "The Street is not geared to provide value," conceded Warren Shaw, director of research at Citicorp. "It has more to do with serving the client base, making a certain number of calls per day, getting on *The Institutional Investor* all-star list, all of which has nothing to do with picking good stocks."[1]

One starts out with this foundation, aware all the while that alterations in the markets and personnel have posed grave challenges to technicians and fundamentalists alike, placing both on the defensive, while those investment agnostics haven't provided a meaningful alternative. Simply stated, the old rules don't apply as they once seemed to, and nothing has appeared to take their places.

FUNDAMENTALISM

Fundamentalists, as the term suggests, like to think they are involved with the basic building blocks of stock analysis. They start out with an exploration of the economy. Are we headed toward a period of growth of recession, inflation or recession, higher or lower interest rates? What is the outlook for fiscal and monetary policy, foreign trade, commodity prices? When all of these and other questions are answered the fundamentalists turns to individual industries. Given this outlook, what might be expected to happen with steel? Computers? Drugs? Retailers? Utilities? Autos? And so on down the line, the object being to locate those industries with better than average prospects for the coming year or so. This done, the fundamentalist investigates companies. After a while he may alight on several that appear headed for better things, *which are not yet reflected in its price.*

He might uncover a "special situation," a stock that looks like a bargain on its own merits, and not necessarily because of the economy or industry. Once these were found by stumbling across

---

[1]*The Institutional Investor*, the closest the Street has to a house organ, compiles annual lists of analysts who in the view of their large clients do the best job. Placement on the first or second team is one key to higher status and income, and the major houses vie with one another to get as many of their people on the list as possible, since this is a major selling point when seeking new business.

a little followed stock or getting a tip from a source. Nowadays these often appear by use of "computer screens." In the data bank is a universe of facts about large numbers of companies. The fundamentalist asks the computer to draw up a list of stocks with certain characteristics—say, selling for P/E ratio of under 10, offering a yield of 6 percent, with earnings growth of 15 percent a year or more, and in the retailing industry. The machine churns out the list, the analyst looks it over, and then might find a particular nugget to recommend.

At this point the fundamentalist may take a position, which will be liquidated when the price reaches what appears to be a reasonable level. On March 29, 1986, *The Economist* offered as good a statement of fundamentalist methodology as might be found:

> First, make your own guesses about the future, whether for the whole economy or a single company: oil prices, interest rates, wages, technology, East-West politics, Ronald Reagan's health— anything that might affect share prices. Then compare your views with those of other people. If you are more optimistic than the consensus, buy and keep buying until the gap closes; if not, sell.

This is the crux of the matter. The fundamentalist believes there are such things as "undervalued situations," and that he is more astute than "the market." Suppose the analyst locates a stock selling for 30, which present values and future prospects indicate should be selling for around 40? The buy might be made. What if the company and industry position remained unchanged and the stock declined to 25? It would be an even bigger bargain, and more shares would be purchased. In fact the fundamentalist would continue buying on the way down until either his perception of the company, industry, or economic prospects are altered or the stock rises to where he thinks it should be. Benjamin Graham, with whom we will shortly be spending a few pages, wrote:

> For 99 issues out of 100 we could say that at some price they are cheap enough to buy and at some other price they would be so

dear that they should be sold. The habit of relating what is paid to what is being offered is an invaluable trait in investment.

Finally, fundamentalists are keenly aware of rewards from alternate investments, particularly bonds and other instruments tied closely to the interest rates; some technicians take account of rates, but most give them short shrift.

Out of all this flows a stream of recommendations, and since investors prefer advice on what to buy rather than what to sell, most of the advisories are based on overly optimistic assessments of results. Zachs Investment Research, which monitors over 1500 analysts and 3000 companies, regularly informs its readers of this fact. "They're constantly revising downward. They're in the game to sell stocks. They're too bullish." This is the conclusion of Ben Zachs, the firm's executive vice president. Other surveys indicate that analysts tend to be better at short run predictions, say quarter-to-quarter, than those over the longer term. "Most analysts don't even have quote machines on their desks," observed Maryann Keller, a money manager for Vilas-Fisher. "You operate in a vacuum. Very often analysts would make recommendations having no idea of what the market will do. Very often anlaysts would be as obtuse as anything you can imagine."

Keller is referring here to fundamentalist behavior. It so happens that she is one of them. Earlier in her career she followed the auto stocks for Paine, Webber. "I knew all about multiple-valve engines and discus couplings. Analysts are repositories of every bit of information that can be relevant to the investment."

THE TECHNICIAN

Not so the technician, who starts out with an entirely different point of view. He cares little for the economy or even the stocks themselves; as one of them once said, "They could be called oranges, apes, or kangaroos instead of GE, Westinghouse, or Consolidated Edison. All I care about is the price action."

The technician starts out with a belief that the action of the market is determined solely by forces of supply and demand, these determined by rational and irrational forces that cannot be fully comprehended, but can be traced. Moreover, they move in patterns; the technician believes that the development of most phenomena runs in cycles. The nuts and bolts of technical analysis will be discussed in the following chapter, but it should be noted here that technicians tend to believe the market sends out a message, which if properly deciphered can be used to predict the future course of prices. For them the market is always right, prices at any given moment are always where they should be, and the economy is irrelevant.

Several years ago, when technician Joe Granville was riding high, Wall Street apparently hanging on his every utterance, I appeared with him on a panel, and asked why the market moved as it did. He replied that everything was volume and price, and could be seen on the tape if one would only look. But what caused volume? Why did investors behave as they did? Granville didn't get the point of the questions. Who cares? Just look at the tape and read its message. I persisted, and then, with a glint of either malice or condescension in his eye, he asked what kind of a car I drove. It was a six-year-old Plymouth. Did I know anything about cars? Yes, I replied, and tinkering with them was always interesting. Granville then gestured to the window, outside of which was parked a Rolls-Royce. "That's mine. All I know about it is how to drive and when to put in gas. You'll probably tell me that's not enough, that I should learn about engines. But why? I know all that is needed. But now tell me this: how come if you know all about markets you are driving a beat-up Plymouth, and I have the Rolls?"

The audience roared. Granville had a point, and every technician will recognize it. Orange, apes, or kangaroos. Who cares? Just chart the action and look for patterns.

Some years later, after a series of very bad calls, a battered Joe Granville appeared on a television program, offering his latest forecast. He spoke of gross national product, profits, international trade, the deficit—sounding very much like a fundamentalist. This is common. When technicians fail, they turn to fundamentalist approaches. Likewise, when fundamentalists are off track, they speak of market volume, short positions, resistance levels—like a technician.

While both fundamentalist and technician are interested in current knowledge regarding the past, the former do so in the belief that such knowledge can form the foundation on which to understand the company's position, while the latter cares only about the distilled statistics which are fed into his brain or computer to churn out the advisory.

Which are you, fundamentalist or technician? Be warned that the reply often is more the residue of personality than intellect.

Though it is always dangerous to generalize, fundamentalists tend to be empiricists; to them the gross national product is a suspect concept; they prefer to study corporate profit and loss statements and take these apart minutely. As might be imagined, fundamentalists are much more comfortable discussing individual stocks than the market as a whole. Fundamentalists may seem to be dull, plodding souls, who latch on to a stock, often fall in love with it, and won't budge until overwhelmed by evidence. They can swamp you with facts, but under it all is a passion as burning as that of any technician for evidence they are right in their assessment of individual stocks or the direction of the market.

Veteran fundamentalists learn to allow for this flaw. One of the best of them from another generation, Gerald Loeb, often conceded that he was thoroughly unreasonable when it came to analyzing Chrysler. Loeb loved the company and its products, to the point where he wheedled invitations to test drive new models. That fellow who believes IBM can do no wrong may be right—but he is a committed fan as well, whose analysis has to be listened to with care. The same goes for that woman who is convinced Apple will dominate the micro market, to whom the stock is always a buy.

Technicians, in contrast, often have mercurial temperaments and are quasiscientific in approach and vocabulary. They are unwilling to sit by and await the main chance, flitting in and out of stocks, never developing the kind of loyalties that mark the fundamentalist. It used to be said that women enjoyed dating technicians—more fun, more imaginative, more impulsive—but wanted to marry successful fundamentalists.

Generally speaking, technicians are in vogue during bull markets, when investors want to believe stocks can soar out of sight and self-fulfilling prophecy is the rule, while fundamentalists develop followings during bear interludes, when their search for undervalued situations can more easily be satisfied. Being a fundamentalist might have taken you out of the market in 1929, 1969, and 1971, before stocks declined sharply, but you would have been on the sidelines in the early 1960s and through most of the bull interludes of the 1970s and 1980s as well.

Even the best of them can blunder. Ben Graham gave out a strong recommendation for bonds in 1972, just in time for one of the worst bear interludes for that market. The reason: bonds were about to enter into a period unlike any other in American history. On the other hand, John Templeton, one of the most successful fundamentalists, tells of buying $100 worth of every stock selling for below a dollar on the Big Board and Curb Exchange in 1939, when the market was depressed. He amassed a pile of stock in 104 companies, of which 34 were bankrupt, at a cost of approximately $10,000. The shares were held for around four years, and Templeton got more than $40,000 for them.

BEN GRAHAM

Each camp has its own collection of gurus, but appropriately, two champions tower over the others. As noted, Graham is generally considered the dominant figure in fundamental analysis, while Charles Dow occupies the same position in the technical pantheon. A good deal of subsequent work has been a commentary and elaboration on their basic insights. While most investors need not know how to apply their techniques—there are dozens of professionals who will do that for you, at little more than the cost of a magazine or newspaper or time to watch a television program —all should have a nodding acquaintance with the methodologies and assumptions underlying them.

Graham arrived in America from England in 1895 at the age of one. His father represented the family firm of Grossbaum & Co., and the name was changed to Graham during World War I to counter anti-German sentiments. Ben graduated from Columbia, where he majored in classical languages and mathematics, in 1914, on which he took a job as messenger at the brokerage firm of Newberger, Henderson & Loeb, where he soon was writing reports on firms and making recommendations. He was good at it, and became a partner in 1920.

Always a person of broad interests with a zest for life, Graham remained as comfortable with the classics and mathematics as with stocks and bonds. And with women. He married three times, after which he lived with a French mistress who had served in the same capacity for one of his sons.

In 1926 Graham formed an investment pool known as the Benjamin Graham Joint Account, managing it with an associate, Jerome Newman. He reaped large profits in the waning months of the bull market, only to be almost wiped out during the 1929–1930 crash. During this period Graham taught a course at Columbia, where he met David Dodd, who was one of his first students and later became a professor at the business school. They wrote their book in 1933 and it appeared the following year, at just the right time. The market crash was over, and a substantial recovery had taken place, which attracted some brave souls to the securities market. Many of these remained only for the rally, and then withdrew to the sidelines. For 1934 as a whole 324 million shares were traded, the lowest in a decade, and the outlook was rather bleak. Graham wasn't preaching to investors or those thinking of entering the market. Rather, together with Dodd he produced a textbook used in business schools by the few students who continued to follow the subject. Interest in the market grew during the next few years, and in this period Graham's message was sent abroad.

It would be nice if one could recommend a careful examination of Graham's classic *Security Analysis*, (New York: McGraw-Hill, 1934) the first edition of which was written with Dodd. Unfortunately, it is a monumentally dull book, compared to which the Seattle telephone directory makes scintillating reading. There is an overly long section—almost 200 pages—on accounting procedures that was and is fascinating to practitioners but which others would find devastating. A good deal of the Graham/Dodd method involves more than a passing knowledge of accounting, since it is grounded in an analysis of the firm's financial position. Graham also coauthored (with Charles McGolrick) another work entitled *The Interpretation of Financial Statements*, deemed a classic in its field. Some accountants are able to infuse their writings on the subject with zest and humor; not these two. On the other hand, Graham's slim volume, *The Intelligent Investor* (New York: Harper & Row, 1965), is accessible, and might be read profitably by any investor, even the newcomers.

Simply stated, Graham preached a super-conservative fundamentalist investment approach. In the preface he wrote of his decision to place "much emphasis . . . upon distinguishing the investment from the speculative approach, upon setting up sound and workable tests of safety, and upon an understanding of the rights and true interests of investors in senior securities and owners of common stocks." In another place he said: "An investment operation is one which, upon thorough analysis, promises safety of principal and an adequate return. Operations not meeting these requirements are speculative."

These were the kinds of words battered investors wanted to read, and those who ventured into *Security Analysis* found much there that fitted with the new conservatism in the market place. Yet Graham was also saying that common stocks could be considered investments, a somewhat daring viewpoint at that time, when other respected analysts were asserting that only bonds, and high grade ones at that, could be bought and held for investment purposes.[2]

Along with all fundamentalists, Graham ever was on the prowl for undervalued situations, this happy circumstance identifiable by statistical means. He looked for a high return on invested capital, a key figure he derived by dividing after tax profit by net worth. This could not be viewed in a vacuum, but rather the figures for the company under investigation had to be compared with others in the industry group. For firms in high growth industries the ratios might be as high as 20 to 30 percent, for average companies the 10 percent figure might be the "norm," while in high turnover low profit margin businesses lower than that might be acceptable.

What Graham looked for was not so much a high level in any given year, but rather stability and moderate growth compared to others in the industry, and a tendency to the upside, combined with a P/E ratio not appreciably higher than similar companies.

Graham was intensely concerned with the corporation's financial strength, not surprising considering the time during which he wrote and the proclivities of his audience. The ratio of current assets to current liabilities was most important; he was loath to consider recommending the purchase of shares in firms with current ratio of less than 2/1, although this varied from industry to industry and even company to company. Graham was wary of companies with a high ratio of debt to equity; the general rule here was that common shares should represent more than half the firm's capitalization.

Graham was well known for his penchant for preferring stocks selling substantially below their net asset (or book) value, or to put it in a more modern fashion, those worth more dead than

---

[2]In *The Intelligent Investor* Graham put it this way: "The most realistic distinction between the investor and the speculator is found in their attitude toward stock market movements. The speculator's primary interest lies in acquiring and holding suitable securities at suitable prices. Market movements are important to him in a practical sense, because they alternately create low price levels at which he would be wise to buy and high price levels at which he certainly should refrain from buying and probably would be wise to sell."

alive. The well-known raiders of our time—Ivan Boesky, Carl Icahn, and T. Boone Pickens among others—won fame and wealth by applying this principal, and their efforts in doing so in 1984–1985 should have alerted astute investors that stocks were undervalued. Of course this was complicated by the way corporations keep their books. The raiders know that excess "good will" can inflate assets, while companies that have written down producing assets to zero (as Disney does with much of its film library) are understating their book values. But for old-line industrials it works pretty well. By and large investors should consider book value, but as Graham observed, changes in book value over time are a better indication of value than simply a larger book value than current stock price.

Graham offered little advice regarding timing, an area which attracted a great deal of interest from technicians, and this often is cited as one of his weaknesses. Not necessarily, since he does make the point that one should buy stocks when they are deemed undervalued and sell when they no longer can be so categorized. Technicians like to follow trends, selling stocks when their prices fall below certain levels and purchasing them on breakouts to the upside. Graham took the opposite approach. "Never buy a stock immediately after a substantial rise or sell one immediately after a substantial drop," he wrote. Oftentimes technicians sell to fundamentalists and vice versa.

Having established this foundation, Graham next turned to the practical matter of stock selection, and here he departed from the concrete, empirical realm and necessarily entered that of conjecture. Graham suggested that investors take into account expected future earnings and dividends, and not pay more than a specific amount—which varied according to editions of the book. However, they were always related to yields available from alternate investments, bonds in particular. Just as consistently, Graham urged investors to adopt a long-term perspective, and not to overreact to short-term developments and market fluctuations, this the hallmark of the fundamentalist.

As is caution. In *The Intelligent Investor* Graham urged readers to assemble a portfolio with four criteria in mind: (1) adequate diversification; (2) for the most part concentrate on stocks of large, prominent companies; (3) stocks with long-time records of paying dividends; and (4) stocks with low P/E ratios. All of which is fine for a bear market, or for investors desiring to preserve their capital.

What about bull markets, when stocks soar and euphoria reigns? Should one ever plunge into stocks that pay no dividends with no immediate prospect to do so, or that pay small dividends in relation to earnings or the price of the stock? Or those that sport high P/E ratios? It can easily be seen that Graham's approach wouldn't do well during the great upwards sweeps the market occasionally experiences, when fundamentalists believe prices are too high, sell, and then watch in dismay as they hit new highs. Graham particularly avoided new issues, observing that when these are in vogue it is a sign the speculative mania has taken hold, and prudent investors should leave the market. In writing of growth stocks, Graham stated, "Obviously stocks of this kind are attractive to buy and to own, *provided the price paid is not excessive*" (emphasis added). The problem lies in just that, of course, since growth stocks have long sold at high prices in relation to current earnings and at much higher multiples of their average profits over a past period. Graham generally shied from the growth field. In *Security Analysis* he and Dodd wrote, "We are haunted as it were by the spectre of growth stocks—by the question of how best to deal with them in the context of our own basic principles."

This isn't to say fundamentalism should be abandoned during bull markets, but rather that its practitioners are constantly seeking to buy low and sell high. So do us all, you might suppose, but think again. If the stock is low, it must be for a reason. Perhaps *then* is the time to sell. And it follows that if a stock is rising rapidly, its price way out of line with what you can see in the balance sheet and profit and loss statement, there must be something happening to push it there, and perhaps it will continue along the same road, which would suggest a buy. Market bottoms and tops are visible only in retrospect; it often makes sense to sell when a stock is falling and buy when it is rising. Does this sound reasonable? If so, you may have the soul of a technician, because that is the way they think.

Modern technicians speak in a jargon, using such terms as oscillators, head-and-shoulders formations, triple tops, advance-decline ratios, and so on, while the vocabulary of fundamentalists contains such comparatively mundane terms as P/E ratios, earnings, profit-and-loss, dividends, interest rates, assets-to-liabilities ratios, and the like. Fundamentalists deal with what they would consider empirical evidence, and so do technicians, but to them the market tells a story of its own, and they seek to translate it into English, but more important, buy and sell orders.

CHARLES DOW

As noted, the father of technical analysis is Charles Dow, also the founder of the Dow Jones & Co., the famous financial publisher best known for two of the nation's most respected newspapers, *The Wall Street Journal* and *Barron's*, and whose stock usually sells at a P/E multiple that appropriately would discourage fundamentalists from considering it. Dow might be as puzzled by those who today claim to be his acolytes as the Wright brothers would be by modern jet passenger planes, for his message was relatively simple, and had more of a relationship with fundamentalism than do the systems of many technicians who followed.

Dow appeared on Wall Street in 1880 as a financial writer and editorialist for the *New York Mail and Express* and the Kiernan News Agency. Almost 30 years old, he had put in time at several Rhode Island newspapers and more recently, he had reported on activities in the wild silver mining areas surrounding Leadville, Colorado. This was a period when investors purchased and held bonds, when gamblers haunted gaming operations, many of them shady, known as "bucket shops," and sudden activity in an issue didn't signify better prospects for the company, but rather that a manipulation was under way. All of this fascinated Dow, who while a quiet and self-effacing individual was quickly caught up in the action.

After two years, Dow decided to venture forth on his own, and joined with another Kiernan employee, Edward Jones, to form Dow Jones & Co., with offices at 15 Wall Street. Functioning as reporters and editorialists, the two men put out *The Customer's Afternoon Letter* which contained closing prices, financial news, and rumors floating around the district. Seven years later this letter was transformed into *The Wall Street Journal.*

As has been noted the investment community was rather small in this period and interest in markets confined to a relatively few individuals. Dow knew his letter wouldn't provide him with much of a sustenance, so he became a partner in a brokerage, Goodbody, Glynn & Dow, which gave him additional insights into the markets, all of which were translated into *Journal* editorials.

Dow offered little hope to those who thought they could beat the market. The professionals are in charge, he wrote, and how could amateurs hope to win in contests against them? Brokers could offer little by way of worthwhile advice. Any of them who claimed special competence was a fool, a fraud, or worse, "because if he could, he would surely trade for himself and would scorn working for ⅛ commission when he could just as well have the whole amount."

What of those brokers who claimed to have inside information regarding speculative pools, and were willing to let their customers in on sure things? Dow scoffed at the idea. "Speculation is not at its best a simple and easy road to wealth, but speculation through people who advertise guaranteed profits and who call for participation in blind pools is as certain a method of losing as could possibly be discovered."

Given this, why should anyone even attempt to speculate or invest in stocks? Said Dow, because there is a rhythm to the market's movements, and even those of individual stocks, which if perceived at least could give the investor a fighting change. Dow wrote of this occasionally in his editorials, and gathered together they form the basis of the Dow Theory, the most famous and lasting technical methodology in history, and the foundation for most others.

In 1899 Dow wrote that there were three basic movements in the stock market. "The first is the narrow movement from day to day, the second is the short swing, running from two weeks to a month or more; the third is the main movement covering at least four years in duration." Daily action reflects activities of speculators and traders, based more on hunches than anything else, while the second derives from the machinations of large pools. The third results from economic forces beyond the control of any individual or group. "Reports from all directions are that business is active, labor is well employed, and businessmen are making money" cause a large scale bull market, while bear markets result from the opposite news." The individual investor cannot hope to make out well by concentrating on the first two movements, because the cards are stacked against him there, but the third is another matter.

Market movements are affected by three forces—sentiment, manipulation, and facts. Of these sentiment, the basis of the third movement, is the most powerful. "When it is widespread [it] will defeat the strongest speculative combinations which may be working against it." Manipulation may move stocks for a few days or even weeks, and new facts are continually being pumped into the system. Sentiment tends to be longer lasting, withstanding factual barrages and even manipulations. When Dow wrote of sentiment he seemed to be thinking of those fundamentalists who find it difficult to accept bad news about a stock with which they were enamored. It takes a lot to transform a bull into a bear, or vice versa.

Dow went on to write that "there is a pronounced difference between bull markets that are made by manipulation and those that are made by the public. The former represent the effort of a small number of persons; the latter reflect the sense of the country on values." Speculators and pool managers may influence price movements for a day or even a week or so, but no longer. "The sentiment that endures and sweeps away the strongest interests which oppose it is invariably founded upon general conditions that are sufficiently universal and sufficiently potent to affect the opinions of practically everybody." Quoting tycoon William Vanderbilt, Dow noted that "everybody is stronger than anybody." This he considered the primary trend.

Such is the link between Dow's version of technical analysis and fundamentalism. The third movement on which he concentrates is the result of the development of the economy reflected in buy and sell orders at the NYSE and other markets. Generally speaking, those involved in speculation and investment are more sensitive to economic activities than most others, since they make their livings from the correct interpretation of what is happening. If they can look ahead and see a robust economy they will buy, with selling taking place in anticipation of a slump. Their beliefs, translated into action, cause prices to rise or fall, usually in advance of the actual economic developments. Thus Dow's famous statement that the relationship of the market to the economy was that of a barometer, not a thermometer.

Dow compared the third movement, or primary trend, with the tide, which may be due to his lifelong love of the sea. Go to the shore at any given moment and watch the waves lapping the beach. Is the tide coming in or going out? One cannot say by watching the terminal point of the first few waves. But after a while it becomes apparent. While each wave may not reach as far as the preceding one, an irregular pattern appears. The individual waves were the actions of the first two movements, but taken in the aggregate one gets the picture of the way the tide is going. Translated into investment terms, one should buy into bull markets and sell into bear markets.

The need for a way to measure the movements led Dow to create an index, which first appeared in the July 3, 1894 issue of *The Customer's Afternoon Letter* and followed irregularly for the next few years. This original Dow Jones Index was comprised of 12 stocks, 10 of them railroads, 2 industrials, which were used to measure the movement of the general market. Two years later Dow improved on the indexes and refined his theory. Now his readers had an industrial and railroad index, and Dow wrote that a third movement cannot be said to have begun until both of them went into new high or low ground. Other refinements followed, and by the turn of the century all of the essentials were in place.

Dow never claimed to have created a magical method for investing. "The first thing that is necessary to note is that in dealing with the stock market there is no way of telling when the top of an advance or the bottom of a decline has been reached until some time after such top or bottom has been made." Dow wrote this in May 1902. He died seven months later, at the age of 52.

Dow wan't the first person to come up with the rudiments of technical analysis; others had constructed indexes, for example. He reached a wider audience, however, and attracted followers who carried on his work. The most important of these was William Peter Hamilton, who became editor of the *Journal* in 1908, and who refined and publicized the theory to the point where it might be called the Gospel According to William. Under Hamilton the *Journal* prospered and grew, both in size and importance. The great bull market of the 1920s helped, of course, with Hamilton becoming a respected and well-regarded forecaster of primary trends. But manipulation and concern with the first two movements prevailed during that decade. Hamilton monitored the action, and on October 25, 1929, came out with his most famous editorial, entitled "A Turn of the Tide," in which he noted that according to the Dow (by then really the Dow-Hamilton) Theory, the market had signaled a reversal to the bear side.

Some Dowists claim that this call vindicated the theory, but such is not so. Hamilton had also called a bear turn in 1926, after which the market tripled. As noted, Dow disclaimed prescience, as did Hamilton. Modern technicians tend to be more sure of themselves, not surprisingly so since technical analysis aspires to scientific status. Should you come across some arrogant technician, ask innocently what is meant by the term "false signal." Better still, read the founders themselves. Hamilton's book, *The Stock*

Market Barometer, first appeared in 1922 and since then has been republished several times, and can be found in many bookstores devoted to business and the securities markets. Also see Robert Rhea, *The Dow Theory: An Explanation of Its Development and an Attempt to Define Its Usefulness as an Aid to Speculation* (Colorado Springs: Robert Rhea, 1932) for a clear and systematic explanation of commentary on the Theory by one who followed Hamilton and carried the torch after him.

Few nowadays take their Dow Theory unalloyed; there have been so many variations that much of the original message has been buried under an overlarding of jargon. More important, Dow's successors have applied his tests to individual stocks, since until recently knowing where the market was heading provided guidance, but didn't tell the technician which issues to buy and sell. This changed with the arrival of index options, which have been alluded to in Chapter 1 and will be discussed fully in Chapter 9.[3] This was inevitable, since today's markets are so different from those of Dow's period as to make most observations obsolete. What remains of consequence is his psychological insights, belief in cyclicality, and attempts to develop indexes to test hypotheses.

Finally, reflect that the community is chock full of technicians who put into effect programmed buying and selling operations, and fundamentalists with huge data bases. It isn't as it was in Dow's day, when a person could relate the market to the rise and fall of the tides, or when Graham was working at it, pouring over corporate reports. So decide whether you are a fundamentalist or a technician, reflect on what it means, and ask yourself how the knowledge will help you in selecting investments.

---

[3]If this seemingly constant referral to other sections of the book is troublesome, consider that investments today is so complicated a matter that to attempt to explore several lines of argument simultaneously would make for a hopeless muddle. It is far better to follow a thread to its conclusion and take up variations on the theme later on.

5 STOCK MARKET PERSPECTIVES: TECHNICAL ANALYSIS AND THE RANDOM WALK

Today's technicians utilize tools derived directly and indirectly from Charles Dow's early work. Most of them draw up several kinds of charts to illustrate price movements, attempt to find in them the kind of patterns of which Dow wrote, and then extrapolate and/or interpret them. At one time this kind of "charting" was the technicians' prime tool, but the coming of computerization and the advent of far more economic information has made them turn increasingly to statistical measurements of behavior or sentiment along with selected business indicators.

THE ANATOMY OF CHARTS

There are several kinds of charts, all easy to construct but difficult to interpret. One is the bar chart, on which are plotted the highs, lows, and closing prices for a stock or index. This is what a typical bar chart looks like (see Figure 5-1).

89

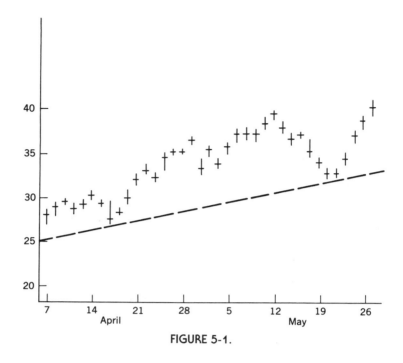

FIGURE 5-1.

Observe that the daily moves seem to form a pattern, not necessarily on a day-to-day basis, but over time. The daily changes are Dow's first movement. The second movement, which continue for several weeks, is commonly known as the secondary trend. The dotted line drawn here is the third movement, or today's primary trend.

Note the primary trend here is to the upside even though there are three secondary trends downward. When might the primary trend be said to have been broken? When another secondary trend upward fails to reach the previous one's level, which is shown in Figure 5-2. At this point the stock (or index) might be said to have given a sell signal. But be warned about those false signals; this might be one of them.

There are a number of complications to ponder. Most technicians take volume into consideration; a reversal on low turnover

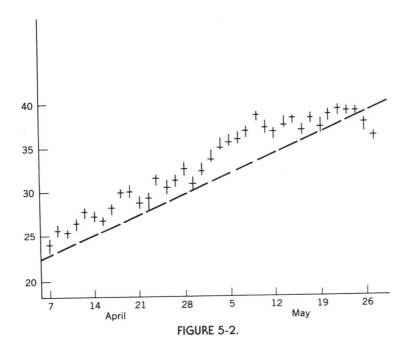

FIGURE 5-2.

signifies less than if the trading was robust. Also, there are many formations—pennants, triangles, wedges, and gaps are the more familiar of these, and are assiduosly dissected and debated by technicians. Lovers of esoterica delight in duplex horizontals, delayed endings, fulcrums, saucers, and so on. Technical "research" abounds, and new methods of diagnoses appear regularly.

Take a look at Figure 5-3. This is a head-and-shoulders formation, drawn with a trend line connecting previous lows. If the price fell under the trend line it would signal a bearish move, but if it bounced back, the way upward would be open. For how long? That depends on the resistance level—or in the case of a downward move, the support level. In Figure 5-4 is a bar chart on which highs and lows are connected to form a "channel." Let the price rise through the support and the move would be bearish; above the resistance, and you have a bullish indicator.

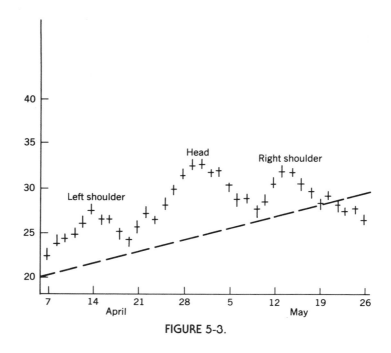

FIGURE 5-3.

Point-and-figure charting is a slightly more complicated variant, which offers a different picture of the movement of a stock or the general market. Entries are made only when the stock or averages rises or falls a predetermined amount. While bar charts map daily movements, point-and-figure ones are concerned only with price changes and ignores time. One technician may mark off only moves of half a point or more, while others consider full point or even two points the meaningful change. In Figure 5-5 we have a chart marked for one point move, starting when the stock was at 50. Note that the stock moved upward (marked by X) to 62, at which point it declined a point, leading the chartist to make a different notation (O) and keeps at it till the next move.

Some of these moves can take place in a day, others may not be changed for weeks, depending on the stock's volatility and the intervals selected. As do bar chartists, point-and-figure fanciers talk

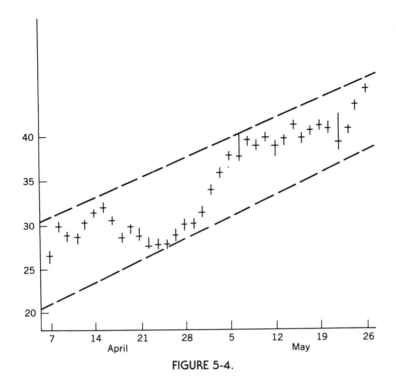

FIGURE 5-4.

about breakouts and resistance levels, but their interpretations can vary widely from their confreres.

Interested? This is meant only as an introduction and illustration. Further and deeper discussion belongs to separate volumes on the subject. A good place to start would be Robert D. Edwards and John Magee, *Technical Analysis of Stock Trends* (Springfield, MA: John Magee, 1967), an old work but still the best introduction to charting. A more recent work that might be explored is C. Colburn Hardy, *Investor's Guide to Technical Analysis* (New York: McGraw-Hill, 1978).

Is there anything to technical analysis? Decide for yourself, but consider the words of John Train, a noted and successful fundamentalist, who advises investors to "forget about technical analy-

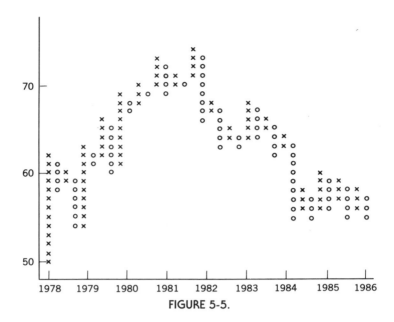

FIGURE 5-5.

sis" altogether. Train wrote that he has a wager open to any technician who opts to accept.

So my bet goes like this: Somebody digs out some charts done on a daily basis from a few years back. He removes any identification and cuts each chart in the middle. He gives the first half to the technician.

All that worthy has to do is tell me, on a $100 bet, whether a stock was higher or lower at any specified point in the second period than at the end of the first. Since he claims the ability to prophecy, and is willing to have the rest of us take a substantial risk on his say-so—paying brokerage and tax whether we win or lose—he should be confident enough of his powers to give modest odds. Three to two seems fair enough.

Train concludes by noting that no technician has ever taken him up on the offer.[1]

---

[1]For a further sample of Train's observations, see his delightful *Dance of the Money Bees* (New York: Harper & Row, 1974).

Long before Train threw down his challenge, William Shakespeare gave his opinion on attempts by soothsayers to discern almost any pattern they wished. In *Hamlet*, Act III, Scene III, the Prince speaks with Polonius:

Hamlet:	Do you see yonder cloud that's almost in shape of a camel?
Polonius:	By th' mass, and 'tis like a camel indeed.
Hamlet:	Methinks it is like a weasel.
Polonius:	It is back'd like a weasel.
Hamlet:	Or like a whale.
Polonius:	Very like a whale.

If Shakespeare were around today as an investor, one suspects he would select the fundamentalist approach.

THE KEY INDICATORS

Now for the indicators, of which as noted there are scads, the major problem being which to take seriously and how much weight to give to them. Begin with the notion that indicators reflect general economic and market conditions, and not the promise for individual stocks. Technicians use indicators to show the direction of the market, and not to locate issues on which to plunk their funds.

How to generate indicators need not bother investors, since the work is done for them by the pros, many of whom put out market letters which they will happily send for a fee. One of the best of these is *Market Logic*, which employs no less than 36 of them, grouped into four categories: fundamentals (which includes the yield on the Dow Industrials and the P/E ratio), monetary (interest rates and the discount rate among others), sentiment (including credit balances and the short interest), and technical (such as total return index and the high/low logic index). At any given time some are bullish, others bearish, and a number of them neutral.

In early 1986, for example, 25 indicators were bullish, 5 bearish, and 6 neutral, which the editors took as a very bullish forecast.

Barron's devotes some space to indicators in each issue, not surprising for a Dow Jones publication. Indeed, this weekly newspaper, which should be required reading for fundamentalists and technicians alike, has created many of the more familiar indicators. Those wishing to have a quick introduction to them could take a look at *Barron's* "Market Laboratory" section. There, under "Week's Market Statistics," are listed close to 50 indicators, and there are at least another 100 monitored by serious technicians, with new ones appearing all the time. Among the more closely watched of the *Barron's* indicators, in no particular order, are: the Low-Priced Stock Index, Buy/Sell, Total Shorts, Specialist Shorts, Net Buy/Sell, Odd Lot Trading, T-Bill/Eurodollar Futures Spread, and Salomon Government/Corporate Yield Spread, some of which will be discussed later, along with others not reported on by *Barron's*.

Some indicators are monitored for decades, others last for only a few years, vanish or fade, or are replaced due to new insights or changes in the economy that make them unreliable. For example, seasonally adjusted freight car loadings used to be considered an important indicator of economic activities, but the relative decline of the freight rail business has made it less popular. At one time production of sulphuric acid, a basic chemical used in many industrial pursuits, was considered interesting if not important; this is no longer the case. The life of a technician, once relatively simple, has become far more difficult.

The most popular genre today are contrary indicators, utilized by those who want to go against the majority. If the crowd says "buy," the assumption is it has done so already, and so there is little buying pressure left, with the next move to the downside. The reverse goes for selling. "Are you a contrarian?" is the kind of question a television interviewer might ask a professional investment advisor so as to establish his credentials. In fact contrarianism has become so popular since 1984 that it became the accepted wisdom, and created a nice paradox. All those contrarians became a majority, which meant that there was no original majority to work against. Or to put it differently, one had to monitor the contrarians, and then become a counter-contrarian.

One of the better known of the contrary indicators deals with odd lots, these being purchases and sales of less than 100 shares of stock, which are "round lots." Odd lot buyers and sellers are usually small investors, who presumably know far less about what is happening than do the professionals. The theory is that they more often than not miss important market turns. Thus odd lotters are heavy sellers at the bottom of a decline and strong buyers as stocks are about to reach their peak.

Every business day *The Wall Street Journal* publishes statistics on odd lot trading. If on a particular session the odd lotters bought 210,564 shares and sold 325,993, the ratio of sales to purchases would be .65 (210,564 divided by 325,993). Watch the indicator for a market cycle and you'll realize it tends to fluctuate between .40 and 1.6. A ratio close to .40 would indicate heavy odd lot selling, and astute investors would take this as a sign to make purchases. Likewise, as the index inches up past 1.3 those in the know would realize that odd lotters are doing a lot of buying, and consider the wisdom of dumping stocks.

While still watched, the Odd Lot Index isn't as important as it used to be, since odd lot sales and purchases today comprise a very small portion of total trading—less than 1 percent—whereas the institutions have expanded enormously, and of course they don't trade in piddling amounts of shares. One of these days the Odd Lot Index probably will go the way of freight car loadings.

A far better predictor is the Odd Lot Short Sales Ratio which measures shorting by small investors.[2] The index is derived by dividing the odd lot short sales by an average of odd lot purchases and total sales, figures available from the NYSE. The index is said

[2]Shorting, or short selling, means the sale of stock not owned, but borrowed from the broker, that has to be replaced later on. One would sell short if believing the stock was due for a decline. Thus the short of a stock at 50 that subsequently declines to 30 would result in a 20 point gain (before commissions and brokerage charges for supplying the stock).

to be in neutral at around 1.2, but has ranged from close to 0 to over 6. The higher the ratio, the more odd lot shorts are being made, and thus the more bullish the outlook. Let the ratio rise above 4 and you have a fine bull signal, and conversely a decline to under 1 may be considered bearish.

At one time or another most investors subscribe to a market letter put out by an investment advisory service, edited by seers who claim special expertise on securities. These letters feature market commentary, recommendations, and ruminations. Few are actively involved in short selling and other bear market techniques, and so the bias toward bullishness is pronounced. The reason can be illustrated by a claim by well-known newspaper columnist Leslie Gould that he had seen the 1929 market collapse coming months before it did. When reminded that he had filed bullish articles that summer and fall, Gould replied, "If I had said 'sell everything' in one article, what could I have written the next day?"

MARKET LETTERS

Thus it is with market letters, whose editors are under pressure to ferret out undiscovered situations that will outperform the market, enable them to advertise their successes, in this way attract new subscribers. *Investor's Intelligence*, a market advisory service itself, monitors the others, and believes it a most bullish sign when 42 percent of them are bearish, this indicating their subscribers are out of the market awaiting reentry, while a decline is in the wings when 17 percent or less are bearish. So market letter advisories can be a pretty good contrary indicator.

This went haywire in 1984. A large majority of the letters were bearish the first part of the year, indicating a rise was in the cards. But they turned bullish, and sharply so, in late summer. In April less than 33 percent of the letters had been bullish; by August more than half of them had sent out buy signals, and the bullish atmosphere continued on in 1985 and 1986. Indeed, by early 1986 all but the most confirmed bears were on the buy side. This was supposed to mean their subscribers were fully invested, thus the next move would be to the downside. Yet the market continued to steam ahead. Clearly this is one indicator that no longer functions as logic and experience once dictated it should.

Most, though not all, market letters aren't worth following much of the time. This isn't because they are edited by fools or charlatans (some are, however) but rather due to the streaky nature of prediction and the simple fact that at times investors should go to the sidelines and wait things out. What is a letter writer to say on such occasions? He is obliged to come out with regular recommendations, usually on a weekly, semimonthly, or monthly basis, and subscribers expect to be told what will going up and what will be going down, not something like, "For the time being, stay in money market funds." So the recommendations come, even though the recommender isn't convinced he had found the pure gold that the readers expect. Had Leslie Gould been a letter writer instead of a columnist, this doubtless is what he would have done.

In any case, a summary of current thought can be obtained by subscribing to *Investor's Intelligence* or *Market Logic. The Hulbert Financial Digest* analyzes recommendations in some 80 of the more prominent newsletters and evaluates their records.

There is a crude rule-of-thumb method used to locate the "hot" letters at any given time. Look at the advertisements in *Barron's,* and seek those crowing over their records. All writers are governed by SEC regulations, and you can be pretty sure the evidence hasn't been fabricated and is reasonably complete. One of the more accessible methods of gauging market sentiment is the number of advertisements of this nature in any given issue. The letter writers with good recent records like to take out ads boasting of them, while the others lay low until experiencing a change. If many of those bulls are proclaiming their prowess it means that a turn to the downside is in the wings. Indeed, whenever *Barron's* has an issue with more than 100 pages it is time to consider some sales.[3]

All of the letter writers have their fallow periods, and should you see one on a TV stock market-oriented show, introduced as being right in the last four or five turns, don't conclude he is a mystic or genius. If you start out with 64 letter writers and half say up and the other half say down, 32 will be right. Now do the same, monitoring the half of the winners who are right on target. After a while you will have 16 who were correct twice in succession. Of these eight say up, eight down, and now. . . . But you get the idea. In the end we are left with a single person, who was on target six times in a row. Now it doesn't work out so neatly, but something like this often is the case.

However, on occasion a really hot letter could be read and followed profitably, due more to the workings of self-fulfilling prophecy than anything else. Let a writer receive a great deal of publicity in a steamy market and his every word will be translated into buy and sell signals. It never lasts for long. Given this kind of success forecasters develop *hubris*, and fall into the trap one of them, Yale Hirsch, has called "the walking on water syndrome," which holds that after a while they believe they are infallible, and confuse self-fulfilling prophecy with genius.[4]

PITY JOE GRANVILLE

As noted in Chapter 4 Joe Granville, that mercurial, charismatic technician who was very much on target in the 1970s, said at the time:

---

[3]Regular *Barron's* readers know that from time to time an advertiser will offer a bundle of trial subscriptions for a modest fee, this being one of the more common methods of promotion utilized by their publishers. Less well known is that almost all of them will send you a free sample issue, for the same reason.

[4]According to *The Hulbert Financial Digest*, only 19 percent of market letters outperformed the NYSE Composite Average in August 1986.

"Technicians look ahead, fundamentalists look backward. The true language of the market is technical. . . . The majority of those involved in the market are bombarded with mis-timed fundamental data which nine times out of 10 haven't a blessed thing to do with where the price of the stock or the market is headed."

Granville's *A Strategy of Daily Stock Market Timing for Maximum Profit* (Englewood Cliffs, N.J.: Prentice-Hall, 1960) is a classic in the area of the use of indicators. He utilized as many as 17 of them, interpreting them with panache, to the delight of his followers. Granville's career vividly illustrates the impact gurus can have if they achieve fame and credence, and are the kind of showman he turned out to be.

On January 6, 1981, at the peak of his popularity, Granville told subscribers to his stock service to sell everything. The next day the Dow declined almost 24 points, shaving $40 billion off stock values on a then-record volume of 92.9 million shares. Later on Granville revealed he had drawn this conclusion from the fact that one of his indicators, based on the relationship between the stock price and the price of its 200 day moving average, flashed a sell signal.[5]

The market indeed did decline irregularly for the next few weeks. Granville received still more publicity, and continued on his whirlwind lecture tour, going on to predict earthquakes, claim to be teaching a simian to drive his car, and engaging in the wild buffoonery for which he had become notorious. By early March, however, while he still called for disaster, the market was above its January high and a month later it crossed the magical 1000 level, followed by a more than 200 point decline.

What turned out to be a major upward sweep began in August 1982; Granville labeled it a "sucker rally." The Dow was over 1000

---

[5]This kind of indicator is most popular and simple to keep. The technician charts the stock by creating an average for the past 200 trading sessions, and then at the close of each session adding that day's close and subtracting the earliest one, thus generating a new figure to be charted and in the process ironing out very short-term movements. So long as the number of stocks selling above the average is expanding a bull move continues, and when it stops or declines, the market is due for a correction. This is what Granville saw that January.

again by November, while he remained bearish, and he continued to call for a collapse as the index crossed over the 1500 level in late 1985.

For that year as a whole the Granville options portfolio ranked lowest in the Hulbert survey. Granville had been generally wrong throughout the 1982–1985 period, continuing to predict the next 1929 was just around the corner, usually doing so on fundamental grounds. Not until early 1986, when the bull market was so well established as to become a cliché, did Granville change his tune.

THE PSYCHOLOGY OF INDICATORS

Some of the indicators have a psychological as well as economic foundation. Lee Idleman of the brokerage house of Neuberger & Berman has assembled what he calls the Greed Index, based perhaps on the old saw that the two primary emotions on the Street are fear and greed, the former propelling bear markets, the latter lubricating bull ones. Idleman uses 10 indicators he believes signal the relationships of fear to greed, such as preference for growth versus defensive stocks, and claims that when the Greed Index goes over 60 it is time to sell, while a fall to under 30 is a buy signal.

Of course this is somewhat personal and cannot be quantified as, say, the short sales can, but the principle is worth considering. When you see wildness developing in markets a sale might be in order, while the onset of sudden fear can be a time to buy. For example, consider stepping in when a foreign crisis suddenly erupts, when a presidential illness is disclosed, or a health scare is announced. Sometimes you'll lose, but more often than not the market (or stocks involved) bounces back after a few sessions. Conversely, sell when all kinds of new issues go to premiums on offering and when stocks appear to be soaring into the stratosphere.

The trouble with the latter position is that by selling you may miss out of some juicy profits. It is of little comfort recalling that Nathan Rothschild claimed his fortune was based on having sold too soon when the stock you bought at 50 goes to 70, you sell, and it is over 100 a month later. Plunging into a bull move is like riding the surf; the trick is knowing when to get out.

There is an old Sicilian tale about a certain wine that leaves a slimy sediment at the bottom of the bottle. The trick is to raise the neck to your lips carefully and drink, knowing the wine is richest the further you go, the best draught coming from the liquid closest to the slime. The last drop of wine is the best; the first of muck is horrid. And so it is with staying the course of a bull move. Use Idleman's Index if you will, or accept the concept and utilize emotions as an excellent contrary indicator.

On the principle that it pays to follow the smart money technicians consider two other indicators. Insiders—meaning company officers, directors, or large stockholders—who purchase or sell shares in companies in which they have interests, are required to report all transactions they make in securities of these companies to the SEC, which reports on them in its "Official Summary of Security Transactions and Holdings." Several university-generated studies have shown that insider buying and selling is an excellent indicator to discover where individual stocks are heading. That this should be so would seem obvious; if five or six insiders were buying and none selling, one might assume they were doing so because of conviction the fortunes of the company they knew so well were advancing, while sales would indicate the opposite.

But not necessarily. In companies where insiders exercise options to buy stock at lower than market value sales might indicate attempts to diversify individual portfolios. Or it might be they need the money for a down payment on a house, or to pay college tuition. After all, insiders are also human. Generally speaking insider sales indicate less than insider purchases. On balance, however, insider transactions is one of the better indicators, though so many astute investors know this as to make it less meaningful than it once had been.

At one time a large short position was taken to indicate that many investors believed the market would decline, and so was interpreted bearishly. On the other hand, those shorts will one day be covered, and so represented a large pool of potential buyers. So rises and falls in the short position were interpreted differently by different people. Now the situation has become even more clouded. In the new market environment short sales no longer mean the investor believes the stock will fall. Rather, these can be entered into as part of a hedge strategy, combined with index futures and options. So a large or small position can reflect programmed speculation, and not bullish or bearish sentiments.

Transactions of specialists, who in a way are also insiders, should be monitored carefully. As noted specialists are charged with maintaining an orderly market, but this does not mean they won't behave in their own interests when the situation dictates. No other people have better "feels" for the issues they follow than do the specialists. If there is a rhythm to the stock, they are ideally positioned to sense it. Also, specialists can have more fundamental information regarding the companies whose stocks they handle than many others, so their actions are worth following.

This explains the popularity of the Specialist Short Sales Ratio. If specialists are actively shorting their stocks, it may mean they expect a decline, and the opposite would be true if the short positions are diminishing. Normally the ratio of specialist short sales to total shorts (SS/TS), is around 55 percent. When specialist shorts rise faster than do those of the public, the ratio will rise. When it gets to 65 percent or so, some technicians would say a market decline is in the making, while a ratio of under 40 percent is deemed bullish. It works out as almost as well as does that for insider transactions.

The Mutual Fund Cash Position is also worth watching, the idea being that when the funds are awash with liquidity they are in a strong position to plunge into the market and so apply buying pressure. But there is another way to look at the situation: if the funds are on the sidelines, these experts/professionals might be telling us that equities aren't attractive at current levels.

In spring 1984 the institutional cash level was high, more than 11 percent of assets, which some took as a signal the market was due for a rise. So it was, caused in part by the flow of these funds into equities. However, late in the year the level fell below 8 percent, which traditionally was a sign the institutions were fully invested, and was interpreted as a sell signal. Yet the market soared through all of 1985, during which the institutional cash level remained below 7 percent. It was under 6 percent in early 1986, and yet the bull market rolled on.

The reason? Some said it was the continual flow of foreign funds, to which was added an enormous amount of money from individual retirement and Keogh accounts—according to some as much as $400 billion. Yet as it turned out most of this went into bond funds, and not equities.

The simple fact of the matter is that this once-useful indicator apparently is now giving off false signals, and might be discarded as once was the car loading figures.

Does it make sense to bet against the "smart money" at such times? The answer is generally "yes." The pros can also be wrong at important market turns, missing bottoms and tops alike. Then too, at times during the 1970s large cash positions signaled that money market instruments, paying double digit yields, were more attractive than stocks. The development of families of swap funds, in which a management has several into which the investor can switch when he feels the time is ripe, means that cash and equivalent ratios have to be higher than before to accommodate sudden mass departures. This isn't to say that the cash and equivalent holdings aren't worth watching, but rather that their importance and significance has changed over the years.

THE FOSBACK APPROACH

Norman Fosback of the Institute for Econometric Research has come up with a more sophisticated version of the Mutual Fund Cash Position. He factors interest rate levels out of the raw data and calculates the percentage of cash relative to total assets so as to better reflect the sentiments of fund managers. He had labeled this "the Fosback Index," and claims it is "a major breakthrough in stock market prediction" and "an exceptionally powerful forecasting tool." The actual method Fosback utilizes is outlined in his book, *Stock Market Logic* (Ft. Lauderdale: Inst. for Economic Research, 1977), and need not concern us here. What Fosback has learned is that when the ratio reaches above 2.5 percent of assets a substantial stock market rally is signaled.

One of the more imaginative technicians, Fosback also has his "three steps and a stumble" indicator, which states that when the Federal Reserve tightens monetary policy by increasing the discount rate, margin requirements, or reserve requirements three times in a row, the market will decline. This is the bearish equivalent of his "two tumbles and a jump" indicator, which holds that when the Fed lowers any of the three rates twice consecutively expect a market rise.

Finally consider the Confidence Index, generated by *Barron's* in 1932 and published weekly in the "Market Laboratory" section. This is simply the relationship of the yields on high grade bonds to those available from intermediate grade bonds. The theory here is that when investors feel the future is bright they will switch funds from high grade bonds to intermediates, bidding up their prices and so causing their yields to come closer to those of the better rated debts. This is another way of saying that when the relative yields are narrow it is a sign that confidence is high, and when they widen confidence is low.

This might appear sensible, but in the unsettled interest rate atmosphere of the 1970s the index gave poor signals; to put it bluntly, few sophisticated investors had much confidence in the Confidence Index, and the situation hasn't changed much since then, despite Dow-Jones' attempts to refine and fine tune it.

As noted, there are scores of indicators, of which these are a representative sample. And we haven't even discussed the most popular of the lot nowadays, the "Wall Street Week Technical Market Index" compiled by Robert Nurock, which is discussed in host Louis Rukeyser's book, *How To Make Money In Wall Street* (Garden City: Doubleday, 1974). In addition to the Odd Lot Short Sales Ratio and the NYSE Specialist Short Sale Ratio, Nurock has eight other indicators—the Advance-Decline Index, the Dow Jones Momentum Ratio, the NYSE High-Low Index, the Institutional Block Ratio, a Low Price Activity Ratio, comparison of activity on the NYSE and American Stock Exchange, an Equity Financing Index, and a bond market index. Nurock has set up the Index to predict intermediate term trends, from three to six months.

Like the others, it isn't consistently dependable and has sent out false signals; knowing this, Nurock occasionally overrides it himself. Indeed, indicators usually conflict with one another. At almost any given time a goodly number of them will point to higher prices, others to lower. This isn't to say that they should be ignored, but rather that their utility is limited.

Confused as to which path to take? You needn't be. Just remember that the decision on fundamentalist and technical analysis is probably bred in the genes, or if not that, at least implanted on personality. Once again, fundamentalists hold that their thoughts as to where prices of stocks and the market as a whole should be are right and the market is wrong, and they act on that assumption, while technicians believe the market tells a story they can interpret and trends they can extrapolate. The fundamentalist studies the economy and individual industries and companies to understand the market, while the technician concentrates on the market and individual stocks, reasoning that from them he can guess what is happening in the economy—but often has little interest in such matters. Both believe the market is rational and understandable, and they search for enlightenment. To use religious terms, fundamentalist and technician believe in God, but worship at different shrines. To carry it further, disillusioned fundamentalists often turn to technical analysis, and vice versa. At one time there was no other church to attend.

Not any more, or at least not necessarily. There is in the world of investment analysis an analogue to the "God Is Dead" move-

ment that shook the religious community in the 1960s and provided grist for TV talk shows for a few seasons. It now is possible
—indeed considered a mark of sophistication—to hold that both
fundamentalists and technicians are wrong: There is no way to
predict prices, for there is no clear relationship of or correlation
between economic data and prices, no pattern to be discerned
and from which to profit.

THE RANDOM WALK

This is most familiarly known as the Random Walk Theory. Ferti-
lized by computerization and hatched out of the universities in
the 1960s, it came of age in the hectic, unique markets of the following decade, when all the rules went awry and technicians and
fundamentalists alike threw up their arms in disbelief. The reasons are those stated in Chapter 1—the power of institutional
forces, the development of new trading vehicles, major alterations in the financial landscape, and the rise of a new class of
money managers and traders for whom the old rules are outmoded, even quaint. Let the computers of a half a dozen fund
managers decide to trigger a buy or sell campaign and the charts
and indicators of most technicians could look rather foolish.

The technicians respond that the mainframes are programmed
with technical data, but they really don't know, for these are
closely guarded secrets. The same would happen to fundamentalists, of course, though their longer time horizons would more
readily accept such fluctuations. This isn't to suggest that the old
versions of fundamentalism and technical analysis have been
abandoned, but rather the world in which they once held sway
has been altered sharply, requiring shifts and changes in both
methods of analysis—and cognizance of the impact of these new
forces.

In its basic version (known among academicians as the "Efficient Market Hypothesis"), the Random Walk Theory holds that
price changes in individual stocks are independent of the se-

quence of previous price changes. At any given moment the quotations for a stock reflect all available knowledge, and since there is no way of knowing what will happen next, investors cannot make meaningful predictions on a consistent basis.

The first statement disposes of the technicians, the second the fundamentalists. To Random Walkers the technicians are akin to bogus seers who claim to possess the power to read palms and forecast events from tea leaves, or like Polonius, see several shapes in cloud configurations. Fundamentalists, they say, are under the delusion that they know more about an individual company than do insiders, who even if correct cannot possibly forecast future developments, and cannot demonstrate clear and precise relationships between economic events and market movements.

There are a number of criticisms of the Random Walk. First of all, while chart-reading often takes on aspects of astrology, several of the indexes, such as the Odd Lot Short Sales Ratio, have consistently demonstrated their predictive qualities, while only the foolhardy would ignore data on insider trading. Even more compelling is the inability of Random Walkers to generate their own theory of causation. Fundamentalists can tell investors *why* stocks can often be underpriced, and technicians have their belief in cycles and patterns. Just as theologians asked the God Is Dead crowd to explain the existence of the universe, life, and the like and received unsatisfactory answers, so the Random Walkers have been unable to offer an alternative investment technique, based on the theory, to guide investors. Yet the concept offers some good ammunition against the technicians in particular, and arguments *they* haven't answered satisfactorily.

The theory is generally traced to the work of a French mathematician, Louis Bachelier, who formulated it in a doctoral dissertation at the turn of the century. Other researchers in the field added to Bachelier's work, generally buttressing his conclusion that the stock market has no memory, and that prices move in a random fashion. Along the way several schools of thought developed. The most orthodox held that at any given time the market reflects *all* information, private as well as public. Others believed that only public information was reflected in prices, while many concluded merely that there was no relationship between past, present, and future stock prices.

All of this work was done among a small coterie of mathematically inclined economists, little known to the general public. One had to read highly abstract academic journals to be au courant with the latest twists and turns the theory was taking.

It awaited the development of two mechanical devices and a bull market to bring the Random Walk to the forefront. The first was the Xerox machine, used by researchers to reproduce Bachelier's long out of print thesis and send it off to their fellows. The second was the computer, which enabled the academicians to test their hypotheses. Finally, the bull market of the 1960s sparked interest in stocks, attracting foundation support.

Well-funded, the academicians fed the raw numbers into their IBM and CDC mainframes and brought forth data to support conclusions. Meanwhile their hitherto esoteric papers and books were parlayed into fine positions at prestigious universities and lucrative Wall Street consultantships. Shallow technicians and plodding fundamentalists alike felt threatened by these professors who carried on research at computer consoles in Cambridge, Chicago, and San Francisco, who spoke in an arcane jargon and seemed so self-confident, who had never engaged in trading or put their own money on the line, and cared little about investor psychology, earnings, wheeling and dealing, and stock rigging.

The technicians in particular lashed out at the Random Walkers. Were they saying that throwing darts at the financial pages was as good a method of selecting securities as any other? They were shocked—and then threatened—when the answer came back: an unqualified "yes." George Goodman, who writes under the name "Adam Smith," related the tale in his 1968 best seller, *The Money Game* (New York: Random House, 1968):

Senator Thomas J. McIntyre, Democrat of New Hampshire and a member of the powerful Senate Banking Committee, brought his dart board in one day. Senator McIntyre had tacked the stock market page onto his dart board and thrown darts at it, and the portfolio picked by the darts outperformed all of the mutual funds. Senator McIntyre's darts thus supported the . . . testimony of Professor Paul Samuelson of MIT and Henry Wallich of Yale. . . .

It became a fad; the irrepressible Malcolm Forbes took out his darts and reported the same result. Customers throughout the country were playing the game, and the technicians were growing increasingly troubled, as some Random Walkers went so far as to accuse them of harboring dark motives. "The point is, the technicians often play an important role in the greening of brokers," wrote Random Walker Professor Burton Malkiel, then of Princeton, in his book, *A Random Walk Down Wall Street* (New York: Norton, 1973).

Chartists recommend trades—almost every technical system involves some degree of in-and-out trading. Trading generates commissions, and commissions are the lifeblood of the brokerage business. The technicians do not help produce yachts for the customers, but they do help generate the trading that provides yachts for the brokers.

Thus technicians emerge as the handmaidens of brokers hoping to churn accounts. Malkiel concluded that "until the public catches on to this bit of trickery, technicians will continue to flourish.

Malkiel and his colleagues were easier on fundamentalists, in part because of evidence that in the long run, stock prices *do* reflect economic changes. One researcher, MIT Professor Paul Cootner, discovered that the Random Walk didn't apply when the past was defined as being longer than 14 weeks, but that it did for more recent information, which seemed to say that "inside" and "hot" intelligence were worth *less* than that which was well known and digested, just the opposite of the conventional wisdom, and in line with much fundamental research. Then too, except for purposes of screening, fundamental information could not be programmed into their computers to generate buy and sell commands. Others note that the general tendency of stock prices over long periods is upward. One Random Walker thought prices moved in a fashion similar to that of a drunk heading toward the front door—you know where he is heading, and suspect he will get there after a while, but there is no way of knowing the direction of the very next step.

Finally, some fundamentalists have come to terms with the Random Walk. In 1976 Ben Graham himself gave the signal, recognizing that alterations in the investment landscape required adjustments to his basic theory. "I am no longer an advocate of elaborate techniques of security analysis in order to find superior value opportunities," he told a seminar.

> This was a rewarding activity, say, forty years ago, when our textbook, "Graham and Dodd," was first published, but the situation has changed a great deal since then. In the old days any well-trained securities analyst could do a good professional job of selecting undervalued issues through detailed studies; but in the light of the enormous amount of research now being carried on, I doubt whether in most cases such extensive efforts will generate sufficiently superior selections to justify their cost. To that very limited extent I'm on the side of the "efficient market" school of thought now generally accepted by the professors.

Graham continued to assert that one should buy stocks in highly liquid companies, whose prices are below their working capital value. This appealed to a number of those Random Walkers. Many of the no-longer impecunious academics found themselves in the happy circumstance of having to invest substantial sums, and it turned out most were closet fundamentalists, this due perhaps to their strong antipathy toward technical analysis. When one was asked if he used a dart board to select stocks he roared, "Do you think I'm foolish enough to risk my own money on mere theories?"

COMMON STOCKS:
6 THE INVESTMENT BATTLEFIELD

Let's suppose you have more than a nodding acquaintance with securities and have decided to enter the investment battlefield. You have gone ahead and located an intelligent, honest full-line broker or have opted to go with a discounter. You have looked at yourself carefully and critically in the financial mirror to calculate just how much risk you can afford in light of age, family, health, general outlook, and so on and have concluded it makes sense to invest directly in stocks, the subject matter of much of this chapter. What's next?

If your account is with a full-line brokerage you will have been placed on its mailing list, and every week or so receive the revealed knowledge pushed out by the research staff. If you deal with a small house, this might be as little as a single page composed by one of the partners; the big wire operations will send off a packet of reading material, some resembling financial magazines, written and edited by a staff that would rival that of *Business Week* and much larger than the handful of people who manage to put together *Barron's* each week. Should your account be at a discounter, you pour through the usual financial magazines and perhaps subscribe to a market letter or two.

To complicate matters you are being whipsawed by conflicting opinions and advice. Being a diligent investor you read all you can about the market and in particular stocks that interest you. The local librarians have come to recognize you as a habitue of the investment section, pouring over the latest issues of *Value Line* and related publications, while there probably is a favorite investment TV program to be watched nightly or weekly.

The trouble is that much of the information is contradictory, and the more you read and hear, the more bewildered you become. Wouldn't it be nice to have the assurance of those pros who pontificate in print and over the tube? But then you note that they tend to be self-congratulatory when their calls work out and forget about failures.

THE SNAKE OIL PEDDLERS

After a while an answer to the dilemma may appear to present itself, or at least so it seems going by anecdotal evidence. You have acquired the habit of listening to a radio market commentator while driving home from work, the kind who accepts telephone queries and tries to offer advice. In our time he has taken on the qualities of a relative who is supposed to know what is going on and stands prepared to share his expertise with you, his favorite nephew or niece. Indeed, one of these pundits even asks to be called "Uncle."

Be warned that such individuals are among the more dangerous threats to your financial health, and since they have become so popular in recent years perhaps merit some extended comment.

If you are on the shady side of 60 you may recall a weekly radio program during the 1930s that dealt with family difficulties. The host was Dr. A. L. Alexander, who listened to heart-rending tales of ungrateful children, cheating spouses, abandoned parents, and so forth. He would hear them out patiently, interrupting occasionally to ask impassioned guests "please don't touch the microphone," and in the end would deliver his verdict along with advice.

Alexander's heirs can be found among today's radio investment advisors, some of whom are former brokers and financial writers; fast-talking, glib, persuasive, and all-knowing. Rarely do any of them admit to uncertainty or lack of knowledge. Callers typically sketch their problem or ask specific questions—about a maturing certificate of deposit, how to invest IRA money, or an inquiry regarding the probable course of interest rates or stocks. A colloquy with the host follows, in which unhedged advice usually is dispensed, and thousands of listeners try to plug that information into their own investment programs.

The practice carries grave risks. Even assuming the hosts know whereof they speak, listeners attempting to apply advice intended for others are akin to those seeking to cure their ailments by dosing themselves with medicines prescribed for others.

How about getting information and advice directly from the kind of person similar to those who sounds so knowing over the airwaves, an individual who presents himself as a "financial advisor"? These hardly existed as recently as the 1970s, but now abound, with several universities offering programs leading to a master's degree in the subject. Know that financial advisors are not licensed, though there are professional associations that set standards. They can't be debarred and don't have to carry malpractice insurance.

Before seeking out a financial advisor (they can be located through ads in telephone yellow pages or by contacting graduate departments of business colleges), consider the following. In the first place, your situation may be so straightforward and uncomplicated it isn't worth the cost, or so complex that you require the help of an accountant, attorney, and trust company officer as well as that of an advisor. Second, the business isn't professionalized to the extent that you can trust anyone with a few certificates on the wall and letters after his name. Finally, there is the risk of running into an advisor with dual loyalties—a person attached to an insurance company or brokerage with reason to steer you in that direction.

RUDIMENTS OF ANALYSIS

Let's assume that you put aside the idea of of using such services and decide to go it alone. You read, ponder, agonize, and in the end get on the phone with the broker, if with a full-line house bandy about ideas, and make your decision: "Buy 200 shares of Minnesota Mining at the market."

You now track the stock, watching it move up, down, and sideways. If it declines you wonder whether you should buy more (as a fundamentalist might) or sell and take your loss (the technical response). Should the stock rise, would it make sense to buy more (technical again) or take profits (as might the fundamentalist). You may have gone through the drill; if so, the feeling is familiar. Moreover, it never goes away, no matter how long you've been an investor.

Perhaps too you have now decided to learn more about the market—or even the economy. After a while many investors decide that to go about it intelligently they need a wide education. How can you know as much as you should about Texas Instruments if you don't know a semiconductor from an integrated circuit? How can you judge Merck without a passing knowledge of pharmacology? Why purchase shares in Newmont until you know a lot about the promise for copper and gold, problems in South Africa, and so on down the line? Indeed, a sensible and informed investor has to be knowledgeable about virtually every subject in the college catalogue. This is why many securities researchers come to their jobs from posts in industry rather than with MBAs in hand. It is much more sensible to train a petrologist in finance than to teach a finance major about the oil industry.

Are you dissuaded, hopelessly confused, and want an alternative to such investing? If so then go to Chapter 10. If not, read on.

What we are left with is what may be the best alternative, that you will have to do much of the work yourself, and absorb the rudiments of economics and financial analysis. More to the point, you will have to go over some of the raw data those analysts look at. There is a catch, however. You need not become an amateur economist, but only understand what they are saying, the relationship between the economy and the markets, and know how *perception* of that impact can affect stocks and other financial instruments. Call it one part economics, one part mass psychology, and one part common sense.

Don't think this an impossible task. Consider what your reaction might be to having been told that you or a close relative requires a complicated surgical procedure. Some might simply take the doctor's word for it, or at best seek out a second opinion. The truly cautious would hie it to the library and engage in a quick directed reading course to learn all possible about the procedure and the latest research in the field.

Of course we are not talking here of a life and death situation, merely your financial security, perhaps a distant secondary consideration, but secondary—no less than that—for most readers. It must be so; otherwise you might not have gone this far in this book.

THE FEAR OF ECONOMICS

It is usually best to begin with fundamental analysis, for this is where most novices get their initiation. (Technical work is left to the more specialized books mentioned earlier.) So first off is that matter of learning something about economics. Does this dismay you? It shouldn't, because I am talking of a variety of economics you can absorb fairly easily, and the exercise might even prove enjoyable. Moreover, the knowledge required is of the kind that will enable you to go through the business magazines without feeling like a clod.

Reflect that others, with more at stake than you, have found themselves in the same situation. Carl Icahn, perhaps the greatest of the corporate raiders, majored in philosophy as a Princeton undergraduate, and broke his mother's heart by quitting medical school in his second year in favor of a Wall Street career. A youth spent in the oil fields, and not in academic groves, prepared T. Boone Pickens for his work in finance. John Gutfreund, labeled "The King of Wall Street" by *Business Week*, was devoted to literature and theater while at Oberlin; the chairman of Salomon Inc. had literary aspirations and hoped for a career as a director in Broadway. His predecessor, Bill Salomon, had forgone higher education for Wall Street.

After raising her children Madelon Talley returned to college, attended Columbia at night, completed her studies at Sarah Lawrence where she took a conventional liberal arts program, and soon was one of the Street's most respected money managers. William Simon, banker and then politician who eventually wound up as Secretary of the Treasury, and later went on to amass a fortune as a private investor, concentrated on swimming and beer (according to his own testimony) as a Lafayette undergraduate. Alan Greenspan, former chairman of the Council of Economic Advisors and before that one of the district's most astute analysts, completed his PhD in the subject *after* his Washington stint was over; one wonders what went through the minds of his examiners at the doctoral defense.

Perhaps the most famous investment banker of our time, Felix Rohatyn, majored in physics and skiing, as he put it, during his stay at Middlebury, and averred that he owed his success at Lazard Freres and on the national scene to the fact that he never had a course in economics. Not unusual; J. P. Morgan too was a physics student, while Sidney Homer, who revolutionized bond analysis, studied philosophy at Harvard and dismayed his opera diva mother, Louise, when telling her of plans to go to the Street. At the height of his career, Homer went to great pains to deny being an economist; "I'm a bond man," he would tell interviewers.

Each of these arrived at the investment arena and became

pros *without* the kind of economics training you might think appropriate. All had what amounted to on-the-job training. No one expects individual investors to aspire to the kind of knowledge these individuals command or commanded, but they either should obtain as much as their needs dictate or stick to simpler, though less rewarding, kinds of investments. It can be done.

Start off with the fact that you will have to absorb a vocabulary and some relatively straightforward concepts. It has been said that all of economics is a commentary on the law of supply and demand. Not quite, but there is enough truth in this to make the claim plausible. The terminology is the problem, along with the difficulty some economists have in making themselves understandable.[1] Just about all you will need can be derived from two extremely well-written books (though of course there are others). Paul Heyne's *The Economic Way of Thinking*, (Chicago: Science Research Associates, 1983) provides a good introduction, while Lawrence S. Ritter and William S. Silber, *Money* (New York: Basic Books, 1984), is a fine dissection of that subject.

If economics were a science, investors would have a much simpler time of it. The fact of the matter is that so many variables are clashing with one another all of the time that it is difficult for the pros to tell what lies ahead, and of course the amateurs should be uneasy when venturing into an arena in which even the superstars have their share of stumbles.

The list of forecasting blunders by top ranked economists is so long that it could literally take up volumes. So just consider that in late 1985 most of the major firms and organizations engaged in doing just that were asked their estimates of growth (or lack of

---

[1]John K. Galbraith once remarked that if an economist can't be understood, its usually because he either has nothing to say or lacks wit and a command of language. Of course Galbraith never suffered from either of these maladies, and his erudition and wit have always been the envy of his less graceful confreres. A handy guide to the terms economists use is Douglas Greenwald and Associates, *The McGraw-Hill Dictionary of Modern Economics: A Handbook of Terms and Organizations* (New York: McGraw-Hill, 1973 and subsequent editions).

same) for the first quarter of 1986. Here are some of the predictions:

Data Resources	−0.3%
Chase Econometrics	1.7
Wharton Econometrics	1.9
Eggert Econometrics	2.5
Georgia State University	2.6
Manufacturers Hanover	2.9
Townsend Greenspan	3.5
Dun & Bradstreet	3.8
Polyconomics	4.0
Morris Cohen & Associates	4.2
Peter L. Bernstein	5.3
Sanford C. Bernstein	7.3

Source: Insight, June 30, 1986, p. 43.

The actual growth figure was 2.9 percent, meaning that Manufacturers Hanover was right on target. What about Data Resources and Sanford C. Bernstein, respected seers both? Well, back to the old drawing board. But also consider that in predicting for the fourth quarter of 1985, in which growth of 0.7 percent was registered, the closest was the same Peter L. Bernstein (0.3 percent), who was so far off base for the first quarter of the following year. Likewise, Manufacturers Hanover, which did so well in the later quarter, thought the last one in 1985 would come to a growth of 3.2 percent, pretty far from the mark. A knowledge of past records of prediction is an uncertain guide to future dependability.

Little wonder that President Reagan seems to derive so much joy in twitting economists; its an old presidential custom. Harry Truman used to plead for a "one armed economist," because his were always saying, "On the other hand . . ." and often were just as wrong as some of those cited previously. John Rutledge, chairman of Claremont Economics Institute, was right on the button when he said, "It's like Beirut. Fourteen different armies are vying for control and no one seems to be winning."

In 1983 Chairman of the Council of Economic Advisors Martin Feldstein, one of the nation's most respected economists, predicted that Reaganomics would cause higher interest rates and general calamity unless there was a tax increase. No increase took place, and rates went down. Salomon Brothers Chief Economist Henry Kaufman is one of the nation's most astute financial analysts. He was generally correct during much of the 1970s and early 1980s, and he too erred in predicting higher rates for 1983–1984, but is still listened to respectfully, by those who value his perspective on the markets. So is Richard J. Hoffman, formerly Merrill Lynch's chief economist who went off on his own in the summer of 1985. At that time he opined the Dow would be under 600 by July 1986; as it turned out, the Dow was more than triple that figure the following summer. Even with the best of intelligence (in both meanings of the word) able practitioners can go wrong. Nobel Laureate Milton Friedman was convinced the Federal Reserve's loose money policy adopted in 1983 would lead to a strong bout of inflation. It didn't happen; inflation declined instead.

It pays to follow the analyses made by such as these, but don't base investment decisions on them. Also, don't think because that forecaster on television has more letters after his name than in it, or is a major Wall Street prognosticator, that he has to do a better job than you. Not necessarily. You will discover this the more you read and hear. The rule is look to economists for insights into the process and analytical methods, but don't take their predictions too seriously—especially when it comes to the market.

GOING IT ALONE

Now for your daily and weekly reading. The financial pages of no daily newspaper, not even *The New York Times* or *The Washington*

Post, can compare with the entirety of *The Wall Street Journal*, one of the jewels of western civilization, easily available in most places in the United States. You won't get any "hot tips" from the *Journal*, and don't think it offers "inside information"; how could this be, given the circulation? But it does contain most of the background material you will need to assess the economy. This should be supplemented by a perusal of magazines mentioned in the first chapter and afterwards—*Barron's*, *Business Week*, *Fortune*, *Forbes*, and for a most perceptive view of the world scene and new perspectives on the United States, *The Economist*.

There is no need to subscribe to all of these and read them cover-to-cover, or even on the date of publication. Since many local libraries get most or all of them, make a habit of stopping by once a week or so to skim through them for articles of interest. An hour spent in this fashion can pay both long- and short-term dividends.

So you have decided to avoid the gurus, listen skeptically to experts, and embark on a reading program of your own. What does all of this mean if you accumulate information but still lack a conceptual framework to channel the knowledge? Here are a few ideas to start you on your way.

You might begin by considering that many on Wall Street believe the business cycle has generally been deemed a good rough indicator of where the economy is headed. Is this really the case? The cycle may be divided into four phases: expansion, leveling out, contraction, and recovery. Contractions, usually known as recessions, run around 11 months on the average, while expansions carry through for a shade less than three years. So a complete cycle lasts around four years. But this is only a rough estimate. During the post-World War II period recessions took place in 1949, 1953–1954, 1957–1958, 1960–1961, 1970, 1974–1975, 1980, and 1981–1982.

Note that there was no dip from 1961 to 1970; cyclists betting on one in mid-decade clearly were disappointed. Also, there was no three-year expansion between the 1957–1958 and 1960–1961 recessions. As stated, the intervals are not carved in stone. Also, recessions and expansions are best identified in retrospect.

These words are being written in summer 1986, when talk is that we are heading toward a recession sometime in 1987. Why? Because, say some economists, the recovery from the sharp 1981–1982 recession is "aged," which is to say a downturn is overdue. If so, such a development would affect your investment decisions. The best time to buy stocks would be at the bottom of major market declines, which took place in 1962, 1966, 1970, 1974, 1978, and 1982. What do these have in common? Three of these were recession years (1970, 1974, and 1982) and three were years of strong economic performance (1962, 1966, 1978).

So much for the pattern.

Is the stock market itself a good economic indicator? Some economists have said the market has predicted 11 out of the last 5 recessions, which is to say it *isn't* reliable. Others claim that the market tries to predict the future, reflecting what the consensus believes will be the economic and financial situation a few months out. Of course, belief and reality are different. The fact is that the record is spotty at best.

We return to the matter of obtaining a view of the economy and where it is headed, and the fact that all of our guides are uncertain. If it makes you any happier remember that professional economists can't offer more than a hedged prediction. If they could, their recommended courses of action would mitigate any problems which might develop. Even undergraduate students know how to head off a recession or at least soften its impact; pump up the money supply, decrease taxes, or increase the level of government spending, or a combination of the three. Do this at the right time and the expansionary policies will soften any future dip. The problem is with the analysis. Suppose it is wrong, and the economy is not about to fall into a recession? Then these policies could cause a major bout of inflation. The economist is a doctor, diagnosing the economy and writing out a prescription. The correct diagnosis can lead to a cure, a wrong one can cripple or maim.

Generally speaking, the market looks ahead from six months to a year. This means that even though the economy is doing well today, earnings are in good shape, and what the Department of

Commerce identifies as the Index of Coincident Indicators is showing up nicely, there may be trouble around the bend.

What should be of greater concern to investors is the Index of Leading Economic Indicators, which purports to show what lies ahead—the area of greatest market concern.[2] This indicator, and a number of others, are monitored carefully by most financial advisors and portfolio managers, which is reason enough for you to do the same. Learning about its message presents no problem; the news appears on financial pages shortly after being released. But this Index and the others are not foolproof. Indeed, nothing in economics is, not even the law of supply and demand.

The Index is flawed in many ways: a sharp jump or decline in one statistic, due to unusual circumstances, can throw a forecast out of kilter. Moreover, the Index doesn't take into account unanticipated events—the Organization of Petroleum Exporting Countries' actions in the 1970s, for example, and revolutions almost anywhere. If peace—real peace—should break out suddenly, markets throughout the world would tumble (the pros don't like the unexpected) though the development would be bullish in the long run.

This doesn't mean you should throw up your arms in resignation and abandon the market, figuring that without a knowledge of what economic shape we will be in a year hence investment decisions are too difficult to contemplate. Not necessarily, for unlike the economist, the investor need not be held accountable to such forecasts. Rather, he should act on what is generally believed, and not what will turn out to be true or false.

A KEY PERSPECTIVE

John Maynard Keynes, the greatest economist of the first half of the century and an astute investor, once observed that the way to

---

[2]This Index, compiled as are the others by the Commerce Department's Bureau of Economic Analysis, is comprised of 47 series, covering marginal employment, industrial production, new and unfilled orders, business enterprise formation, inventories, money and credit flows, and even stock prices.

select the winner in a beauty contest was to study the judges, and not the contestants, for they will determine who takes the prize. It is a message investors should take to heart. The way to invest in the future of the economy is not to ponder what will transpire, but merely the kind of assessments institutional managers are acting on. Do they think a military buildup is in the making? If so, they may stock up on General Dynamics, Northrop, Lockheed, United Technologies, and scores of smaller firms, and watch their prices rise. Is it important that they are right or wrong? Yes if one is to understand the economy. No if all one cares about is investments.

We have observed that the investment arena is one in which self-fulfilling prophecy reigns. Let it appear a medical breakthrough is in the works and one group of stocks will rise and others fall, and the same holds true for speculations regarding revolutions in South Africa and Latin America, new oil and natural gas finds, rumors of action against car makers, and so on down the line. Is there talk of a cancer cure coming out of one of the drug houses? Its stock will soar, as analysts scramble to figure out which other firms will win and which will lose. What if the rumor is false? Then the stocks will eventually fall, and all the while industry insiders know that a cure for acne would bring in much more earnings than might one for cancer, but would not rate such headlines. When the situation in Libya heated up in April 1986, astute investors considered the impact on foreign travel, concluded it would be down, and bought heavily in such domestically oriented stocks as Disney, Marriott, and Holiday Inns. The stocks rose, but not because of the economic outlook for these companies, but rather the conclusions of investors regarding this outlook. Simply stated, the supply of stock remained constant, the demand rose, and this pushed their prices upward. Self-fulfilling prophecy did the trick.

The money supply figures, which the Fed releases every Thursday after the market closes, is deemed one of the better indicators, and other example of self-fulfilling prophecy at work. Everyone *knows* (or just as good, acts as though they know) that higher than anticipated increases are bearish, for that means the central bank will soon tighten money, causing financial stringency. Likewise, lower than expected rises or declines are deemed bullish, because the next step will be a loosening of rates, which Wall Street likes. So if the supply is up, chances are good the market will decline the next session, and then a rise will follow a lower than expected increase.

Do weekly figures *really* matter? No, not really; it's the pattern that counts, and this develops over many weeks, even months. Why does the market behave as it does in the light of the figures? Self-fulfilling prophecy.

By now you may be thinking that much of this is irrational. So it is, and the trick is to guess how others will react to news all agree is not that meaningful, and then take actions before they can.

Money is a serious business, but it is a game as well.

What it comes down to, then, is that you should understand economic forces but be modest about your abilities to use present information to forecast future developments, and consider how others will interpret news they think means something.

In time you will learn that the experts' predictions aren't all that good, but it matters little, since the generality of investors are at a loss without some guru or another to follow. Do you *really* think that any economic model can tell you what the unemployment and inflation rates will be next year at this time? Most are wrong; the few that are close to target receive publicity, but chances are they will be off base next time out. It does make sense to watch the forecasts carefully, because once again, others will act on them. For example, if a respected group of experts predicts higher interest rates they may indeed rise—because borrowers will hasten to the market to get money before the prices rise, and by their actions cause the advance.

Be warned, however, that the profession is getting wise to this. There is a group of economists known as the "Rational Expectations School," which holds that individuals behave according to their rational expectations. According to some members, the reason long-term interest rates remained high in the 1983–1985 period when conventional wisdom indicated they should have fallen was because large investors expected it wouldn't last, that inflation would return, and so refused to lend at the lower rates, thus obliging borrowers to up their bids.

It works for the market as well as the economy, though in a somewhat different fashion. If most experts predict—as they did in late 1985—that after a correction of around 100 points stocks will resume their upward move, there probably won't be a correction, since the "smart money" will be in there on the buy side when anything like it seems to be taking place.

Now none of this is your problem, but you do have to make investment decisions, which means taking a point of view on the economy.

So start out by asking yourself—right now—where you think the economy is going, and also what you think the experts will be saying. If you assume prosperity will continue or is on the way, look to certain industries and instruments for investment ideas. Should you conclude we are headed toward recession, different ones should be considered. Finally, there are some industries which are "recession resistant," in that they grow no matter what happens to the economy short of disaster.

THINKING ABOUT INDUSTRIES

You don't have to know much about investments to figure out which industries are sensitive to the business cycle and those that are not. We all have to eat, for example, so stocks in food companies generally tend to ignore the pressures of economic expansion and contraction. So do soft drinks, electric utilities, and others dealing with what many deem necessities. But you can't expect to outperform the market with them, unless the industry is revitalized, takeovers transpire, or the company changes its spots.

Yet secular growth is the rule in the American economy. At all times be aware of the vitality and creativity of capitalism, a system in which new products and industries are born with astonishing regularity, while old ones fade and vanish. Last decade's growth industry may be this one's mature area, and a declining business in the early twenty-first century. More often than not, industries and companies don't die—they metamorphize. The radio manufacturers, to cite an obvious example, became major forces in television receivers, while the major radio networks became big players in television programming. Not all are that obvious. The Studebaker brothers were among those buggy manufacturers who recognized the automobile would put them out of business, and made the switch. IBM was the nation's most important manufacturer of large calculators, and scrapped that business to go into computers. Minnesota Mining & Manufacturing does this sort of thing on a regular basis. In fact this is one of the more important attributes to look for in an industry and its companies.

But you probably are already aware of the phenomenon of origination and growth. If you are 30 years old you will recall the birth of the microcomputer industry, videocassettes, cable TV, digital instrumentation, the spate of new energy sources that came with the oil crisis, the rebirth of automobiles and the emergence of genetic engineering, fast food health stores, pet rocks, Cabbage Patch dolls, low-priced airline tickets, and computerized chess players, just to mention a few that come to mind. At the same time there was the continued erosion of the old steel industry (but the concomitant birth of a new one), the decline of the cigarette industry, the failure of American firms to hold on in consumer electronics, struggles in semiconductors, the crash and revival of mobile homes, and many other changes. When looking at an industry it is well to figure out just where they are in developmental terms.

The rule here is to give the matter some thought, that industrial America is ever evolving and we have to be on guard against generalizations.

Even then there are difficulties in predicting developments in growth industries, many of which, after all, do not have much of a track record since they are so new. For example, did you ever think McDonald's, Piccadilly Cafeterias, and Ponderosa would suffer during recessions? At one time the conventional wisdom held that spending on fast foods was discretionary, but nowadays a different view is held. With Americans edging to the point where they consume half their meals away from home, fast food has entered the stage where it resembles coffee more than a Caribbean cruise, which is to say it is nondiscretionary. Rather than eliminating them, during bad times many Americans switch from more expensive eateries to the less costly ones. Eventually fast foods may be looked on as beneficiaries of recessions, not victims. Similarly, the general view was that the fast food chains would do poorly during the fuel crises of the 1970s, since so many of their patrons arrived by auto. It didn't happen; after the fact analysts reflected that the restaurants have become so ubiquitous that almost all Americans can get to one or more with little expenditure of fuel.

Beware the sin of extrapolation, assuming that if a company or industry has expanded by a certain percentage for the past few years it is bound to continue. Remember video games, both in arcades and at home? That was supposed to become a permanent, multibillion dollar industry. It vanished in smoke after about three years. How about microcomputers? In 1983, two years after IBM introduced its PC and set the industry on fire, the wise heads had it that in a very short time most American homes would have one or more, and given the rapid technological changes and price cutting, would trade them in on a regular basis. It didn't happen; in 1984 and 1985 many small and medium-sized manufacturers went belly up.

Get into the habit of trying to assess the qualities of industries, companies, and products. If you could have gotten into Coleco and Warner Communications before the height of the video game boom and sold out before it crashed, you would have done very well. In all such things, be on guard.

Monitor the American scene, with an eye to changing social customs and the nature of the population. The best stock picker I ever knew was a nice old lady who didn't own a single share, and in fact never read the business section. In the 1950s, when automatic pin spotters first appeared in bowling alleys, the then mother of three and her husband moved to suburbia, frequented drive-in theaters, and joined a bowling league. Anyone who purchased AMF and Brunswick, the two leading factors in the industry, would have done very well. When the government released evidence on a link between cigarette smoking and cancer, she switched to the high-filtration Kents; that year its manufacturer, Lorillard, was one of the market stars. At about the same time the Soviets launched sputnik, leading to an orgy of national criticism about the evils of materialism. She purchased a new car that year—a Rambler American—as though to demonstrate her willingness to live a more spartan existence, and American Motors led the pack at the NYSE.

That woman and her husband are in a retirement home today, and her daughter is married, has two children and a job, and little time for household work. So the kids go to a local Kinder Care while she drops by fast food operations and supermarket salad bars for dinners for the family. And nursing home, child care, and fast foods outperformed the market.

Incidentally, this is one of the reasons for the decline of Avon Products. Avon did very well when housewives wanted part time work to earn a few extra dollars, doing so by calling on other housewives to sell their cosmetics. The Avon lady now has a full time, better paying job, and the fewer housewives mean that much fewer "Avon calling" rung doorbells.

There is a moral to this: demography is destiny, and investors would do well to keep this in mind when considering new and declining industries.

Some economic historians have concluded that just as there is a business cycle—crude and unpredictable in prospect though it may be—industries too go through several stages, which they label birth, development, growth, maturity, and decline. Keep in mind, however, that this categorization is meant to be suggestive, and there are plenty of exceptions to what isn't even meant to be considered a rule. As you read, reflect that all of this has an investment component which should recall the "triangle of investment" discussed at the beginning of Chapter 2.

Industries in the birth stage are noted by easy entry, less than onerous capital requirements, rapid change, and constant product alteration. Such was the case with automobiles at the turn of the century, fast foods in the 1950s, and electronics and microcomputers in more recent years. Solar energy falls into this category, to cite an example of an industry that may never make it. Or to put it differently, for each emerging industry (and company, for that matter) that survives and flourishes, there are dozens that remain concepts and little else (remember citizen band radios?). Truly growing industries often shuck off the business cycle, expanding in bad times as well as good.

Is there any way to distinguish between winners and losers? The former fill a felt need or help create one. Fast foods came along when Americans had already started eating out or taking in prepared food more than in the past; the hamburger joints of the 1930s appeared when few could afford on a regular basis what was close to being a luxury. Microcomputers arrived after two generations of office workers had become acclimated to the larger machines. Airline travel wasn't much in the 1920s and 1930s, for safety, comfort, and financial reasons; it became important after World War II when these problems were overcome.

Developing industries are identifiable by high initial prices of products that decline regularly—like the Model T Ford did in almost every year of its existence, or microcomputers today and TV sets in the 1950s and 1960s. Indeed, when prices remain stable and tend to rise, one can safely conclude that the great development phase is about to end or has already done so. Industries in the developmental stage are also noted for rapid technological change; today's McDonald's are different from those of the 1950s, and the menus change with regularity (remember the ballyhoo regarding fast food breakfasts?).

Look for combinations. In 1985, for example, there were 203 mergers and takeovers in the computer industry, versus 118 the previous year. Generally speaking developing industries are stormy places which one enters with some trepidation. Take positions in the right stocks in them and you'll do very well indeed, but there always is the danger of failure. You might not make a fortune by purchasing shares in an electric utility (a mature industry) but the electric company probably won't go bankrupt either, and until fairly recently wouldn't cut its dividend. Not so a start-up electronics operation.

Which is another hallmark of developing industries; stocks in companies operating within them generally don't pay dividends, since they need all the funds they can get for expansion in the rugged battleground of the marketplace.

The growth phase may be said to have begun once the shake-outs are just about over, and at this point the product or service is no longer novel, those consumers and business customers which simply *must* have them are sated, and companies start thinking more about bringing them to the masses from the base already established in a specialized segment of the market.

Since there is no clear demarcation between development and growth stages, one must make judgment calls. One sign that growth has commenced is the higher ratings given bonds issued by the surviving firms, the greater familiarity of the product and service, and toward the end, lower percentage increases in the rate of expansion. A second is the withdrawal of the entrepreneurs and their replacement by managers. Once a firm reaches a certain size professional management is required, and often the imaginative, innovative originators of the company find that they lack the talents and interests to manage the operations and make strategic plans for what now is a multidivisional corporation. Another sign is the initiation of cash dividends, which the companies now can afford.

Maturity arrives when managers come to realize that their capacity to produce has become much greater than the markets can bear, and that in the future growth will have to come from enlarging market share at the expense of others. Capital costs are now high, and these factors make entry by new players difficult, though not impossible. Advertising and promotional competition now becomes more common, especially since product prices have stabilized. Insofar as the companies are concerned, the survivors are large, move more sluggishly, and bureaucratic atherosclerosis has become a major problem, to which managements devote a great deal of time attempting to overcome. At this point too the market no longer provides the firm with astronomic P/E ratios, while dividends continue to increase. The result is that the yields from their stocks often become attractive.

There was a time when automobiles and television receivers were growth industries, oblivious to the vagaries of the business cycle. Not so today, when cars and TVs are among the more cyclical products and industries. The same is true of housing, one of the most complex and important industries, since it involves lumber and appliance companies, savings and loan associations, movers, manufacturers of carpeting and furniture, and even fertilizer producers (for new lawns), and the dinnerware companies, not to mention department stores. In boom periods people have more money, and given an optimistic point of view might go into the market for homes—that's the positive view. The negative is that this is also the time that interest rates tend to rise, as to mortgage charges, which can price housing out of the market. Similarly, mortgage rates decline during recessions—when lower house prices might attract buyers—who are wary of such commitments at these times.

By now you probably have thought of dozens of companies that don't fall into these categories. For example, in computer mainframes IBM has avoided the maturity phase and often prances around like a colt. Consider that in 1980 IBM wasn't even a factor in the microcomputer field, and that today its Entry Systems Division, charged with that market segment, would be the world's fourth largest computer firm (behind IBM, Burroughs and Digital Equipment) if a separate firm. Others in the industry seem positively middle-aged—Control Data and Honeywell come to mind. Tobacco is a mature industry, but in the late 1970s Philip Morris behaved like a growth company. There is little need to go into the amazing revival at Chrysler at a time when the domestic auto industry was in a state of malaise. Again, there are plenty of other examples one could cite to indicate just how complex the matter is.

Now for some general rules—or perhaps a better way to put it, observations:

1. Unless you are familiar with a new, young, industry from personal or business experience, refrain from buying stocks in individual companies: there are better ways to participate, specifically through purchases of specialty mutual funds, more on which in Chapter 10.

2. When seeking stocks in growth industries look to management rather than products. The ability to adjust to new circumstances, to capitalize on opportunities, is a crucial element in the capitalist environment. Does the CEO of a company who has demonstrated such abilities get $1 million a year in compensation? He may be underpaid. Similarly, the CEO who works for a dollar a year and runs his company to the ground is overcompensated. Admittedly this is a difficult matter to assess, but in this stage good management is the *sine qua non* for success.

3. In mature industries by wary about going against the leaders. Do you really believe a new department store chain can compete with Macy's and Federated, that secondary operations can become major players? In this industry, and other mature ones, investors should look for firms making end runs around the leaders by entering specialty fields. General Electric and RCA failed in their attempts to go head-to-head against IBM; Apple, Digital Equipment, and Cray did well in specialized parts of the industry. The same is true for pharmaceuticals, foods, and other mature industries.

Armed with this approach, you are now ready to consider assessing individual companies. Be forewarned: it isn't a simple matter, and even if you are prepared to do so, and possess the requisite knowledge, it may not be the best way to go. Here's how to start, and if you get discouraged along the way, cheer up: there is a simpler and preferred way out, discussed in the concluding chapter.

We have no further need to catalogue the many publications in the investment field, so consider what you can do on your own.

CONTACTING THE COMPANY

The best way to start is with materials put out by the company in which you are interested and are easily available to shareholders. Obtaining annual reports poses no great problem. Each spring leading newspapers and business magazines carry several pages of ads paid for by participating firms offering to send you copies of their annuals. Select those of interest, or simply write "all" across the coupon at the bottom of the page, mail it to the box number indicated, and in a few weeks you'll start getting a steady stream of them (along with dirty looks from your mailcarrier).

For the others contact the company directly. Most large enterprises have staffs whose sole occupation is stockholder relations and you, as a present or potential stockholder, have access to them. So go to the local library and look up the latest Standard & Poor's report on the company, and after reading it turn to the bottom of the second page, where you will find its headquarters, a listing of officers, and a telephone number. If the firm has an officer in charge of shareholder relations, telephone and ask to speak with that person; if not, try the president or chairperson.[3]

No, you probably won't get to speak with him, but rather a secretary. Tell that individual you would like to receive the latest copies of the annual report, the 10-K, the most recent quarterly report and 10-Q, and any other material that might be of interest to a stockholder. If the person on the other end sounds reluctant, mention casually that under law this material must be provided, and you will be told it will be dispatched as soon as possible. Al-

---

[3]The big firms have toll-free 800 numbers, one of the great inventions of our time.

low for delays and the like, and it may be necessary to call again, but probably not; companies are pretty good about such matters.[4]

The next step is to read the reports, attempting to obtain an impression of the firm. A great deal of information can be obtained from the annuals, if you take the time to read it carefully. You might be surprised at how few stockholders even bother to go through the materials. A survey taken in 1983 indicated that half of them only skimmed reports or simply threw them away, and of those who read them, only 55 percent found them useful in making investment decisions.

These reports are scanned by investment professionals, those analysts (especially the fundamentalists) who offer advice for a fee. Here is what they found useful in them, in order of importance:

	Section	Importance Rating
1.	Financial statements	95%
2.	Business segment information	93
3.	Financial review	87
4.	Five- or ten-year financial summaries	87
5.	Management's analysis	81
6.	Review of the year	78
7.	Quarterly summaries	74
8.	Statement of accounting policies	73
9.	Financial highlights	70
10.	Letter to shareholders	69
11.	Dividend payments (two years)	54
12.	Stock price history (two years)	43
13.	Inflation accounting (effects of changing prices)	39

[4]If you would rather not wait, try a private concern, Disclosure Inc. (5161 River Road, Bethesda, MD 20816, 800-638-8241), which is in the business of providing them to interested parties, and will send microfiches to you at a modest fee in a matter of days. Most local libraries have microfiche readers for your use.

Note the importance of understanding financial statements. This presents a problem unless you possess a knowledge of accounting—indeed even BBAs in accounting have difficulty in getting to the root of some reports. But then you have to go on to the 10-Ks and 10-Qs. These are filings with the Securities and Exchange Commission, mandated by the Securities Exchange Act of 1934, which contain more information, usually of a financial nature, that may be of use.[5]

The next step is to ask your broker to call up the stock on his computer to see if there has been any important news on it during the past few months. All full-line brokerages subscribe to one or more information retrieval services; to no surprise, one of the favorites is Dow-Jones, and such a search can save many hours in the library. Most general statistical material can be found in Value Line, Moody's Handbook, Moody's manuals, the S&P manuals, and while their advisories should be taken lightly, the statistics can be important.

By now you may be wondering how to analyze and interpret those financial statements. Instruction in such matters is best left to other books, for to attempt to do so here would require several hundred pages. In any case it may not be necessary, given the time constraints most investors operate under. Moreover, you will need several works, perhaps even a college course, because it is such a complicated matter. One way to start would be a careful reading of one of the best in a large field in Joel G. Siegel, *How to Analyze Businesses, Financial Statements and the Quality of Earnings* (Englewood Cliffs, N.J.: Prentice-Hall, 1982). Appreciate, however, that while Siegel knows whereof he writes and does so clearly, it will be tough sledding at times.

Perhaps by now you have suspected it might make better sense to try some other, simpler kind of investment method. Or if it *really* takes all that time and effort to do a good job with stocks, perhaps you should use that energy for some other potentially more rewarding investment area.

---

[5]Thornton O'glove with Robert Sobel, *The Quality of Earnings* (New York: Free Press, 1987) deals with the analysis of such public documents.

THE POTENTIAL OF INSURANCE

Most of us don't think of insurance as an investment. This is unfortunate, since some of the newer policies make a bit of sense, especially for high bracket taxpayers who are troubled by the vagaries of the new tax law. Many of these have been created by insurance companies but are offered through stock brokerages, and merit investigation.

One of the newer and more interesting products, sold by several companies, combines insurance with payment of tax-free income at a better than average rate—upward of 7 percent.

These come with different names, like "Future Plus" or "The Money Tree." Call your broker, describe it to him, and he will probably know what you mean, and have a policy to offer. It goes like this, an example taken from an offering made by the North Atlantic Life Insurance Company.

Consider the situation of a 55-year-old male who takes out one of these plans. The first year he puts down $25,000, which immediately gives him an insurance policy with a $111,460 death benefit a surrender value of $22,292—but no income.

For each of the next four years he pays premiums of $3841. The death benefit remains constant, but the surrender value of the policy rises to $51,124. Since the policyholder has put in a total of $40,364, it is a decent but not particularly terrific growth record.

Now the fun begins. The policy is now fully paid, and in the sixth year the policyholder receives $3841 tax free in the form of a policy loan, and this will continue for the rest of his life. The death benefit declines by that amount the first year, but the cash value of the policy changes, depending on the current interest rate. In autumn 1986 that was 10 percent, and the cash value would be $53,391.

So it goes until the eleventh year, by which time the insurance coverage is down to $83,286 for our 66 year old, the surrender value, $64,164. At this point the additional interest on the policy's cash value goes to purchase more insurance, and that figure starts to rise, to $84,786 in year 12, $86,863 in year 13, and so on. By the time the policyholder is 72 years old, he will be covered to the extent of $92,467, while the surrender value will be $73,447 (again, assuming a 10 percent interest rate). And all the while those annual checks for a tax-free $3841 will continue to arrive.

If this is not wholly satisfying, consider the following: the policyholder can borrow against the cash value at low rates. Also, the policy can be terminated at any time for the surrender value.

As noted, this kind of policy is offered by many insurance companies, through stock brokerages. We are currently in a period in which new financial instruments are being created with astonishing regularity, and investors must remain flexible and open minded to make sensible choices.

A generation ago that 55-year-old male would have thought the time for life insurance had passed him by—and he might have been wrong. Today some investors, especially wealthy ones, couldn't be more off base. This isn't to say that such insurance is for everyone. But some variants certainly merit investigation.

Others such as Universal policies are fine surrogates for stocks and bonds. At this writing earnings on reserves are sheltered as well as any individual retirement account or Keogh plan, and some policies can even offer protection against inflation, linked as they are to the Consumer Price Index. The insurance industry had undergone nothing less than a revolution in outlook since the old days when the basic choice seemed to be between term, whole life, ordinary, limited payment, endowment, and other familiar plans. Universal Life, Future Plus, and single premium deferred annuities can make more sense for some investors than equities or debts, and new products come out all the time. Imagination and innovation, which at one time was limited to marketing, is now concentrated in product design. This is one of the more important secrets investors should explore.

But there is a problem. Far too many insurance brokers are wedded to the hard sell, and giving them a ring and asking for information can lead to months of telephone calls from oleaginous types who once having seen a flicker of interest won't let go. Unfortunately the insurance industry's new imaginative approach in its products hasn't extended to sales, which is why you might try going through a stock broker. What is needed is an insurance equivalent of a no-load mutual fund. Once these could be found in savings bank life insurance, but sadly, the banks don't offer the more imaginative products, though at this writing several are nibbling at them.

This book does not deal with insurance, and this is about as far as can be gone in the matter without the author's venturing into what for him are relatively uncertain waters.[6]

IS REAL ESTATE FOR YOU?

Real estate presents different difficulties. Stated simply, wheeling and dealing in residential and commercial properties can be far more financially rewarding than securities with less risk, not the least of which being due to peculiarities in the tax laws, some of which remain even after tax reform. Again, this isn't the place to investigate real estate, but there is no shortage of books and seminars in the field. For the former, simply peruse the best seller lists; works on how to double your money in properties are as common as those diet books promising a sleek figure in nothing flat. But consider that in addition to a knowledge of techniques real estate investment requires a different kind of temperament than does buying and selling securities. In contrast to properties, securities are "clean," in that they are readily marketable and liquid. Anyone can sell a round lot of GE any business day at around the same price of the last trade; the same isn't true for a rental or commercial property. Purchasing a municipal bond doesn't require too much knowledge; buying a stake in a mini-mall calls for expertise in law and accounting as well as real estate, and in addition an entree to local banks and S&Ls can be useful. This is to suggest that one gets more bang out of the real estate buck, but at a price.

---

[6]Those interested in a good introduction to the subject might consult Robert I. Mehr, *Fundamentals of Insurance* (Homewood, IL: Irwin, 1983.)

Then too it is less messy to conduct research on securities than real estate. Amateurs can do fairly well in the securities market; real estate is for those forceful, intelligent, hardworking, and gutsy individuals willing, able, and daring enough to enter the field.

One final nonsecurities form of investment, and we can turn to methods of analyzing securities and shortening the odds against you when engaging in duels with the high stakes players. That is your own business. Most people work for others, but more new businesses are opening in America than ever before, and even though most fail, others do succeed. If you are in business for yourself, or are a franchisee, securities investments shouldn't appear attractive. Indeed, if they are, then perhaps something is wrong with your business.

More small companies fail due to lack of capital than any other reason. So be prepared to plow back earnings, and let accumulating that portfolio of stocks and bonds wait until a later time. When would that be? Once again, your instincts will provide a signal. When the time comes that you yearn for dividends and interest and tire of the business, the time may have come to get out. If you are a small operator, a partnership might be the answer, meaning you might seek out someone willing take a share of the business for a cash consideration. Larger businesspeople would want to think about a public offering, a matter for investment bankers. But those who have achieved this status already know what to do, so we need not dally here any longer.

So we return to stocks, still one of the better vehicles much of the time, for most small investors. But let us recapitulate the problems investment in equities pose:

The investment arena is dominated by heavy hitters, who know much more than you and work at it full-time.

The development of index options and related instruments mean the market can turn more on arbitrage and related operations than economic or business intelligence.

Interest rate fluctuations can alter perceptions of securities in a twinkling.

Alternate investments easily switched can disrupt equities.

New instruments more appropriate than stocks are being created regularly, and it takes an expert merely to keep up with them.

International markets have become more accessible, but is this the place for you? And if so, where will you get the needed information?

Keep this in mind the next time you think you know what's going on in the economy, industry, and the company that looks so good. How will it be impacted by options expirations the third Friday of the month? Or the Triple Witching Hour four times a year? If your information is good, how can you explain the fact that you may have indirectly purchased the stock from an institution that presumably knows it better? If Henry Kaufman has spells of wrong calls how can you have all that confidence in your abilities? Are you willing to spend the time and make the effort to learn about hedging with options? Do you want to learn about the mechanics of Ginnie Maes and more important, when to buy and sell them? Finally, how conversant are you with the Hong Kong and London markets?

Now put it all together. If you are a fundamentalist, ask yourself if the stock's promise over a reasonable period, say six months or so, is reflected in the price. If not consider buying. Should you be technically inclined, none of this will mean very much, but even so reflect it's nice to have fundamental reinforcement for the charts. But as you do, think about alternatives— bonds/fixed income securities in particular.

7 CORPORATE FIXED INCOME SECURITIES: THEIR WORD IS YOUR BOND

Note that in the last sentence in the preceding chapter reference was made to "bonds/fixed income securities." This was done deliberately, because different individuals use each term to describe what they think of as essentially the same kinds of instruments, namely debts, which is probably the broadest and more accurate classification of all.

In fact not all fixed income paper are bonds as the term is conventionally used, while not all bonds offer fixed income. Yet all, in one way or another, represent a financial obligation owed by a borrower to a lender, which with some exceptions must be paid in full at a specified time unless the borrower intends to go into default and have assets seized or face legal action.

Perhaps this is too fundamental. Perhaps not. Go through the shelves of bookstores (or those of libraries) and you'll find scores of investment-oriented books that deal exclusively with stocks or give debts short shrift. There is a good reason for this; the kinds of people who buy investment books tend to be oriented in that direction, and authors and publishers go fishing where the fish are to be found. Moreover, the world of the small investor is geared to stocks. Finally, one might trade in stocks to make a bundle, but while killings can be made with debts, generally speaking—most of the time—these instruments are for the investor, not the speculator. Hence the decision to cover more bases in this chapter than has been done with stocks.

Investment guides written a generation or so ago would make a careful distinction between bonds backed by the corporation's total assets and those with a call on specified holdings. In addition there were debts founded on the company's general credit, and several others that were not. There would be a long section in such works on the differences between these, in particular on how debentures, a call on the firm's general credit, are of a lower quality than bonds, which are liens on specific properties, such as a freight car or machine tool. Since debentures were riskier, they provided higher yields.

These differences matter little nowadays in the corporate sector, and some textbooks in corporate finance and investments don't even cover the subject (though as will be seen they are extremely important when it comes to the tax-frees in the municipal and state bond field). Generally speaking, if you are troubled about the viability of the firm that issued the bond, as an investor (as opposed to speculator) you probably should avoid all of its debt issues.

THE REVIVAL OF BONDS

During the 1960s bull market debts were about as boring a set of instruments as might be considered, and for good reason. For the most part they were purchased by institutions, placed in portfolios, where they remained until maturity. Stocks performed spectacularly; in the relatively stable interest rate environment, bonds languished. The Dow rose from 535.76 in June 1962 to peak at 994.20 in January 1966, in one of the most sustained bull moves in American history. In the same period the Dow Bonds rose from 86.07 to 87.12, hardly a thrilling performance.

Many studies indicate that the long-term total return from common stocks is higher than that from bonds, not surprising given the fact that bonds offer less risk than equities of the same company. "Stocks are like the 'fast woman' you found thrilling, but dangerous," said one male chauvinist financial writer, while bonds were the kind of person with whom you "settled down and raised a family." "Make your money with common stocks," he concluded, but then "switch to bonds and collect interest."[1]

As had so many other aspects of the investment scene, this changed during the 1970s, when investors became highly sensitized to interest rates and many discovered or returned to the old debt markets, while new instruments appeared early in the decade to dazzle and intrigue them.

For example, bonds with floating interest rates became the rage in the late 1970s and early 1980s, when uncertain markets made it extremely difficult to sell long-term bonds, and it continues to the present. So it was that in late 1985 Chrysler issued $200 million of 10-year floating rate extendible notes, paying interest quarterly, at an adjustable rate based upon the London Interbank Offered Rate (LIBOR) quotations for three-month Eurodollar deposits prevailing two business days prior to the beginning of each interest rate period and a spread of ⅜ of 1 percent.[2] Bonds that paid no interest for a specified amount of years and then went to a fixed (or variable) amount thereafter came to the market. Packagers would take a low coupon long-term bond, selling at a large discount, affix a "put" to it enabling the purchaser to redeem it at par within a few years, and so transformed a 3 percent bond maturing in 2006 selling at around 60 into a 3 percent bond maturing in 1990, going

---

[1]Interest, not dividends, an important distinction, and not only for when you make out your IRS forms. Stockholders may receive dividends, returns on their equity. Bondholders get interest on money they lend the company or government.

[2]You didn't follow that one? No matter, it really isn't important. Those bonds were marketed to institutions, not individuals. The example was presented simply to demonstrate the complications of the market today.

for over 90. A wide variety of convertibles came to market, some backed by stock of other than the issuing company.

So it went, as the bright young men and women at the bond houses sat around dreaming up new products for their dazzled customers.

High yields helped. At times in this period investors could purchase virtually risk-free one-year notes and certificates of deposit paying 18 percent and more. One might have reflected that in order to do as well in stocks one would have to purchase shares selling for 50 with a $3 dividend and see it go to 56 within a year. Little wonder then, that money flowed out of equities and into debts.

Equities-oriented analysts had been in great demand for a generation, and brokers knew their clients required up to date expertise on hot stocks. Now this started to change and interest in debts picked up as the decade wore on. Today's investors know that there are times when representation in debts makes good sense. But it took a dramatic move in early 1986 to alter the perception of debts convincingly. At the time Wall Street was certain that plunging interest rates would convert many owners of individual retirement accounts from long-term certificates of deposit to stocks. It didn't happen to the extent anticipated. Rather, IRA accounts switched from prime quality debts paying 8 percent to chancier paper with yields of around 12 percent. "Junk bonds," including those issued to pay for leveraged buyouts, became a surrogate for stocks in the eyes of many investors.

How long will it last? At least as long as the yield on intermediate-term bonds remains more than 4 percent higher than the inflation rate. As the United States continues to feed on foreign capital, in part the result of the deficit, expect rates to continue on this way. Also, while the equities market rode high in 1982–1986, corporate profits languished. Faced with the choice between secure bonds paying high interest in a noninflationary environment and stocks that have risen substantially but without a concomitant increase in earnings, investors flocked to the bond market.

Before plunging into the complexities of today's debt market it might be prudent to take note of some of the more important factors investors have to keep in mind before making commitments.

THINKING ABOUT BONDS

First put aside all of those thoughts regarding fundamentalism, technical analysis, and the random walk; such methods of analysis will have no place here. When analyzing a stock like General Motors one has to take into consideration such considerations as the economy, government regulations, foreign competition, and so forth. You can afford to ignore such matters too. In looking at IBM stock you have to assess the future prospects of computers; this need not worry you when it comes to IBM bonds. Indeed, if both IBM and General Motors had bonds that offered identical payouts and maturities, it is likely they would sell at pretty much the same price. As an investor, whether you owned one or the other wouldn't matter very much. So in this respect bonds are much easier to evaluate than are stocks.

Moreover, they are also more "forgiving." Bonds reflect political, market, and interest rate risks, as do stocks, but at the same time they also represent simpler and safer investments than stocks of the same companies, even though in most cases rewards are not as potentially great. Should you purchase shares of stock in a company at the price of $10, you would have no idea of what it would be in January 1995. But the purchase of the firm's bond maturing that month would carry with it the assurance that if the firm is still solvent on that date, you will be paid the face value.

In addition, the stockholder would have no certain dividend, while the bondholder's interest would come in regularly at whatever dates were on the face of the bond. This is another reason many investors, won over to certificates of deposit in the 1970s, have gone to bonds in the 1980s. Why purchase shares in a chancy new electronics firm at 10 in the hope of seeing it double, when you could get a bond selling at 72 with a 4¾ percent coupon maturing in 1994, which translates into a 6.55 percent current yield and a yield of approximately 9.7 percent to maturity (assuming the company is still around seven years hence)?[3]

Now for some definitions. Like stocks, bonds have a par value, and coupon rates indicating the amount of interest due on them. Most corporate bonds which are dealt with in this chapter are issued in denominations of $1000, which is to say if you see a Kraft 7.6 percent bond maturing in 2007 quoted at 88, it means it sold for $880, paid $76 in interest per year, and would be redeemed at par, $1000, in the year 2007. In Chapter 8 we will see that most new municipal and state bonds trade in units of $5,000 or $10,000, so that a 5 percent corporate bond maturing in 2000 selling at 60 would mean $3000 for a $5000 face value bond, paying $250 a year in interest, and returning $5000 in the year 2000.

Until fairly recently almost all bonds were issued at par, which is to say a new offering of Ford bonds would cost $10,000 for $10,000 worth in face value. In the past few years some corporations for various reasons sold them at discounts from par, which is to say $10,000 face value bonds maturing in 2006 with a 5 percent coupon might be offered for $5000. In this case the purchaser would receive a 10 percent yield on his investment of $5000, and a capital gain of $5000 on maturity.

Which leads to another matter, that of calculating expected returns on bonds. Scan the NYSE Bond Trading list in your newspaper and you might find this kind of entry:

AT&T 7s01	9.1	157	77¼	76⅝	77	+ 1

This means that American Telephone & Telegraph's 7 percent bonds maturing in 2001 have a current yield of 9.1 percent, and that $157,000 face value of them traded the previous session, with a high of 77¼ (or $772.50 for a face value $1000 bond), a low of $76 ⅝, and a close of 77, for a gain of 1 point (or $10).

The bondholder knows that in 2001 he will get $1000 for each

---

[3]If you don't understand how these figures were derived, rest assured the method will be explained in a few pages.

bond he purchased yesterday for $770. Assume the maturity is 14 years from now. A *rough* method to calculate total yield would be to consider that at maturity that particular bond would have gone from $770 to $1000, or increased in value by $230, which comes to an average of $16.43 a year. So every year the owner would receive $91 in interest and on the average, $16.43 in unrealised capital appreciation, for a total of $107.42 on an investment of $770, which comes to 13.9 percent.

This approximation can be made with the aid of a hand calculator, but there is a simpler way: ask your broker, who can provide the figures from his tables or more likely now, computer. If and when you purchase bonds the information will be noted on the confirmation slip as well. At this point simply reflect that bonds selling for under par (at a discount) will return current income plus capital (gains), while those selling at par offer only the former. Finally, bonds selling for over par, for example a 13 percent AT&T of 1991 going for 107, will be redeemed at par in 1991.

The four elements investors should consider in the case of an individual bond are (1) rating, which is to say, degree of safety; (2) maturity, meaning the date at which the bond is redeemed for face value; (3) yield, sometimes known as the "coupon," which is the amount of interest paid, usually twice a year; and (4) call provisions.

Some bonds have call provisions, meaning that under specified circumstances the issuer has the right to redeem them at a fixed price on a stated date. Thus, an 8 percent bond issued now with a maturity date of 2016 might be redeemed at 103 on January 2, 1996. What might lead the corporation to do so? Lower interest rates at that time would be the most obvious reason. If the financial climate had changed so that the firm could issue a similar bond, perhaps also maturing in 2016, with a 6 percent coupon, it well might call in the old bond and issue the new one, thus saving itself 2 percentage points in interest, or to use a term more commonly heard on the Street, 200 "basis points," each basis point being 1/100th of a percent.

Examples of this abounded in 1985 and 1986, as issuers rushed to market to call in high yield instruments sold to investors in the 1970s. In 1986 the Intermountain Power Agency placed $4.224 billion of new debt to replace old, and by so doing succeeded in lowering its borrowing costs from 11.31 percent to 9.46 percent, saving over $1.1 billion over the life of its bond program. Purchasers of the old bonds should have known they could be called. They profited from holding double digit highly rated debt for a few years, but now had to settle for less. The following day AT&T retired $600 million of 10-year 13¼ percent notes issued in 1976 and $400 million of 14¼ percent debentures issued in 1978. "Given the lower interest rates now available, retirement of high-coupon debt is a topic that comes up with every company we cover," noted Reed Parker of Duff & Phelps, one of the smaller bond rating firms. Indeed, while the eyes of many investors were affixed on the continuing bull market in stocks, billions of dollars of refinancings were occurring on the bond market, not only many times the volume of new stock offerings, but more than the total worth of stocks traded on the NYSE and Amex.

Investors should know whether or not there are restrictions and conditions on the bonds they are considering. For example, income bonds are debts on which payments will be made *only* if earned in that year. Convertible bonds are a special case; these are debts that can be converted into common stock either at the option of the owner or under some special circumstance. Some bonds have sinking fund provisions, meaning that after a date fixed under terms of the offering the company will refund a specified number of bonds, usually selected at random. But all of these are the finer points, matters to be considered after the Big Four: rating, maturity, yield and call.

Consider the question of quality. In stocks one has to rely on individuals or teams of analysts who may differ on the subject. Several large organizations such as Value Line and the big wire houses have attempted to assess short- and long-term promise in terms of a rating system, but there is little science to this.

RATING THE ISSUES

Not so the agencies that rate bonds, the two most prominent being Standard & Poor's and Moody's, the former a subsidiary of McGraw-Hill, the latter of Dun & Bradstreet. Both look into such matters as financial strength, flow of funds, coverage of interest, and the like. However, not all bonds are rated since to do so would tax even their facilities, considering the enormous number of issues.[4] While these two services do a meticulous job of rating new bonds, they are less careful in monitoring changes in the corporation's fortunes. Thus there is a degree of inefficiency in the market. The bonds of a company might be better or worse than the designation indicates, and astute bond buyers occasionally can profit therefrom.

Standard & Poor's rates bonds in declining order of merit, as AAA (extremely strong), AA (high quality, a shade under AAA), A (strong, but could be affected by extremely adverse conditions), BBB (somewhat less than A), BB (speculative, with protection of interest and principal only moderate), B (assurance of interest and principal in doubt), CCC (an element of risk present, and bonds may be in default), CC (more speculative), C (in default with little promise of recovery, D (pretty hopeless). Moody's ratings are Aaa, Aa, A, Baa, Ba, B, Caa, Ca, C, with no D rating. More often than not, the two services will agree on the ratings they assign to bonds covered. For both the top two are high grade, A and BBB medium grade, BB and B speculative, and the others of interest only to speculators.

Those speculative bonds captured a good deal of attention in the 1984–1985 period, when leveraged buyouts were the rage.[5] A

---

[4]Mention should be made of Fitch Investor Services, which specializes in bank securities, and the aforementioned Duff & Phelps.

[5]A leveraged buyout transpires when individuals, often insiders, succeed in purchasing a company by issuing bonds which are exchanged for stock. What emerges is a private company with a heavy debt. Then, on occasion, the new owners will sell off assets for cash, using this to retire debt.

veritable flood of "junk bonds" emerged from several investment banking houses, led by Drexel Burnham Lambert. Rated BB and B, they sported high yields and attracted the attention of gamesters. More than a dozen mutual funds based on the bonds made their appearances as well, gaining devotees eager for high returns as interest rates declined. Thus many bondholders met the decline in rates by switching from good quality paper to that with lower ratings, in this way maintaining their return.

Drexel Burnham and others argued that even if some of the bonds went into default, the returns were so high as to compensate for failures. For a while this view enjoyed a vogue. Then came the collapse of oil prices in late 1985, followed by the failure of several petroleum and petroleum-based firms. Four companies in the business went into Chapter 11 bankruptcy that year, with Global Marine alone accounting for $340 million of the more than $1 billion in arrears. As though to sooth fears, Drexel announced that its index of 110 high yielding issues produced an impressive return of 22.5 percent in 1985—this followed by a note from another banker that the total return on completely safe Treasury bonds came to 31.5 percent in the same year.

Are junk bonds for you? Perhaps, but not if you are the kind of person ordinarily attracted to bonds. On the other hand, individuals used to taking crap shoots in speculative stocks might take a whirl in this market instead. In early 1985 the default rate was 1.22 percent—up from the 0.54 percent of the previous year, but not yet at disaster levels.

How safe is safe? Are you fearful that your AAA-rated IBM or GM 20-year bonds will default or fail to pay principal? Ask yourself what it would take to cause this to happen, and reflect that if the country ever found itself in such a mess, obtaining bond interest would be among your less pressing problems.[6] For all in-

---

[6]During the 1962 Cuban Missile Crisis I ran into a friend who confided that he was selling all of his stocks and bonds and buying gold, in the expectation of atomic war. Who would care about the value of gold in case of atomic destruction? If he meant what he said the man was behaving irrationally. But in fact, stocks and bonds did decline and the gold he purchased overseas rose. What he really did, I suspect, was to gauge how the markets would react and speculate accordingly, not unlike Keynes and the beauty contest judges.

tents and purposes, AAA and AA bonds are so safe as to obviate the need for concern. Barring another Great Depression, the same holds true for A and even BBB. Since depending on markets the spread between AAA and BBB bonds can be 150 basis points, one should consider carefully the merits of purchasing the latter and obtaining a much higher yield. That 150 basis points might not sound like much—an 11½ percent yield rather than 10 percent. Reflect that 11½ percent is 15 percent more than 10 percent, and you'll see why the risk might be worth the reward. Especially for short and intermediate maturities, the former generally considered five years or less, the latter five to seven or so years.[7]

THE YIELD CURVE

This brings us to the matter of the yield curve, a means of charting yield over time. Figure 7-1 illustrates what it looked like in early 1986.

What might happen if after a while investors decided that inflation will be less of a threat in the future than it has been in the recent past? They would settle for lower yields, causing the curve to "flatten," as seen in the dotted line drawn in Figure 7-1.

Note that both curves shown here indicate higher returns the longer the bond is to run. For example, five-year maturities offer yields of 7 percent, 10-year 9 percent, and 20-year 10 percent. The curve has had something like this shape for so long that many investors (and newcomers to bonds) can't recall a time when it looked like the one presented in Figure 7-2:

Consider the assumptions behind each curve. Figure 7-1 indicates there is a greater return for longer than shorter maturities because investors think inflation will erode the principal and make future interest payments worth less than those at present, and so they won't buy a bond whose price doesn't take this into

[7]At this writing AAA rated industrial bonds are yielding 10.19 percent, AAs 10.13 percent, As 10.2 percent, and BBBs 11.19 percent.

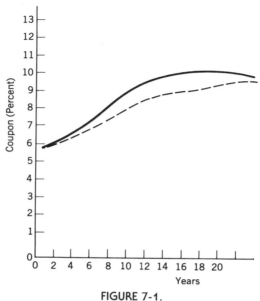

FIGURE 7-1.

consideration. Inflationary expectations are a part of the conventional investment wisdom of our times, so this kind of curve has become "normal." The curve in Figure 7-2 indicates that longer bonds yield less than shorter ones, reflecting a belief, not much in evidence now, that prolonged deflation is occurring or is on investors' minds, so they are willing to accept lower long-term rates than short-term ones in order to "lock in" a return a bit higher than they anticipate will be the case in a few years or even months.

Inflation is the devil for bond investors, one reason why interest rates are so high in the mid-1980s. Traditionally, interest rates used to be the inflation rate plus 3 to 4 percent, so that a 2 percent inflation would indicate long-term bond yields of approximately 6 percent. We have seen inflation rates of 2 percent coinciding with long-term rates of 9 percent. Old timers look at this with some amazement, as though an elephant was floating overhead. How did it get there, but more to the point, why doesn't it come crashing down? The reason is inflationary expectations.

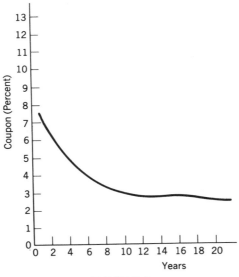

FIGURE 7-2.

Suppose you are faced with this situation today (as it is when these words are being written): what would be the prudent course of action? Clearly to buy long-term bonds, because if and when inflationary expectations are dispelled, the long-term rates will decline, perhaps from 9 percent to 5 percent or so, presenting bond holders with nice profits—but only (as will be seen) if they purchased the right ones in terms of yield and price. For now the rule is this: during periods of uncertainty, the yield curve rises sharply, and it levels off when the outlook improves. If you expect a great deal of inflation, insist on a very high return on long-term bonds, or ignore them completely and stick to shorter maturities. If the long-term yield is very attractive and you think the market is wrong about rates, by all means go with the longer term bonds. In the late 1970s some BBBs maturing in 15 years were returning high double digit rates, only to decline sharply within a few years, presenting their owners with excellent capital gains and interest in a period when common stocks were weak.

SELECTIVITY

Now for some actual examples, that will illustrate some of the complexities of the bond market.

REPRESENTATIVE BONDS AND THEIR S&P RATINGS

	Company	Bond	Price	Current Yield	Yield to Maturity
AAA	Amoco	6s 98	76	7.90	9.38
AA	Northwest Fin.	12s 98	106⅞	11.23	9.63
A	General Foods	6s 01	68¼	8.79	10.10
BBB	SCM	10s 96	91⅞	10.88	11.35
BB	La. Power	10s 08	81⅝	12.25	12.44
B	ARA Holdings	12s 92	98⅜	12.15	12.27
CCC	Petro Lewis	11s 97	57	19.30	20.90

Source: Standard & Poor's Bond Guide, Year End 1985.

Observe that the shorter the term of the bonds, the smaller the percentage spread between yield and yield to maturity. The reason should be obvious: the closer one gets to the day the bond can be turned in and paid off, the closer its price will be to the par value. A 3 percent bond maturing in 2026 might sell for 40, since it won't be redeemed at par for another 30 years. But in the year 2025 it could be going for around 98 or 99.

Note too another relationship between current yield and yield to maturity: the higher the former (taking into account the rating), the lower will be the latter. A bond offering a current yield of 8 percent and a yield to maturity of 10 percent and one offering a current yield of 6 percent and a yield to maturity of 12 percent might be of a similar quality.

It works in reverse as well. Observe that Northwest Financial's 12s of 98 sells for 6⅞ points over par, meaning it will be redeemed at a lower price than it can be purchased, and the IRS won't consider this a capital loss, since the purchase was made in the expectation of the decline. The yield is 11.23 percent, high for the quality bond at the current writing, but the yield to maturity is 9.63, which is low.

The rule is that investors who are willing to sacrifice current yield usually are rewarded by higher yields to maturity and vice versa.

There is another point we might as well talk about here. Some bond buyers hate to purchase even uncallable debts far above par, knowing they will be redeemed at the face value. Thus a bond maturing 10 years hence selling today for 110 will decline to 100 at the end of its run, on the average of a point per year. If you paid 110 for the bond now it was because its coupon was higher than comparable bonds issued now, and so the current yield would be better. On the other hand, the yield to maturity would be lower. So some bond holders eschew them, seeking instead bonds selling for under par.

Does this make sense? Consider these two bonds, which happen to be tax exempts, and their prices in early 1986. The first is a New York NHA guaranteed bond with a 5.375 percent coupon, maturing in 2006, the second a Northwest Bergen County 10.25 percent also maturing in 2006. Both are rated AAA.

You can see that the New York issue offers a higher yield to maturity, but a far lower current yield. Year-in, year-out, the New York issue will pay $537.50 a year, the Northwest Bergen $1025. Of course there is the danger of a call, but such is not the case with this particular NW Bergen bond. So which would you rather have for the next two decades?

Bond	Yield to Maturity	Current Yield	Price
New York 2006	7.60	6.95	77⅜
New Bergen 2006	7.25	8.56	119¾

ZEROS

Let us return to the matter of sacrificing current yield for yield to maturity, which in spite of this example may make sense for many investors. The most obvious and logical end result of this are zero coupon notes and bonds. In this case the corporation issues original issue discounted debts maturing at the specified time without interest payments.[8] One of the companies that did this is Allied Corp., which at this writing has zeros ranging in maturity from 1987 to 2009, all rated A. The 1987s are going for 88, with a yield to maturity of 8.24 percent, while the 2009s are selling for 8¼, with a yield to maturity of 10.89. Consider that General Foods 6s 01 in the table, selling at 68¼ for a yield of 8.79 percent and a yield to maturity of 10.10 percent. The Allied zeros that mature in 1997 have no current yield and at its price of 28 offer a yield to maturity of 11.30.

Zeros, especially those with long maturities, can move quickly on interest rate changes. One purchased in 1985 with maturity sometime in the early years of the twenty-first century more than tripled in price in half a year as interest rates plummeted. Of course such bonds could go the other way should rates turn around and head north.

Which would you prefer, zeros or deep discounts? Before answering, add this to the equation: the IRS taxes corporate zeros as though the interest had been paid, this done by amortizing the anticipated gain over the life of the bond. So if a $1000 face value zero maturing in 2007 were to be issued in 1987 at 10, the assumption would be that over 20 years it would increase by $900, this being $45 a year, on which the holder would be taxed, even though the funds were not received. Buy the General Foods issue and you'll receive income (on which you would be taxed) for the rest of the century, and at the end have a capital gain of 31¾

---

[8]In Chapter 8 you will be introduced to the more popular government zeros—CATs, TIGRs, RATs, GATORs, and other fancifully labeled debts, which are more familiar and popular.

points. With the Allied you will have no income, pay taxes along the way, and in 1997, a capital gain of 72 points, the net yield to maturity being 120 basis points more than with the General Foods issue.

Zeros such as this would make sense for a person in the low or no tax situation. A parent might purchase zeros that mature at age 18 for a new-born child, in the knowledge that as long as the child's total income from all sources falls below the first tax bracket none would be paid. In fact this is one of the more common uses for zeros, others being in corporate accounts, individual retirement accounts, Keoghs, and the like. For others who like the concept of zeros, deep discounted low coupon bonds make more sense. At this writing Texas Electric Service's A-rated 4½s of 1995 are selling for 67⅜, offering a current yield of 6.68 percent and a yield to maturity of 10.06 percent. This might be very appealing for an individual in a high tax bracket who expects to retire in a few years, and would like to have that long-term capital gains when his income is lower.

We already have seen that at one time rising interest rates would depress bonds while accompanying advances in stocks. The rationale was simple enough: interest rates rose during period of economic expansion, which implied higher corporate earnings and so better stock prices as well. At the same time new bonds would come to market with more attractive coupons than carried by the old, causing the latter to decline in price. To illustrate the principle, suppose you owned a bond selling at par, paying 10 percent ($100 on a $1000 maturity value) maturing in 2010, and a new bond of the same quality, coming due in the same year, came out with a 12 percent coupon, this being 20 percent more than your 10 percent. The sensible thing to do would be to sell the old bond and buy the new one, which would result in a decline in price for the old to the point where its yield would be the same as that of the new issue. How far would it fall? To around 85. But consider that the bond market would have anticipated this, and the decline would have begun much earlier, perhaps even before interest rates started to rise.

Until recently investors would switch from stocks to bonds during uncertain periods, and take to equities once the outlook appeared fine. This is no longer the case. In our times, when central banks can and often do manipulate money supply to attempt to influence interest rates, the market has come to believe that inflation harms stocks as well as bonds while lower interest rates redounds to both of their benefits. The result is that they move together, or to be more accurate, during recent years a belief that lower rates were on the way would cause bonds to rise, and this would be taken as a signal for an advance in stocks. Of course stocks can move either way for a variety of other reasons, but in our present environment, when as several analysts put it "money moves the markets," bond tend to lead stocks.

USING BOND SALESMEN

Now that we have this out of the way, let's return to the transaction. Assume you are prepared to make your purchases. You call your broker and tell him that you are interested in placing funds in bonds. From that point on the drill differs considerably from the mechanics of buying stocks.

In the case of stocks, whether you use either a full service or discount broker, your order will be taken to the market and shares purchased from a specialist (on the NYSE and Amex) or dealer (OTC), individuals who make markets in the shares. Suppose the stock is going for 45 bid 45½ ask. You probably will get it at 45½, to which the broker's commission will be added. If you deal with a full service broker you might ask for his thoughts on the stocks that interest you, and receive some information from researchers, perhaps a report as well.

It can be done that way with bonds as well. As previously noted bonds are traded at the New York and American Stock Exchanges, and may be followed in some of the larger newspapers. Do so for a while and you'll realize the price swings are much larger than that for stocks. The reason is usually that the market for listed bonds is relatively thin. A bond might not trade for more than a week or two, during which its bid and ask prices are changed with no transaction taking place. When one does, it reflects interest rate moves and other changes that have occurred since the last trade. Hence those wide swings. If you buy or sell a listed bond, you will be charged a commission such as with stocks, one difference being that you will receive or pay accrued interest. Thus, should you purchase a 12 percent bond that pays $60 semiannually 30 days after the last payment you will have to pay $10 in accrued interest, which will go to the seller. Likewise, if you sold that bond, you would receive the accrued interest.

The vast majority of bonds are traded OTC, however, with most dealings taking place to and from the broker's inventory. It works something like this:

You call the broker and tell him that you are interested, say, in $10,000 face value of AAs maturing around 1994, and ask what is in the inventory. He might then call up the list on the computer screen and rattle it off. He might say, "We don't have anything like that, but I can get you a Texas-New Mexico Power single A maturing in '95 with an 4.95 percent coupon for 68. The yield is 7.2 percent and the yield to maturity comes to 10.12. Or how about an Amoco triple A 6 of '98 going for 75⅞, with a 7.91 yield and 9.38 to maturity? I could look up some more if you like, but these seem closest to what you want."

When a dealer buys bonds they go into the firm's portfolio from which the sales are made. The purchases are from individuals and institutions, as are the sales. Because of this the bond experts at the brokerages are important individuals, since they act in ways similar to those of specialists, in that they set prices, adjusting them when necessary to "move or attract the goods."

The brokerage hopes to make money from profits on its portfolio, the differential between the interest earned on the holdings and the costs of tying up funds in maintaining the portfolio, and of course the spread between the price paid for the bonds and the price for which they are sold. This means that the dealer might have paid 74 yesterday for that Amoco bond offered to you today at 77⅞, and that if you wanted to sell it back in a week or so you might be offered 74 or 75. It also means the firm's bond man has to actively manage the portfolio, for if he purchased a bond for 87 and interest rates rise, he might not be able to sell it for more than 85, suffering a loss. There are no such problems on the firm's equity side, where the broker acts as an intermediary between you and the specialist or dealer, and generally does not maintain an inventory.

Well and good. You tell the broker that you are interested in the Texas-New Mexicos and ask how much he has, the answer being around $50,000 face value, meaning that you will have no trouble getting your $10,000 for $6,800 plus accrued interest. If that seems right, you might place the order, or you might tell the broker you'll call back in a few minutes and get on the telephone to another broker and discover what is in his inventory. You do this, and after a few calls come up with the following list:

Bond	Rating	Price	Yield	Yield to Maturity
Texas-NM 6s 95	A	68	7.2	10.12
Central Tels 8s 94	A	89¾	8.91	9.80
West Penn Power 4⅜s 92	AA	74	5.91	9.66
Beneficial 12⅜s 95	A	113⅞	10.87	10.12
Pru Rlty Sec 0s 94	AAA	37⅜	0	12.16

Which would you buy? The answer, of course, depends on what you had in mind when making the first telephone call. Should your goal be current income, the Beneficials might be fine, but the price including accrued interest would be over $11,900, while the Texas-New Mexicos would cost somewhat over $6,800, with the same yield to maturity though a lower current yield. On the other hand, at maturity you would have to pay capital gains on 32 points. If you didn't need current income the Prudential Realtys might be attractive—a higher rating combined with a nice yield to maturity. But you look into yourself and make the choice. The once fact that wouldn't matter too much was the issuer—the rating is more important here.

TRADING BONDS

You have now made your first bond purchase, followed by a second and a third. By now you realize that unlike your stocks, you have no idea of your profit and loss situation. None of the three bonds are listed on the NYSE or Amex, and while you think you are doing fine since interest rates are falling, you aren't sure.

There are two ways to get the price. The first will require some effort and give you an approximate price. It involves an equation:

$$V = \sum_{t=1}^{n} \frac{C_t}{(1 + i)^t} + \frac{P_n}{(1 + i)^n}$$

V = Market value of price of the bond
n = Number of interest periods
t = Each period
C_t = Interest payment for each period
P_n = Par value
i = Current market interest rate

If this doesn't interest you (and why should it?) there is a simpler way to go, namely call your broker, tell him what you have, and ask for a quote, which will be obtained from his bond expert. Don't do this too often, especially if you have a small, relatively inactive account. But it is one way to go. Another might be to use the tables in the *Thorndike Encyclopedia of Banking and Financial Tables* (New York: Warren, Gorham and Lamont) which can be found in some of the larger libraries.

Some stockholders like to assemble a diversified portfolio to hedge their bets, while others plunge in with a major commitment to one or two issues alone, or concentrate on several industry groups. The same is true for bondholders. Some will want only long maturities, others intermediate or short; some will stick with AAAs and AAs alone, while others want the better yields and can take the risks associated with BBBs and lower. There is no way of prescribing in general for bonds, just as one cannot locate the right stock for *everyone.*

There are differences as well. Some bondholders intend to trade, while others expect to hold to maturity. Sidney Homer once suggested that a long-term bond is like a house you purchase while a short-term one is akin to a rented apartment. But this is only for those who expect to hold on to their debts until maturity. For such individuals, interest rate movements count for little; they are content to collect interest and cash in or roll over their bonds as they mature.

This could prove short sighted. Sharp advances or declines in interest rates can alter the value of the portfolio and its constituents, and given investment objectives, call for sales or purchases. Generally speaking, the shorter the term and the higher the coupon, the less the fluctuation. If there is a move of 200 basis points in interest rates a 10 percent bond maturing in 1990 might move up a trifle, but not much, since maturity is just around the corner. Similarly, a bond with a call provision may hardly budge on news of rate declines, since it is assumed it will be called. But 4 percent bonds maturing in 2015 could move as much as 33 percent on a 200 basis point decline. And the owner might not realize it, since prices are not quoted in the financial press. So the rule is to keep tabs on prices, even if it means calling your broker when rates move to get those quotes.

Fundamentalists generally sell a stock when its prospects are improving and buy when the reverse seems to be the situation. Technicians buy and sell on signals given out by the market or the stock. This is not necessarily the case with bonds. Begin with the commonly recognized view that the bond market is not as efficient as the stock market due to the nature and volume of trading. Also consider that the price of the bond depends on rating, maturity, yield and yield to maturity, and call provisions, and that a willingness to accept a less attractive form of either results in benefits in other areas. Reflect that given the kind of investment outlook we have today, a 5 percent bond maturing in 1995 sells for a higher price than a 5 percent bond of the same quality maturing in 2010. Or that a 6 percent AA maturing in 2000 can sell for approximately the same price as a 7 percent A maturing the same year. Or that by accepting a 30 basis point lower current yield you might get a 15 basis point higher yield to maturity. There can be other combinations as well.

So be prepared to enter into "swaps," especially if they can result in a tax advantage. It would be sensible to exchange one bond for another to establish a tax loss in the former, with no loss of quality or current yield and yield to maturity. Much of this happens at the end of the year, for obvious reasons. But most exchanges take place because markets or investor preferences have changed.

Assume, for example, you owned Bond I, $10,000 face value of a BBB-rated 8⅜s of 2006 which due to declining interest rates had gone from 50 to 68 in a few months, and now offers a current yield of 12.32 percent and a yield to maturity of 12.83 percent. When purchased the current yield was 16.75, and you would like to cash in and obtain a higher current return. Your broker has Bond II, a 9¼ of 1997, rated B, selling at 66¾, with a current yield of 13.86 and yield to maturity of 15.66, and suggests a swap. Consider what this means:

Bond	Price	Rating	Maturity	Yield	Yield to Maturity
I	68	BBB	2006	12.32	12.83
II	66¾	B	1997	13.86	15.66

If you made the swap, you would receive $125 in cash (plus or minus accrued interest differentials), get a lower rated bond but an earlier maturity, and obtain a higher yield and yield to maturity. Of course it could work the other way; you might have owned Bond II, and to obtain a higher rating be willing to pay a small sum and accept a longer maturity and lower yields. In this case you would want to consider such matters as the spread between BBBs and Bs (are they higher or lower than usual?), the yield curve (are longer maturities going for an unusually high or low yield?), and other factors involving your personal requirements. Such matters involve more study; this is only an introduction.

If the subject intrigues you, consider a careful reading of the classic work in the field, *Inside the Yield Book: New Tools for the Bond Market Strategy* (Englewood Cliffs, NJ: Prentice-Hall, 1972) by the aforementioned Sidney Homer and Martin Liebowitz. More on the subject will appear in Chapter 8 which deals with other aspects of the debt market.[9]

---

[9]As noted, the literature on bonds is skimpier than for stocks. But also see Gifford H. Fong, *Bond Portfolio Analysis* (Charlottesville, Va.: Financial Analysts Research Foundation, 1980), and Peter L. Bernstein, ed., *The Theory and Practice of Bond Portfolio Management* (New York: Institutional Investor, 1980).

8 THE MANIA FOR GOVERNMENTS

In 1819, as the nation suffered through its first important financial panic, Daniel Webster and Luther Martin crossed verbal swords in a Supreme Court case (to be known as *McCullough* v. *Maryland*) that directly or indirectly affects all investors more than a century and a half later, and was of infinitely greater importance than the economic disruption then taking place.

The issues were simple enough. The recently rechartered Bank of the United States (BUS) had been strongly opposed in the south and the west, where it was viewed as an octopus whose head was on Philadelphia's Walnut Street, then the nation's financial center. To them the Bank of the United States was an agent of an Eastern money power that meant to dominate the rest of the country.

Several states attempted to prevent the BUS from operating within its borders, either by prohibiting entry or through the levy of exorbitant taxes. Maryland was one of the latter, in 1818 passing legislation to impose heavy levees on the Baltimore branch, where James McCullough was a clerk. The BUS refused to pay, a suit was initiated, and the case was heard by the Supreme Court the following year.

Webster argued for the BUS and Martin for Maryland, doing so before a packed courtroom whose onlookers knew that on the decision would rest the future of federal-state relations. If Maryland prevailed, the states would be seen as sovereign within their borders, while a decision for McCullough would place the federal government over the states in spheres where they collided. Or at least, that was the view as the justices met to decide the case.

The primary direct issue was the constitutionality of the BUS, and speaking for a unanimous court, Chief Justice John Marshall declared that the federal government was within its rights to charter such institutions. Marshall said that Maryland had no right to tax the BUS as it did, for "the power to tax involves the power to destroy." He added that the American people, in their Constitution, "did not design to make their government dependent upon the states." The decision in *McCullough* v. *Maryland* was taken as a clear victory for federal power, and as such led to a spate of litigation, legislation, conflict, and eventually, the constitutional arguments that culminated in and had to be decided by the Civil War.

Lost in all of this was the matter of taxation. Marshall's decision was interpreted as meaning that the states could not tax federal properties and securities—and that likewise, the federal government did not have the right to tax those of the states. This counted for little at a time of low taxes. The total federal take in 1819 had been $24.6 million, and of this amount $20.3 million came from tariffs. What mattered was that the principal was established, and reestablished by subsequent court decisions such as *Pollack* v. *Farmer's Loan and Trust* in 1895, and more recently in court decisions in 1916, 1928, 1937, and 1965.

What this means is that the states are not able to tax today's Treasury bills, notes, and bonds, but more important for investors, interest on state, municipal, and local debts are free from federal income taxes, and really from all taxes since the issuing governments wouldn't tax them if held by residents. This is why a New Yorker would not have to pay taxes on New York debts, but would be obliged to pay state taxes on debts issued by any other state. Not on those issued by Puerto Rico, however, which due to its unique status is able to issue debts free from federal and state income taxes no matter who is the owner.

End of history lesson and start of investment analysis.

FEDERAL OBLIGATIONS

Federal obligations comprise the largest single segment of the securities market, dwarfing equities, corporate bonds, and securities issued by local and state governments. One of these years the mortgage-backed securities market, in its entirety and alone, may become bigger, but not in the foreseeable future.

Large as it is, the government market is simpler to understand than almost any other. In the first place, the national debt you may worry so much about is represented by Treasury bills, notes, and bonds. Bills are short-term obligations which run for a maximum of one year and are sold on a discount basis. This is to say that the interest is represented by the difference the purchaser pays and the maturity value, which is $10,000. Treasury bills come to market as a result of an auction, so that if the bid is $9200 for a one year bill the interest rate would be 8.7 percent.[1] The return on Treasury bills may seem like capital gains, but not to the IRS, which taxes it as interest. As indicated, this return is not taxed by states and municipalities. As this is being written the yield on one week bills is 5.88 percent and for 11 months and 1 week, 6.37 percent.[2]

[1]The investor would be receiving $800 interest on an outlay of $9,200, and my trusty calculator tells me $800 represents a yield of 8.69565 percent. Don't think those thousands of a percentage point are piddling. Big institutions seeking to park funds for short periods may invest several hundreds of millions of dollars in them, and slight rate shifts can represent substantial gains or losses.

[2]Note that the prices quoted in the newspapers are in 32nd of a point, so that if the bid is 100.6 and the ask 100.10, it means 100 6/32 and 100 10/32.

Buying bills is simple enough; a call to your local Federal Reserve bank will give you guidance as to the time of the next auction and information on how to obtain bills directly. A more convenient if somewhat more expensive way to go would be to make the purchase through your broker or bank, where the charge will be around $25.

A number of small investors became involved with the Treasury bill market in the 1970s, when they purchased the short-term paper as a surrogate for savings accounts paying less than 6 percent. But there really is no compelling reason why they should remain involved with them today. Some money market mutuals invest solely in short-term Treasuries. "Super Now" bank and S&L accounts, and other instruments, are just as liquid, virtually as safe, and even handier. Their charges are lower than those of brokerages and banks for Treasury bills, and everything can be done by mail; instead of waiting for maturity or selling the bill you simply write a check for redemption.

Notes and bonds are longer term obligations, with maturities of from 1 to 7 years for the former and from 7 to 25 years or longer for bonds. These are auctioned on set dates in units of $1000, and are like conventional corporates in that they are sold at par with a specified interest rate. My morning newspaper informs me that the 11¼ percent of 2015 goes for 117.27 for a yield of 9.43 percent. Some bonds are callable at par in the last five years of their run. This is noted in the newspaper as, say, "May 94-99 8½," meaning the maturity for an 8½ percent coupon issue is in 1999 and the call, 1994.

Federal agency bonds can be a fine alternative to Treasury notes and bonds. Since they are not issued directly by the Treasury, and some are liable for state and local taxes, institutional investors assign them slightly higher yields. For all practical purposes they are just as safe, however, and individuals interested in Treasury paper should become conversant with this often overlooked area. Some of these agencies are: the Federal Home Loan Bank, the Federal Land Bank, the Federal Intermediate Credit Bank, the Inter-American Development Bank, the Export-Import

Bank, and the U.S. Postal Service. The prices of some agency issues are reported in *The Wall Street Journal* and other large newspapers, as well as *Barron's*.

MEET GINNIE MAE

In recent years many former Treasury note and bond devotees
have been drawn to Ginnie Maes, which have become what are
arguably the best known of federal obligations. Stockholders have
taken to them as well, as have institutional investors. Indeed, by
the early 1980s it appeared the entire investment world had gone
Ginnie Mae crazy, and the thrift institutions and the investment
banks were working overtime to give new twists to old ones.

Mention has been made of Ginnie Maes in earlier chapters, but
the instruments were not defined on those occasions in the belief
that readers would as much require this as they might a descrip-
tion of stocks and bonds. Not quite perhaps, because Ginnie
Maes are much more complicated. That omission will be rectified
here. First some background to provide perspective.

It began with the Federal National Mortgage Association, created in 1938 to purchase and market Federal Housing Administra-
tion-insured mortgages from the savings and loan institutions
and so increase liquidity in that beseiged industry. "Fannie Mae"
balances were not considered part of the national debt, permitting
President Franklin Roosevelt and his successors to expand into
the area without having borrowings appear as deficit spending.
In 1969, after the courts ruled that Fannie Mae operations had to
be considered part of the federal budget, Congress passed and
President Nixon signed an amendment to the Housing Act, under which the agency was transformed into a publicly owned corporation, with the ability to raise funds on the open market and
an implied mandate to do so and to expand operations signifi-
cantly.

This left a gap to be filled by the new Government National
Mortgage Association, which was to perform for the federal gov-

ernment some of the activities previously done by Fannie Mae. This entity, soon to be known as Ginnie Mae, developed the "pass through certificate" for which it would become famous a decade later. Ginnie Mae would purchase Federal Housing Administration and Veteran's Administration mortgages, and assemble them in units to be offered for sale to investors. Keep in mind these were insured mortgages, complete with the government agency's promise to pay principal and interest if they went into default. In effect, they were as safe as Treasury paper.

The initial Ginnie Maes were assembled in December 1970. By mid-decade the certificates were being sold to a wide variety of institutional clients.

Now all the pieces were in place, and the S&Ls and those institutional investors who understood the securities—only a few at the time—were prepared for what has been called the "securitization" of the mortgage market, which means the transformation of the familiar illiquid mortgages into a security which might be purchased or sold by brokers and clients with what most in the nascent industry hoped would be a great deal of liquidity.

By 1975 some $7.4 billion worth of mortgages were being packaged and sold, the figure for the following year was $13.5 billion, of which approximately half went to large institutions, especially pension funds, with the rest held by the thrifts. In 1976 over $15 billion in mortgage-backed securities were sold—compared to $30.6 billion in corporate bonds and $33.9 billion in municipal paper. From out of nowhere mortgage securities were becoming an important competitor ot the older form of fixed income vehicles.

The mechanics of the situation are simple. Your local thrift institution takes in short-term deposits and lends much of them out in the form of long-term mortgages. The homebuyer winds up with the house plus the insured mortgage, say, at 10 percent, while the thrift institution can hold the mortgage, and in addition has taken in a substantial sum of money in the form of origination and related fees.

Thirty or so years ago it would remain at that. Each month the homeowner would mail a check to the thrift consisting of a sum for principal and another for interest, doing so until either the mortgage term was completed or the mortgage paid off early, usually through sale of the house. But with the interest rate and deregulation scares of the 1970s to remind them of the dangers of holding on to such paper for long, the thrifts became eager to sell the mortgage to someone else.

So they do. The GNMA purchases mortgages and then sells them through investment bankers to the public and to institutions. The "bundle" may consist of $50 million in mortgages in a particular part of California, for example. The underwriter will make the offering, and the individual investor can take whatever chunk of it he wants, as long as the amount is over $25,000. So the thrift gets its money and the investor is left owning a portion of a mortgage pool. In effect the owner of the Ginnie Mae has become a surrogate for the bank, obtaining interest on loans from homeowners, but also running the interest rate risk. As for the thrifts, they originate the mortgage, take in the fees, and then sell the mortgage to the packager. At one time the rationale of the S&L was to provide loans for potential homeowners. Now it has become a broker between the mortgagee and the investor.

Each month the investor will receive a check for interest plus a portion of the principal, which is to say that $25,000 investment will be nibbled into with each payout. Along with the check will come a statement of the principal remaining and other information. The Ginnie Mae certificate is fully negotiable and insured; the investor can find a ready and liquid market for the paper, along with quotations for representative pools printed in some financial pages and in the weekly *Barron's*.

For some, the Ginnie Mae is preferable to government bonds, in the sense that they are just as safe and do offer higher yields. But there is no way of knowing how long they will run. Today you might purchase an old Ginnie Mae carrying the equivalent of a 12 percent coupon, meaning that the mortgages in the pool are somewhat above that figure. Now such mortgage holders probably are thinking of refinancing, and each time they do, the amount of principal paid out to the owner will increase. It is not unusual for owners of very high yielding Ginnie Maes to find themselves liquidated in a matter of less than a year.

In 1984 the Street's researchers were saying that the life expectancy of a new Ginnie Mae was between seven and eight years. Then interest rates declined, and uncertainties in mid-1986 made it appear that massive refinancing would remain the order of the day until there was a significant move to higher rates.

The owner of a 20-year industrial or municipal bond knows its maturity and call dates and so could "lock in" rates when this seemed desirable, while making plans based on redemption schedules. Not so the possessor of a mortgage-backed security, who couldn't be certain just when it would be emptied of all mortgages, due to home sales and refinancings.

Novice Ginnie Mae investors often place the greatest stress on yield, trying to get the highest return. Those high yields often mean the mortgages in the package are likely to be redeemed shortly. It might pay to give up even 100 basis points in order to lengthen the term of the paper. So experienced investors tend to go with the lower coupon paper, sometimes selling at a discount. Perhaps the return is a trifle less attractive, but the chance of the mortgages being paid off prior to maturity are much slimmer. Bondholders might think of this ploy as akin to purchasing discounted bonds to protect against a call.

Ginnie Maes are most appealing in periods of fairly stable interest rates. When rates are steadily rising the prices of Ginnie Maes, like those of most debt securities, decline so as to make their yields competitive with those pegged for newly issued paper. When rates decline owners of bonds can congratulate themselves on having "locked in" the former high yields, while at the same time the prices of their holdings will advance. Not so those who hold Ginnie Maes, for on such occasions the owners of mortgages tend to refinance.

Keep this in mind when considering Ginnie Maes in place of Treasury paper or highly rated bonds. There is a reason for the higher yield; as with all such things, it is because the risk (of redemption) is always present. But if this element of uncertainty doesn't bother you, then Ginnie Maes rather than Treasury notes and bonds may be the way to go.

Lebenthal & Co., one of the more original purveyors of Ginnie Maes, has developed a strategy for those investors who are bothered by the fact that once the Ginnie Mae is paid off there is nothing left, and who find the idea of spending both principal and interest irresistible. Lebenthal suggests purchasing a Ginnie Mae for, say, $25,000, and simultaneously buying a $25,000 zero coupon bond running for around as long as you think the Ginnie Mae will last. Both principal and interest from the Ginnie Mae might then be spent. At the end of that time, says Lebenthal, the investor would have a matured $25,000 bond, so the entire package would not be unlike the purchase of a single Treasury note or bond. It sounds nice and neat, but then came the collapse of mortgage rates in early 1986, and homeowners rushed to refinance. Ginnie Maes purchased in 1984 with the expectation of running until 1992 were quickly liquidated. By spring 1986 Ginnie Mae researchers were advising clients to consider the instruments surrogates for three-year Treasury notes.

What it comes down to is this: at one time the Street assumed that given time, Ginnie Maes would become more predictable instruments. It now appears that such will not be so. We seem destined for a lifetime of fluctuating rates, and as long as this is the case, Ginnie Maes will be relatively unpredictable. This has a negative connotation for investors, but a positive one as well. It means that yields will continue to be higher than Treasury bills and notes, a situation that might have changed had Ginnie Mae maturities stabilized.

Finally, those who are put off by the $25,000 minimum for new Ginnie Maes might consider purchasing an old one, for which part or even most of the principal has been eroded, or better still, a Ginnie Mae mutual fund, of which there are scores. Not only will this provide diversification and professional management, but the funds may be redeemed at net asset value, and in addition most of them pay out only interest, retaining principal to be used for additional purchases. Individuals who are bothered by the erosion of principal might go that way.

Most individual investors have never considered purchasing foreign bonds, at least not since they were stars of the 1920s bull market. Certainly news of third world debt problems, fears of revolution and repudiation on the Cuba model and the like, haven't helped. Yet some of the foreign issues should be investigated, since they offer safety and—due to the aforementioned fears—a higher yield than comparable American paper. These are sold here by foreign governments and in some cases, companies as well. In addition there are international agency issues worth considering. There is no currency risk; interest and principal are paid in dollars.[3]

SOME ESOTERICA

However, just about all of these bonds and notes are thinly traded. If they interest you, the way to go would be to tell your broker of this and ask him or her to keep a wether eye on them for you. At one point or other you might receive a call with an offer to sell a Kingdom of Sweden, Asian Development Bank, Hydro Quebec, or some other issue. Compare these with similar American bonds and see if the premium makes them worthwhile. If so go ahead and buy, in the almost certain knowledge that they are as safe as their high ratings indicate. For swingers, there are defaulted Cuban bonds and such, while Mexico debts may be safer than they seem. In early 1986 you could have purchased Mexico 8⅛s of '97 at 65, for a current yield of 12½ percent and a yield to maturity of 14.42 percent.

---

[3]At the end of 1985 the United States became the world's largest debtor nation, meaning that foreigners owned a great deal of what to them were foreign bonds. But there was a difference: these were dollar denominated, to the tune of more than $100 billion. This demonstrates the trust foreigners have in dollars. Would you purchase a franc-denominated bond? Or one in Mexican pesos?

As indicated, the greater the risk the greater the reward.

Mention has been made of TIGRs, CATs, GATORs, RATs, and other acronymic wildlife thought up by imaginative investment bankers.[4] These are Treasury notes and bills stripped of their coupons and sold as zeros, the coupons marketed separately to those wishing a stream of income. In 1985 the Treasury got into the game on its own by issuing zeros on an original basis. Zeros trade on the OTC for the most part, though some are listed on the NYSE, generally at somewhat higher prices, so it pays to go OTC with these.

As with corporate zeros, these can be fine in IRAs and Keoghs, and as gifts for minors. It should be noted that zeros are not particularly liquid, that price fluctuations can be strong in either direction, and they may not be suitable for those who do not intend to hold till maturity and want a locked in rate. Long-term zeros can swing to 10 percent in a session without much trouble. Individuals who purchased maturities in the late 1990s in 1984 were delighted to see them double in less than a year, far outpacing stocks. But it can go the other way as well. Suffice it to say that zeros could prove a terrific speculation on declining interest rates, but they have to be watched carefully.

SAVINGS BONDS

With some exceptions small investors might consider ignoring the Treasury market entirely, and take an alternate route if so high a degree of safety is desired. The most accessible government paper is available at your local bank or S&L. A generation of Americans who came of age during World War II can recall the Series E bonds, the least expensive of which sold for $18.75 to mature in 10 years to $25. The Es (and their cousins, the Hs) were replaced by EEs and HHs in 1980, and these are more interesting vehicles,

[4]TIGR is Merrill Lynch's "Treasury Investment Growth Receipt," and A. G. Becker stretches matters a trifle with its COUGAR, standing for "Certificate on Government Receipts."

and in some markets, the kind even sophisticated investors might prefer.

EEs are issued in denominations from $25 to $10,000 and are purchased at 50 percent of the face value. Thus a $10,000 EE would sell for $5,000, and initially matures in 11 years. These pay interest equal to 85 percent of the five-year U.S. government securities rate, with a guarantee of at least 6 percent. In addition, the interest is taxed at maturity, not as accrued. EEs cannot be redeemed before five years, but this might be a piddling matter for some investors. So an investor wanting to defer interest to a time when his taxable income is lower than presently, and at the same time believes rates will decline to under 6 percent, could do well with EEs.

In addition, EEs can be rolled over into HHs without the taxes being paid. HHs are issued for EEs at face value in denominations of from $500 to $10,000, and have an initial maturity of 10 years. These pay 6 percent, which like corporates comes in the form of a semiannual check to be taxed as current income. Unlike the EEs, HHs can be redeemed anytime after six months.

Look on the EEs as five-year Treasury notes extendible at the option of the holder with a minimum payout of 6 percent, and you'll see why they can be attractive. The only drawback could be the possibility of higher rates in instruments as appealing as these, and renewed inflation that would make most fixed income bills and notes less interesting. Remember, however, that the rate can go over 6 percent—the EEs would be transformed into variable rate paper should this transpire.

While individual investors need know little more about the federal debt market, many can never learn enough about municipal and state obligations.[5] Most municipals come in denominations of $5,000 and $10,000 face value, but bonds buyers and sellers generally deal in units of $10,000. Occasionally a dealer will purchase a lot of, say, $55,000, and after disposing of $50,000 will be

---

[5]For the sake of simplicity, all state, city, county, parish, etc. bonds and notes will be referred to as municipals (munis).

left with that sole $5,000 bond, which may be offered at a slightly better yield just to get rid of it. The general rule is that while odd lots in stocks cost a trifle more than a round lot (100 shares), their equivalents in bonds are less expensive. If you don't mind this, and especially if you intend to hold the bond to maturity (and not get a lower price when selling) consider buying in $5,000 denominations.

One of the first questions to consider is whether it makes more sense to own munis than corporates or federal obligations. The decision depends to a great extent on the spread between interest paid on munis and similarly rated corporates maturing at the same time. Since 1971 the spread for Aas has fluctuated between 2.29 percent (1972) and 4.44 percent (1980). The narrower the spread, the more attractive are the munis. For example, in 1972 the Aa munis offered 5.19 percent, the corporates 7.48 percent. For a person in the 35 percent marginal tax (total for federal, state, and city) bracket, that 7.48 percent translated into 4.86 percent, and so he would have been better off with munis. On the other hand in 1980 the munis offered 8.06, the corporates, 12.50, the latter coming to 8.12 in the 35 percent bracket, making corporates the better buy. So when considering bonds, check the spread in yields. This means you should calculate your total marginal tax rates, which will include state and local taxes as well as the federal.

SOME TAX CONSEQUENCES

Time was when advisors could say that if you were in the 40 percent bracket (combined federal and state) or over, chances are you'd be better off with munis. This is no longer so, given the narrowing of the spread between munis and corporates and passage of the new tax code. Checking total tax take against spreads would be the sensible thing to do if you moved from a state with a high tax load to one with a lower one. Here are some comparisons to make things easier for you:

COMPARABLE YIELD ON TAXABLE INVESTMENT IN PERCENT
FOR EACH MARGINAL TAX BRACKET

Yield on Municipals (percent)	36%	40%	45%
6.0	9.3	10.0	10.9
7.0	10.9	11.7	12.7
8.0	12.5	13.3	14.5
9.0	14.0	15.0	16.4
10.0	15.4	16.6	18.2
11.0	16.9	18.3	20.0
12.0	18.5	20.0	21.8

This suggests that if you are in the 40 percent marginal tax bracket and own bonds offering a yield of less than 13.3 percent and you can get 8 percent munis of the same quality and maturity, you would be better off going the tax-free route, and the same would hold true for one in the 45 percent bracket getting less than 14.5 percent.

At one time all bonds consisted of a "corpus," or body, and a string of coupons, each with a date, amount, and the name of the bank at which it would be redeemed. The holder would clip the coupon and present it to the bank at the proper time to receive cash, while the corpus was turned in on the redemption date for payment in full. This paper is known as the "bearer bond," since the owner's name does not appear anywhere on the corpus or elsewhere, and if lost owners would have a difficult time substantiating their claim.[6] Owners of coupon bonds generally keep them in safe deposit boxes along with a pair of scissors, clip at the proper time, place the coupons in envelopes provided by their

[6]Too much is made of this. All coupon bonds are numbered, not only on the corpus but the coupons as well. Assuming the owner has a record of the purchase, and the selling bond house a record of the number, the coupon and corpus could be traced when redeemed.

banks, and cash or deposit them as they might a check. Some banks and S&Ls charge small fees for this service, others do not, while most will forego charges for customers with large accounts.

All bonds issued nowadays come in fully registered form, as do corporates, meaning that they are registered and interest is sent on to the owners by mail. They are just as tax exempt as their comparable coupon bonds.

Some investors prefer registered bonds—and of course, purchasers of new issues have no choice. The reason is convenience and the certainty that if lost they can be replaced without too much difficulty. Others, more secretive souls, seek out old coupon bonds, their thought being to pass them on to heirs, or sell to third parties, without government or bank interference or knowledge. So the person purchasing a 3 percent coupon bond maturing in 2005 may have thoughts of stripping them of all or most coupons, using them as an annuity, and presenting the corpus to an heir, who sometime in the next century will come into an inheritance without the government's participation. In this way, they are creating their own tax-free zeros.

This can be a dangerous practice. In the first place the heir would be liable for capital gains taxes at maturity, when the redeemer might want to see the sales slip. Of course the heir might attempt a fast one and try to get away with it by claiming the purchase took place a quarter of a century or so ago and the confirmation slip had been lost. But given the electronic capabilities of governments today, and what they might be in the early twenty-first century, such practices could lead to a date in tax court. Nonetheless, many investors still prefer coupon bonds for this reason and tradition. Tellers working in banks in retirement communities know that come early January and June, when the interest on many coupon bonds come due, swarms of senior citizens descend on the safe deposit boxes and emerge envelopes in hand. And that visits to the vault often precede those by grandchildren, who leave for home with envelopes in their pockets.

All right. You decide that part or perhaps all of your bond portfolio should be in munis, and now would like to learn something about what to look for in them. First off, much of what you already know about corporates will apply here. Like them munis have to be considered in terms of maturity, quality, yield, and call. But the situation is more complex in this segment of the debt market. Moody's puts out a two-volume manual in which are described the more than 16,000 municipalities and public projects that have bonds and notes outstanding. Some are recognizable— the states and large cities, for example. But what about pollution control bonds issued by a small town in Missouri for an industrial firm? Or school bonds issued by a union free district on Long Island? Or a turnpike project in New Jersey? For that matter, why did the Missouri town issue the bonds for the company, and what on earth is a free district?

Investors in the stock of an electronics company whose products they have never seen have few qualms, because as technicians they may like its chart or as fundamentalists they think it undervalued in terms of earnings and prospects. But the same individuals sometimes feel uneasy about lending money for 20 years for the garbage burning incinerator of a village in the upper peninsula of Michigan.

They needn't be; as with corporates, the ratings offer an indication of quality, and the investor should also know that if the village reneged on its bond interest, it would have to forego the use of the incinerator. More important its rating would collapse, and future borrowings for virtually any purpose would be close to impossible. In addition, that borrowing might have been predicated on state aid, and those moneys would be available for the payouts. Finally, the courts might decide the village had no right to pass the interest. But if this is troublesome, consider investing in bonds guaranteed by an insurer.

INSURED BONDS

The two leading insurers are American Municipal Bond Assurance Corporation (AMBAC) and the Municipal Bond Insurance

Association (MBIA), which for a fee insures the bonds of an issuer prior to their being offered to the public. In most cases this will result in a AAA rating, so the issuer can sell them with a lower interest rate. The cost of the insurance is more than compensated for by the lower rate paid, so everyone wins on this one. But the weakness of several minor insurers has cast doubt on the worth and quality of insurance. What might happen if many municipalities were unable to pay at the same time? Would the insurers be able to make good on *their* pledges? They seem strong enough, but then again, so do many of the municipalities whose paper they insure. Consider that refusal to pay interest on a sewer loan might mean the sewer would be seized; how long could that go on? A small company in which you own stock can go belly up and only the employees, suppliers, customers, and stockholders will suffer. Not so a small town, in which all the inhabitants would be faced with the loss of vital services or more, depending on the nature of the bond.

This isn't to say it can't happen, but that munis often are much safer than their ratings might indicate. Indeed, it often seems that many municipalities who obtain insurance are stronger than their insurers. But if it makes you feel more secure to have insured bonds, by all means get them.

Generally speaking, the BBB bonds of a large city may be as safe as insured AAAs of small municipalities, for the simple reason that a bailout by the state or federal government would be likely, if only for political reasons. This would apply to general obligation bonds, and not many of the revenue bonds and some hybrids that have made their way to the market in recent years.[7]

---

[7]One of these is the so-called moral obligation bonds, concocted by John Mitchell, who in his time was one of the most respected and imaginative attorneys in the financial district. These were created to enable New York Governor Nelson Rockefeller to engage in some of his more grandiose construction projects after the voters turned them down. The bonds were backed solely by the moral obligation to pay, which turned out to be insufficient. Mitchell went on to become President Richard Nixon's attorney general, of course, and spent some time in prison as a result of his participation in the Watergate affair. There are investors who think he should have gone to the slammer for his role in creating those bonds.

To those interested in the municipal market the distinction between them is of paramount importance.

As the term suggests, general obligation bonds (sometimes also
known by the equally descriptive term, "full faith and credit"),
are secured by the power of the issuer to raise taxes on real estate,
sales, and in other ways to pay interest and principal. Do you
think Philadelphia will renege on its bonds? If not, you can get a
bit more interest by purchasing bonds of that city, rated BBB+,
than you can, say, of Altoona, rated AAA.

PITFALLS REAL AND IMAGINED

General obligations got a bad name due to the 1975 New York
City default, an event that even now is misunderstood by bondholders. A few words regarding this and other situations might
be useful at this point, if only to indicate just how strong the guarantees can be and inefficiences in the market investors might ponder to their profit.

As some may recall, that April New York refused to redeem
various issues of its notes, issued with full faith and credit guarantees. There was near-panic in the municipal market, as perfectly sound governments and agencies found themselves paying
an additional 200 basis points and more in interest due to investor
fears, while New York paper—not only city, but state as well—
fell precipitously. On November 15 the state legislature seemed to
legitimize the action by passing the Emergency Moratorium Act,
under the terms of which the city was permitted to suspend payments for three years. It seemed reasonable enough; after all, the
city hardly could do without police, fire, sanitation, and other services. But full faith and credit meant that the debts had to be paid
before a cent could become available for anything else. Immediately the investment community realized the matter would have
to be settled in the courts.

So it was. While this was happening some of the note owners
went to court to test the constitutionality of the moratorium—and
won by a vote of five to one. In the decision are these words: "A
pledge of the city's faith and credit is both a commitment to pay

and a commitment of the city's revenue generating power to produce the funds to pay."

The final settlement involved the creation of the Municipal Assistance Corporation (MAC), whose bonds were exchanged for the notes. In fact the noteholders did well; for their anguish they received a short-term capital loss and 8 percent bonds maturing in 1986, which within a few years went to par, for a long-term capital gain. Indeed, some adventuresome souls plunged into the market and purchased the depressed New York paper, for the same reason they would do the same when Chrysler seemed to totter on the edge of insolvency five years later; in our time we cannot afford to see a major city or corporation go under, for the repercussions would shake the very foundations of government.

By the early 1980s New York was well on its way to solvency. Soon after it was able to sell debts once again, but fears remain. So do scars in the form of ratings—BBB + for paper which had it been of a different municipality in the same financial shape would have been A or even AA. New York bonds offer high yields in view of the true quality. But try telling that to individuals and institutions who remember 1975.

What this comes down to is the simple fact that it is difficult for issuers to renege, and that government assistance in case they try to do so is probable. Indeed, there were surprisingly few defaults even during the Great Depression. When corporate America was unraveling the municipalities and states continued to pay interest and principal on their obligations. Permanent defaults came to less than one percent of the average debt outstanding in 1929–1937, and late payments to under 2 percent.

If this reasoning sounds plausible, the BBB + rated bonds of some large cities might be worth investigating.

General obligations are straightforward; not so revenue bonds, one of the more complicated and interesting parts of the municipal market.

Revenue bonds are backed by a stream of earnings generated by projects entered into by government or, in some cases, by private companies backed by governments. It could be a turnpike that uses tolls for that purpose, homeowners paying sewer and school taxes, airlines paying landing fees for airport bonds, patient payments for municipal and other hospitals supported by the municipality, charges to students using dormatories supported by the state, and so forth.

These can be tricky, for the project providing funds for debt service have to analysed in somewhat the same way you might any business venture, which is to say check on coverage of interest and consider the general viability of the operation, and its importance to the community. While the threat of cutting off service would prevent a town from failing to make interest payments on its sewer bonds, payments on other revenue bonds might be passed more easily. Turnpike bonds can be troublesome; alternate means of travel can be found. Several roads that have failed to collect sufficient tolls to service debts have gone in and out of arrears. Theoretically bondholders could take control, but toward what end? Far better to let the turnpike operate in the hope that one day payouts will be made and arrearages cleared up. Hospital bonds without state or other guarantees often have low ratings, and if they are used to erect, say, nurses' residences, can go into default without seriously imparing operations. Even should the hospital have to close down chances are there would be other facilities in the area to take up the slack. The same is true of bonds issued to construct parking facilities and dormatories, especially those with state aid for private colleges. Take more care when looking at revenue bonds that you would with GOs, but at the same time consider that when the revenues are raised for some monopolistic enterprise run by the municipality that fills an urgent need, chances are good they will be paid, if not by the issuer, then through a bailout by some other government agency. This certainly is the case for sewer, water, and even public school bonds.

WHOOPS

One of the more spectacular episodes concerning revenue bonds now being played out involves those issued by the Washington Public Power Supply System, more familiarly known as WHOOPS, which in 1982 had $8.1 billion in debt outstanding. The funds borrowed were being used to erect five huge nuclear stations in the northwest, owned by a group of utilities and municipalities there and administered by the Bonneville Power Administration. The project was botched, and it now appears only one of the stations will ever come into service.

As of summer 1986 $2.25 billion of these bonds, for Projects 4 and 5, are in default, while interest on the others—Projects 1-3—is being paid, the funds raised by Bonneville by billing customers for debt service.

There is some question as to whether the bondholders can successfully demand interest payments under the term of the indenture. The matter is complicated by the fact that these bonds are also secured by $19 billion of power bonds from other agencies. The legal ramifications are intriguing, and need not concern us here. Suffice it to say that Chemical Bank, the trustee for a number of bondholders, has taken WHOOPs to court, and has a good chance of winning. Still, prices on the bonds plummeted when rumors of default surfaced, and those with passed interest fell further when the actual action was taken. At this writing the defaulted paper is selling for from $130 to $180 per $1000 face value —while those WHOOPS bonds still paying interest are yielding from 9 to 11 percent, depending on maturity. But at times in 1984–1985, when new rumors of default were making their way through the investment community, the yields were as much as 300 basis points higher than those of comparable issues. WHOOPs 1, 2, and 3 are good grade, and 4 and 5 interesting speculations for those interested in such things.

THE MECHANICS

Your broker at the major wire house, who carries an inventory of corporate bonds, also has one for tax exempts, and I have no quarrel with those who want to use their services. But there are "boutiques" that concentrate on serving small accounts in the municipal area that should be considered. Several specialize on double tax exempts of those of the state in which they are located. So a bond house in Minneapolis will have a substantial stock of Minnesota bonds, a Los Angeles dealer will concentrate on California's, and a Boston on Massachusetts' paper. Investors residing in high tax states and in municipalities with their own income taxes will be particularly interested in triple tax exempts, New York City being an obvious example, and they would be well advised to seek out boutiques. So deal with that large wire house if you will, but also consider an account at a local bond house, compare offerings, and you may find the latter may have a larger inventory and better prices.

An alternative would be the municipal bond unit at a large bank or important regional one. One way to find them would be to make calls, and ask if this bank or that buys and sells munis. Some advertise in the newspapers, and that would be another way of locating them.

Reflect that the broker at the boutique or the officer at the bank deals only in municipals, and probably knows that market better than does his counterpart at the wire house. Generally speaking, they are more able and willing to assist in your education, an important consideration given the growing complexities of this investment sector. Take into account one additional factor when selecting a bond house; there are many that are little more than shoestring operations, and while all will deliver purchases bonds in line with the law, some have failed, leaving their clients in distress. Your best bet would be to look for a bond house that has been in business for a number of years.

Since municipal bond buyers are interested in avoiding local as well as federal taxes, especially in places with high rates, bond dealers tend to play down paper from other states. Should a client in Atlanta want to sell some New Mexico bonds, the dealer will oblige, but knowing its clientele, will offer a somewhat lower price than the seller might have received in Santa Fe. These will go into his inventory to be offered at a lower price than similar

Georgia bonds. You might think the sensible thing to do would be to try to sell them to a dealer in New Mexico, but in practice this does not happen. So consider opening accounts in and getting on mailing lists of bond houses in other states, since a Miami investor might find similar Florida bonds offered in Maine to be at somewhat lower prices than they are in his city.

Some investors would do well to construct their own bond portfolios, in somewhat the same way they might go about doing so with stocks. Just as diversification makes sense to spread risks with equities, so it does with bonds. A person in his fifties might purchase bonds due to mature after retirement, when presumably income will be diminished and he would fall into a lower tax bracket. It might make sense to string out maturities, say over a 10-year period or so, to assure a steady stream of cash from redemptions. Whether or not you should consider lower rated bonds is a matter of personal judgment, but there surely is less danger from a BBB maturing in 5 years than one doing so in 20. Keep in mind what was mentioned in the first sentences of Chapter 7, namely that ownership of bonds of GM and IBM does not represent the kind of diversification as it would with their stocks. The same is true, but to a lesser extent, of bonds of New York City and Puerto Rico. In other words, diversification with a municipal bond portfolio should be by rating and maturity.

Others who may wish to diversify but avoid the trouble of establishing and monitoring a portfolio, might consider unit trusts and mutual funds, both of which have gained in popularity in recent years.

SPREADING RISK

Tax exempt unit trusts were first introduced in the early 1960s. These were simply a bundle of tax exempts—often but not always a diversified portfolio—offered by packagers, who take a cut off the top (and an annual fee) and stand prepared to repurchase the units at net market prices. Unlike the mutual funds the unit trusts are passive, that is to say, not actively managed, though most permit trustees to sell off individual bonds if they believe them to be in trouble or to pay for redemptions.

Unit trusts can be most attractive. They offer diversification, professional selection and oversight, and monthly rather than semiannual income such as that provided by individual bonds. The trustee gathers all of the interest, clips coupons when necessary, and sends on a single check. Owners can call for quotes and sell the trusts easily enough.

There are scores of companies that put together unit trusts, including virtually all of the major wire houses. If you give one of them a call the prospectuses of new trusts will be sent on, and quotes for established ones provided.

One of the first things noticed will be that unlike bonds, trusts are not quoted in terms of yields to maturity, only current yields, the obvious reason being that the portfolio contains bonds that mature at different times, and when they do, the owner received a share of the principal in the mail. Thus a trust offered at $975 paying $72 annually will have a current yield of 7.38 percent.

Most unit trusts are initially offered in demoninations of $1000 face value, and this includes the sales charge, which ranges from 3.5 to 5 percent. Suppose you are told a new trust is coming to market priced at $1000. What you will get is paper backed by, say, $995.20 in bonds to reflect a 4 percent commission (4 percent of $995.20 equals $39.80, and $1000 minus $39.80 equals $995.20). Note that this is higher than the commission charged by discount brokers for stocks. Putting together unit trusts is a lucrative business, which is why so many players have entered the game. Still, to get the combination of diversification and management, the fee may be considered justifiable.

There is a usually unmentioned problem with some unit trusts that should be mentioned, even though there really is no way to guard against it. Many of those wire houses have tag ends of underwritings and bonds that come across their desks that are difficult to market. These might be thrown into a new unit trust and disposed of in this way. This isn't to suggest anything underhanded about the practice, which is impossible to detect, for it would have to go into the matter of motives that could not be proved. In any case, the offering prospectus will inform you of the composition of the portfolio, and if you see bonds there you deem inappropriate due to quality, consider (1) not making the purchase, or (2) they may be perfectly fine bonds of which you happen to know little.

One way to find some peace of mind on this score would be to go with insured trusts. Insurers provide coverage for trusts as they do for individual bond issues, though of course the yields on these are somewhat lower than on the uninsured portfolios.

The greatest impact in this market is being made by trusts containing bonds free of both state and federal taxes. So there are trust designed for New Yorkers, Californians, and others in high tax states. Some trusts have long-term bonds, others short-term ones, so it is possible to buy a long-term New York trust, for example, knowing that it can be easily redeemed.

The mutual funds got into the act in 1976, and now one can also buy mutuals—many of them without commissions—based on tax frees. We will be exploring mutuals in Chapter 10, but here let it be noted that there are a wide variety of tax-exempt mutuals, more even than the trusts. Some concentrate on low rated issues, for example, that offer much higher yields than might be found in the BBB and over segment. In theory the professional managers can ferret out debts that are really better than their ratings would indicate, while owners are willing to accept more risk for greater rewards. Likewise, higher yields can be obtained from long-term bond funds than from the shorts. There are tax-free extremely short-term money market funds whose prices don't fluctuate and offer the familiar withdrawal by check privilege.

When considering whether to go the unit trust or mutual fund route take into account the matter of commissions and fees—the former higher in trusts, the latter higher in funds. What should *not* be a prime consideration is the ability of the manager to trade the portfolio. As noted, bonds are traded more on interest rate expectations than anything else, and while stock portfolio managers might easily have an annual 100 percent turnover, in a period of stable rates and no significant alterations in quality of holdings the bond man might not make a single move. If you expect to be a trader, go with the funds, and if you want to hold on for a while, the trusts might be better.

9 THE ANATOMY OF OPTIONS

This section begins with a warning. There is no simple way to describe options operations and strategies, and some investors throw up their hands after reading about them even in magazine articles geared to the unsophisticated. So be prepared for some tough sledding, in what is easily the most difficult part of the book to understand. We will start out with the easier material, and then advance to the more complex.

Forwarned is forearmed.

THE FUNDAMENTALS

In Chapter 1 we saw that an option gives the owner the right to buy or sell a fixed amount of something on or before a specified date at an agreed on price to the person from whom he purchased the instrument. A call is the right to buy the security, while a put enables its owner to sell—always a specific amount—before a stated date.

No one really knows when options first appeared, but it seems probable prehistoric farmers sold portions of their crops this way, and herdsmen did the same for their flocks. Grain futures were known in Ethiopia as early as 1000 B.C., and were utilized in dealings throughout Roman and European history. In 1570 a commodities futures market was established in London, and others soon were organized in Europe.

To stretch a point somewhat, one might consider that Jacob purchased an option on Esau's birthright by paying him a mess of pottage.

There are options on securities as well. These were employed in London in the seventeenth century, when they were known as "privileges." They appeared in New York during the mid-1800s, now called "papers."

Russell Sage, a wily and imaginative Connecticut grocer turned banker who arrived on Wall Street shortly after the Civil War and soon became one of its more colorful and powerful figures, made his initial impact as an options dealer. Seeing activity in a stock along with a warming of interest and upward movement, Sage would offer to sell a call on it at a specified level within a fixed period, usually six months. A speculator might have thought the stock was due for a fall, in which case he would purchase a "put" from Sage, which gave him the right to sell the stock at a stated price on or before the expiration date.

The purchaser might be an individual wanting to wager a small sum on the stock's performance. Most options buyers of the time were seeking ways to profit from rises or falls in stocks, as an alternative to buying on margin, which was in great vogue. Indeed, margin dealings were the rule, when speculation and gambling were more common than investment in the stock market, and in fact most individuals who bought shares did so on margin. They reasoned that if you thought a stock would rise from 80 to 100 in the next six months, you might purchase 100 shares for $8000 plus commission. Or you could buy it on margin, as much as 90 percent. This meant the buyer put up $800, borrowed the rest ($7200) from the broker at an agreed on interest rate, with the stock held as collateral for the loan. Then, if the stock fell to 72, the investor would be effectively wiped out, the broker selling to recoup his loan. On the other hand, should the stock go to 88, the owner might sell for $8800, repay the $7200 loan, and be left with $1600, for a 100 percent profit on a 10 percent move. Thus "leverage" as it was called could wipe out a position or double it on that 10 percent move in one direction or another.

Options were a better way to do the same thing. The gambler would buy a call to purchase the stock at 80, this known as the "strike price," at any time during the next six months, for which he might pay $500 or so. That was the limit of his liability. If the stock fell, he would be out that $500. Should it rise to between a fraction over 80 but under 85, he would exercise the option but still be a loser. For example, buying the stock at 80 when its market price was 83 would yield a $300 gain, but since the option cost $500, the total loss would come to $200. On the other hand, a rise to 90 would double his money, since the option was exercised at 80 for a 10 point gain, while the option accounted for 5 points, leaving 5, or $500.

Some options buyers so acted in order to hedge on their investments. Thus the owner of a stock purchased at 50, which had gone to 80 like a rocket, might be a trifle edgy. He might want to hold on for the ride, but be afraid of being caught in a free fall should a dip take place. This investor could place a stop loss order with his broker, saying that he should sell if the stock fell to the price of 75 or wherever else he would want to get out. In this way he was assured a profit and protected against a major decline.

A preferable way to go might be to purchase a put option, which would give him the right to sell the stock at 75 at any time before a specified date. In such a case he would have a satisfactory hedge, which is one of the functions of options. So long as the stock remained above 75, the option would have no intrinsic value; why exercise the option and sell the stock at 75 when the open market value was over that sum, say 79? If and when the stock declined to under 75, the option would acquire intrinsic value,or as the term is used, be "in the money."

Let's assume the investor's worst fears are realized, and the stock declined to 20. He would simply exercise the option before it expired, and sell the stock at 75 to the person who sold him the option.

The intrinsic value of this option would rise in direct proportion to the decline in the stock's price when it fell to under 75. Thus a decline from that level to 70 would mean the owner had lost 5 points on the stock. But the option, which gave him the right to sell it at 75, would now be worth that 5 points. Let the stock recover to 75 and the owner would have a gain of 5 on it, but the option's intrinsic value would decline a like amount, to zero. Such investors looked on options as a form of insurance, and so it was.

Using put options in this kind of situation is vastly better than short selling—the sale of a stock one doesn't own, borrowing it from the broker for a fee, in the belief it will go down, after which it will be purchased at the lower price and return to the lender. In shorting the investor might have borrowed the stock from the broker when it was 80, sold it at that price and then, if he were right, bought it back at 50, return the security, and come out with a 30 point gain. But what if he guessed wrong? In such a situation the potential loss was unlimited. The stock could go to 1000 or more, and still the short seller would have to cover. Theoretically there is an infinite potential loss on a short sale.

The shorts went through just such a wringer in 1901, when J. P. Morgan and Kuhn Loeb battled for control of the Northern Pacific. The stock had risen from 57 on November 5, 1900 to 85 on January 2, 1901, and on to 115 by May 1, as both sides bought steadily. Not knowing what was happening, some outsiders shorted the stock at 100, thinking to cover their positions when it fell back to the high 50s. Then the bidding intensified; on May 9, Northern Pacific closed at 325, up 165 for the session. And there were those poor souls, short at 100, who knew they would have to purchase the shares at that level—and higher, if necessary. Needless to say, this caused a panic at the NYSE, as the shorts contemplated their ruin.

Suppose that instead of shorting they had purchased put options at 100 for around five points, or $500 per 100 shares? This would have given them the right to sell the stock at the agreed on price, representing a wager that the Northern Pacific would decline to under 95 (100 minus the price of the option). Of course it wouldn't have been exercised in this case, but the options owner would have lost that $500, and no more.

SOME HISTORY

The allure of options gradually became obvious to speculators. Consider that the average American held no stocks in the late nineteenth century, that the markets were arenas for professionals, with tycoons plunging into the arena to seize control of a company, bands of manipulators organizing pools to shoot prices down or push them up, while lesser fry speculated as they might on a lottery ticket.

The business was brisk; would be buyers and sellers learned of options from advertisements on the financial pages or simply by walking into the offices of the 50 or so dealers in business at the turn of the century. Buying a put or call was not forever, but it did lock one into a position. There was no aftermarket. An individual who purchased a put or call had no place where it might be sold prior to expiration or execution. Individuals who purchased puts or calls understood they would be held until execution or expiration. The owner of shares of Northern Pacific could always get a quote on them at the NYSE. Not so the individual who had purchased a call on the stock.

At the time options were a minor instrument that provided some additional liquidity in the primary markets, and was an interesting device for use by small investors and few others. After a while big investors realized that they could be used in their campaigns as well, and their activities caused ripples in the primary market.

This was the situation during the bull market of the 1920s, when options were popular. Everything fell apart during the Depression, of course, and options didn't revive much in the immediate post-World War II years; there were only 15 or so dealers in business in the early 1950s. Their organization, the Put and Call Brokers and Dealers Association, was an inbred, chummy group, with father and son shops predominating. They had small client lists and little thought of expansion. Options were for pros; the little guy was more concerned with mutual funds and blue chips in those years.

The situation hardly changed during the bull market that followed; not even in the wild days of the 1960s was any important interest generated in the paper. The individual dealers used to advertise the options they had available, and interested parties might call to place orders. The offerings were limited; a speculator expecting a rise in Polaroid might learn there were no calls available, and those that existed were either for too short or long a time period, or for a strike price not to his liking. So long as this situation prevailed options would remain an esoteric vehicle.

The reason was clear enough: lack of marketability and liquidity. Who would buy stocks if there was no aftermarket at the NYSE, Amex, or the OTC market? one asked. So it seemed to follow that for the same reason few would buy options. To individuals who argued that the situation demanded an aftermarket, the old timers at the Put and Call Dealers replied that by their very nature options were short-term paper, expiring in months, and so didn't lend themselves to trading. Besides interest was so limited that no exchange could ever pay its way. Or at least this was the view of those Wall Streeters who knew the paper best.

THE CBOE

The situation was different in Chicago where traders on LaSalle Street were far more familiar with options, since these were the prime paper at the commodities market for which Chicago had long been the dominant center. The Chicago Board of Trade (CBOT) was to commodity options—on grains, meat, and other products—what New York was to stocks. True, there were commodities markets in lower Manhattan, the New York Commodity Exchange and the New York Mercantile Exchange, and Chicago had its Midwest Stock Exchange, which in the 1920s made a futile attempt to seize domination from the NYSE, but this was the traditional division of power.

In 1969, when the commodities markets were sluggish, the CBOT commissioned a report on whether or not it made sense to open a stock options exchange. This was simply a search for new business, a way to utilize existing expertise. The New York securities markets were going wild, with much action centered on the more speculative, low-priced issued traded over-the-counter or on the Amex. The CBOT reasoned that the kind of speculator who liked to dabble in stocks of relatively unknown enterprises selling for around $5 might prefer to do the same with options on IBM, GE, and GM, also traded at low prices, and for which there was a good deal of price action. In addition, plungers in commodities futures might like to deal in what looked like futures contracts in stocks. Out of this came the Chicago Board Options Exchange (CBOE), which opened for business in 1973.

The CBOE was far superior than the old Put and Call Dealers Association. To begin with, as in the case of commodities options, there were uniform expiration dates, the third Friday in every month. As it stands now the CBOE has three cycles: (1) July/October/January; (2) August/November/February; and (3) September/December/March. When the July options expire, that cycle adds Aprils, when the Augusts expire, Mays are added, and Junes are added when September expire.[1] All stocks of the initial list fell into one of the three. For example, on the third Friday in January the Eastman Kodak options for that month would expire, and the CBOE would add its October options to the list. Those

---

[1] The options exchanges are experimenting with monthly expirations, and in 1986, it was possible to buy and sell options for some stocks expiring the third Friday in each month.

stocks whose options were accepted and approved were assigned to one of the cycles. Thus Eastman Kodak was in the first cycle, General Foods in the second, and IBM in the third.

The strike prices were standardized, at $5 intervals for stocks under 100, and 10 for those over that price. As the underlying price moved up or down, options with new strike prices were added. So if a stock selling at 50 rose to 51½, the CBOE would create a 55 option.[2] Likewise, should it fall to 47½, a 45 option would go on the list. Those perusing the options section in their daily newspapers soon became aware that the longer the list of entries for any stock, the more volatile had been its swings over the past nine months or so, since additional options were being created.

The CBOE was followed by other options exchanges— Philadelphia, the Pacific Coast, and Amex. The Midwest Stock Exchange dabbled with options for a while, but soon was happy to merge these operations with the CBOE. the NYSE alone failed to get into the hottest new trading vehicle of the century. Not until 1985 did the NYSE make the move, and by then it was too late to expect much from its small venture.

New stocks were added on regular intervals, and in the 1980s came financial options of various kinds as well as options on stock indexes—the Value Line, Standard & Poor's NYSE Composite, and a Major Market Index. There also are options on bonds, foreign currencies and the dollar, and the European Currency Unit (ECU). Do you think the high technology segment is due for a rise or a fall? Then consider using the computer technology index. There are indexes on gold and silver, and more, with ingenious men and women thinking up new trading vehicles all the time. Indices on mutual funds appear to be on the way, and there is even talk of options on options.

Options interested relatively few brokers and customers, for a reason you are discovering: they were more complex instruments

---

[2]Options are created by the exchanges, not by the companies, a matter some investors find hard to accept. Think of them as wagers. If you bet your friend $5 that the Mets would win a game the team would have nothing to do with it. Likewise, the purchase of an IBM put or call from someone else does not involve IBM in the slightest.

than most of them had experienced. It wasn't unusual for a brokerage office to have one registered representative who was conversant with the instruments and strategies, the others giving him their business for a share of the action. The vagueness on the subject continues; it is surprising to discover how many brokers, even now, assume options are for the speculative few, that prudent investors should stay away from them. A number of them remain unaware of the wide variety of options in existence, and how they might be used by their customers. Until recently they weren't even discussed in any detail in college-level finance courses. In fact the 1978 edition of one of the more popular texts, which runs 745 pages, devotes the grand total of four pages to options, and the 1984 edition of another text, with 26 chapters, has only 12 pages out of 662 on the subject, in a grab-bag chapter entitled: "Leverage-Inherent Securities."

The literature on options is growing, and research in the field is intense. For additional material and information readers really should go to works devoted to the subject. Henry Clasing, *The Dow Jones-Irwin Guide to Put and Call Options* (Homewood, IL: Dow Jones-Irwin, 1975) would be a good start. For those wanting a short, journalistic introduction, an article entitled "How To Play the Options Game" in the December 22, 1980 issue of *Business Week* is worth a look. The best single source, however, is a pamphlet given away free by most brokerages, and sent on to all who open options accounts, called "Characteristics and Risks of Standardized Options," put out by all of the options exchanges and the Options Clearing House.

PITFALLS

Anyone thinking of a Wall Street career might consider that options are a "hot" area. The simple fact of the matter is that we still don't know very much about how options affect the prices of underlying stocks, or have a truly scientific method of determining when the price of an option is attractive in relation to that stock.

Those who can address such subjects intelligently and develop new valuation and trading techniques can write their own tickets at major investment banks.

By now small investors know that the wild gyrations that suddenly hit the markets, like a Kansas twister, can often be ascribed to programmed buying related to index options. If the spread between the S&P Index and the underlying stocks narrows or broadens beyond specified programmed levels, the computer in an office somewhere might set off a buy or sell, and then the operator rushes in to do so in the options or the underlying stocks. This is a game for big players; it takes around $5 million for starters. Then, the movement generated by one program can trigger a second, and then a third. We are now at the stage where 30–40 point moves in the Dow scarcely stifles yawns, since they represent small percentage rises or falls, and certainly have nothing to do with the economy or politics.

Options have brought about many changes in the primary market—the NYSE in particular—and most independent observers agree that few of them are for the good. Take a situation where the option can be exercised at 50, and the stock closes at 49 a few sessions prior to expiration on what has come to be known as "Frightening Friday." Big players might enter the market and purchase stock in the hope of boosting its price to a level where they would have major gains in the options, while others, whose profits would be realized if the stock remained below 50, would come in on the other side. The battles between these forces can be interesting to observers but destructive to small investors in the issues, who have no way of knowing what is happening.

The matter becomes even more complicated on the third Fridays in March, June, September, and December, when options on stocks, indexes, and index futures expire on the same day, with most of the action taking place just before the final bell, this being the reason it is called the "Triple Witching Hour." This is when some of the more important call option owners start purchasing the underling stock, hoping to drive it up to the point where the option can be exercised profitably. And for owners of puts try to thwart them, while those involved in the indexes and index futures join in.

In recent times large investment banks and other big players have gotten into the game and further distorted the market. An investment group with a substantial position in options may purchase the underlying shares if the "spread" is right, or do the opposite if not. Big time speculators are having a field day with options on the Standard & Poor's, Value Line, and NYSE indexes, especially when "divergences" appear between the contract and the underlying stocks. At such times they will engage in large scale arbitrage operations, purchasing or selling the options and then doing the reverse for the underlying stocks. Titanic struggles can ensue, while the little guy with 100 shares or so watches in bewilderment, as powerless to do anything as he might in the midst of a hurricane. Moreover, the resolution of such struggles not only can't be predicted, but their direction is always uncertain. "Trying to profit from Frightening Friday is like trying to catch a screwball," said one such dealer. "In both, you never know the direction in which it will break."

In mid-March 1986, the options exchanges released a special report that confirmed this. The investigators, headed by Hans Stoll of Vanderbilt University, also discovered that stock trading volume in the last hour of Frightening Fridays was nearly triple that of nonexpiration Fridays.

Scarcely a week later Wall Street had another Triple Witching Hour. The Dow, which the previous session had closed above 1800 for the first time, opened lower, rallied, declined, and two hours before the close rallied once again, on near-record volume. All knew the arbitrageurs were engaged in massive buying and selling programs; rumor had it that Salomon Brothers was in on the sell side, while Morgan Stanley was buying. At one point, less than an hour before the final bell, the Dow was off less than 10 points. Then prices cracked; the bears won, and the blue chips that comprised the Dow collapsed. Due to heavy volume the tape was almost a half an hour late at the close, but even before then it was evident the decline was substantial. As it turned out the Dow lost 35.68 points to close at 1768.56, on a volume of a shade under 200 million shares, making it the fourth busiest session in Exchange history. One seasoned trader remarked, "Are there rules? There are no rules. You dodge the bullets," while another observed, "If the pros don't understand the market after a day like this, what does that say for the little guy?"[3]

By May the district and the SEC combined to create a study group with a mandate to discover some means of reforming the system. The talk at the time was that the index options might expire on Thursday evening, or perhaps Friday morning, since the markets seemed to work better in the early hours of trading. The hope was that a change could be recommended and put into place soon—preferably before the next Triple Witching Hour in June.

Sure enough, on Tuesday, June 10, the Dow collapsed by a record 45.75 points, with every stock comprising the average falling. The reason? Most commentators thought it had something to do with the approach of the Triple Witching Hour. It began with a swift decline in index options, followed by programmed selloffs in the underlying stocks. There were other sweeping moves in the sessions that followed, but calm as the big day—June 20—approached. Some thought the "arbs" had "wound down" their positions and would be on the sidelines, but most had to admit they really didn't know what would happen.

Stocks opened slightly higher that session, on low volume, and meandered in mid-afternoon. By then it appeared the arbs indeed had abandoned the market, and talk on the floor turned to weekend plans. The Dow was up by only 2 points with half an hour of trading to go when the big rush began. On volume of more than 50 million shares prices skyrocketed, rising on large-scale buy programs from the major houses, to close up 23.68 points on the day. The Triple Witching Hour had claimed additional victims.

Such is the impact of options, especially index options and options futures, and programs. They can devastate the blue chips that comprise the popular averages, or do the opposite by causing

---

[3]Sterngold, James, "Witching Hour Havoc," *New York Times*, March 22, 1986.

them to soar. Yet the rest of the market can be unaffected. When the Dow collapsed on March 21, 1020 issues advanced while 925 declined, and prices on the American Stock Exchange actually rose. It was the blue chips that underwent the trauma. Indeed, mutual funds concentrating on small stocks were up on the day, while those based on heavily capitalized issues declined.

This resulted in a strange alteration in the way some investors looked at their stocks. Time was when the little guy was attracted to the big blue chips, because they were "safe." The OTC market was shunned, because companies whose shares were listed there were supposedly riskier. Now, however, the arbs do their work on the blue chips, and ignore the lesser fry. So investors who fear the Triple Witching Hour are attracted to the OTC.

Analysts who had cut their teeth on stocks and bonds now found they either had to learn the new ways or go to the discard bin. In spring 1986 28-year-old Steven Gruber, a 5-year veteran investment banker at Lehman Brothers, reflected on the difference between his education and that of the older men and women—in their 30s and 40s. "I studied options theory at school," he noted. "People who came here 15 years ago studied balance sheets."

This need not overly concern the average long-term investor, because things tend to settle down after Frightening Fridays. The district has become accustomed to them and their severity may be less in the future, and the community and the SEC may make changes to mitigate any abuses. Most investors should look upon options either as vehicles to enhance income from a portfolio or speculate on rises and falls in stocks or the market as a whole.

OPTIONS AND THE CONSERVATIVE INVESTOR

Options appeal essentially to conservative investors and daring speculators interested in leveraging their bets. Generally speaking, the former sell call options to the latter, such as institutions and conservative investors. Mutual funds wanting to increase their earnings will also sell options. That prudent investor living off dividends would do well to think about entering the game, in effect booking the bet of the speculator, knowing in advance that no matter what happens, he will come out ahead. Options also provide the means for conservative players to purchase some stocks in what they may deem a safer way than simply placing an order at the market. Through the use of options, investors who know they are klutzes at selecting individual stocks but pretty good at calling market turns can capitalize on their talents. All of which calls for some explanation.

Consider the following scene.

Three months ago Sam closed on the new house, for which he paid $150,000, putting down $50,000 and assuming a $100,000 mortgage. Then he and his family moved in, and after a hectic two and a half months of decorating, putting in new shrubs, arranging and rearranging the furniture, Sam had some of his friends over for the first party in the new place.

All went well. The weather was fine, the caterer performed superbly, and the next door neighbors didn't blast away on their stereo. Sam and his close buddy Frank are standing on the veranda, looking at the stars, and talking about the house. Sam is particularly concerned about Frank's opinion, since he supposedly knows quite a bit about real estate.

"You have a really nice place here," says Frank, and he seems to be sincere, not simply trying to make Sam feel good about it. So Sam opens up. Perhaps he did pay a bit more than it was worth, and maybe if he had shown more patience he could have gotten the seller down a few thousand. But real estate prices are rising, Sam tells Frank, and if he holds on for a few years he might sell for a nice profit. So it not only is a fine place in which to live, but a good investment.

"How much *did* you pay?" Frank asks, and Sam tells him—the whole, unvarnished truth—$150,000 for the house plus another $10,000 in decoration costs.

"It's a bargain" says Frank, to Sam's vast relief. "I'll bet that within a year or so you'll be able to sell it for over $200,000."

Now that seems too good to be true, and Sam observes that the house down the street, with a swimming pool and add-on wing (Sam's has neither) had gone for $190,000 only a year earlier. Frank persists. A small argument begins, and as such things often do, ends with a wager.

"Tell you what," says Frank. "I'll bet the price will go to $200,000 within a year, and here's how we'll do it. You can sell me the right to buy the house for $200,000 at any time up to a year from today, for $10,000."

By now you realize that Frank wants Sam to sell an option. Should Sam do it? If Frank doesn't exercise the option, Sam would be ahead $10,000. What if Frank did buy Sam out? Sam would have had a profit of $40,000 (the house cost $150,000 plus $10,000 in decorating expenses), this being a 26.6 percent return, with the $10,000 for the option making it $50,000, or 33.3 percent. Not bad, Sam might think. Whether or not the option were exercised he would come out ahead. Then Sam considers that his real investment was the $50,000 down plus the decoration expenses of $10,000, for a total of $60,000, and that would mean a profit on investment would be 83.3 percent.[4] So Sam goes ahead and sells the option.

Suppose Frank knows something Sam does not—a large company is thinking about moving into the area, and if it does real estate prices will soar. If this happens he might get as much as $260,000 for the house. That would yield him a profit of $50,000 —the cost would be the $200,000 for the house plus the $10,000 for the option. A $50,000 profit on a $10,000 investment is 500 percent.

How would Sam feel in such a situation (besides never seeing Frank again, that is)? If Sam felt like kicking himself remember that he did pretty well. In fact, both sides won on this deal.

Now think about the attitudes on both sides. In this case Sam was a conservative investor, willing to sell the option so as to make some extra money, while Frank was a gambler, putting

---

[4]As can be seen, buying a house with a mortgage is really a leveraging operation, akin to buying stock on margin.

down a $10,000 bet, knowing he could lose it all, but of course hoping to win big.

That is the way it is with options, As noted, the gamblers buy from conservative investors. And if Sam considered himself in the latter category, he should also think about selling stock options. What this means is that the widow and orphan whose only important financial asset is a bundle of AT&T stock should sell options on it to enhance their total return. If they do it right, they will never be called out of the stock. In fact, it's the closest thing to a free lunch on Wall Street. But that comes a little later, after we set the ground work.

Now for the mechanics of the operations and some basic strategies. Be warned again that this can be heavy sledding, and somewhere along the line—perhaps in the very next page—you may feel bewildered. It could be you already are dismayed. Don't be overly concerned. Rather, go back and reread the paragraphs that are troublesome, reflecting all the while that others far less intelligent than you have mastered the rudiments of options. Also keep in mind that the rewards for understanding are worth the time and effort.

Start out with entries for options on a particular stock, such as the one shown here for General Electric on June 30, 1986.

CALL OPTIONS FOR GENERAL ELECTRIC, JUNE 30, 1986

Stock Price	Strike Price	Calls		
		Sept.	Dec.	Mar.
80¾	65	16½	s	s
	70	11¾	13	s
	75	7¾	9	10
	80	4⅛	6¼	7½

s means no option exists at that price.

Note that calls are available at strike prices of 65, 70, 75, and 80. From this you can tell that the price range for GE over the past three quarters was approximately 62 to 82 (in fact, it was 63 to 82¼). GE's current price was 80¾ meaning that owners of all the options could exercise them on that day and realize a profit—which is to say they are all "in the money." The 65 call option could be exercised to purchase GE at that price, and the stock simultaneously sold at the market price of 80¾ for a profit of 15¾ points before deducting for commissions.[5]

It really wouldn't pay to do this, since the option is selling for 16½, or ¾ over the 15¾ point profit that could be realized through the exercise. So the owner would do better by selling the option than exercising it.

Note that if the owner of the 80 September call exercised it, he would have a profit of ¾. But the option could be sold for 4⅛, or 3⅜ higher. The general rule is that the closer the option is to the strike price (or to put if differently, the line between being in and out of the money) the greater the differential between the exercise value and the market value. This is known as the *speculative premium*, or *time premium*. The extra-3⅜ points was the amount the owner was willing to risk in order to have a call on the stock at that price until the third Friday in December. The closer one gets to the expiration date, the less time the owner has to hope for the stock to rise, so the time premium declines as the date nears.

There are two and a half months between June 30 and the expiration of the September contracts. A person purchasing the September call at 4⅛ was betting GE common would rise to over 84⅛ (the strike price plus the price of the call) in that amount of time. Suppose he was right: on the expiration day GE was selling for 90 as a result of some good corporate news. He would exercise the call and get $1000 for his investment of $412.50. Not bad for an in-

---

[5]This is not to suggest that commissions *can* be ignored. We are dealing here with relatively low priced instruments, and the commissions can mount. But this section of the chapter is concerned with the principles of options, and not the bricks and mortar. The matter of commissions is no small matter, and will be discussed at the close of the chapter.

vestment for less than three months. If he was wrong, all that would be lost would be the $412.50.

Now you can see why gamblers love to buy call options, and why individuals with inside information can use them to multiply profits. And why the market goes crazy just prior to options expiration, when arbitrageurs and others attempt to "move" GE and like issues to make the options good or worthless. Finally, you can now understand that the more volatile the stock (the higher its beta) the more speculative it is, the higher the time premiums will be.

Note too that the further out the call, the higher the speculative premium. If GE wound up six months to the day at the very same price it was on June, you can be fairly certain that March call, now 7½ with almost nine months to go, would decline to around 4 now that there was only three months remaining. How can you know? Because the September 80, with three months remaining, is 4⅛.

Before turning to basic strategies, remember that an option does not represent ownership of a stock, but only a right to buy it at a specified price on or before a certain date. The owner of the stock retains all other rights, including those to receive dividends. So the owner could sell an option on his dividend-paying stock six months out, receive the price of the option, plus two dividends before having to make a decision as to the next course of action.

You already have seen why speculators like to use options: so as to obtain leverage and previously determined risk levels. And buying options *are* risky, make no mistake about that. Data indicate that relatively few options are ever exercised. The buyer of the option wants it to sell at a future date, prior to expiration, when he expects it will be higher. As expiration approaches many sellers, wanting to hold on to their stocks, will purchase in the money calls on them they had sold months before so as to "even out" their positions. The data indicates that around 15 percent of all call options, and less than 7 percent of the puts, are exercised. Moreover, in 1983, a year when the market performed well, 22 percent of all calls expired worthless, which is to say under their strike prices. Naturally, in years the market performed poorly, that figure will rise substantially.

BASIC STRATEGIES

Start out with a simple strategy. Scan the options list in *The Wall Street Journal* to locate stocks you find interesting. Ideally they will be prominent issues that "move" at least as fast as the market itself, this the bait to attract speculators. Since Merck fills most of the criteria, let us use that one. Here are the Merck calls on April 25, 1986:

CALL OPTIONS FOR MERCK, APRIL 25, 1986

Stock Price	Strike Price	Calls		
		July	Oct.	Jan.
155½	120	37¼	38	s
	125	r	32½	s
	135	21⅝	23	r
	140	16¾	r	r
	145	13	15½	19
	150	8¼	12½	r
	155	5¾	10	12⅞
	160	3¾	8	10½

r means option was not traded; s means no option exists at that price.

You can see by the options offered that Merck participated fully in the great bull move of the period. The range for the past year was 98¼–157⅞, and the 160 option was created when the stock crossed the 157½ level.

Merck closed that day at 155½. Suppose an investor decided to purchase a round lot of Merck. He would pay $15,550 plus commissions (which will be ignored for the sake of simplicity, but are charges that will lower the results). Simultaneously, that individual might sell the January 160 call for 10½, receiving $1050. The total outlay would be $14,450.

If on the third Friday in January, Merck wound up at, say, 144½, for a decline of 10½ points during the 10 months, our investor would have been even—no loss, no gain, even though the price of the stock had fallen sharply.[6] The corollary of this is that should the stock stand still—end up at 155½—the investor would have made $10,050 (received for the option) plus three quarterly dividends of $90, for a total of $1320 over a 10-month span. Annualized this comes to a $1584 on an investment of $15,550, or better than 10 percent. Compare this to the 2.3 percent the investor would have received without the option sale.

Of course, the investor had to give up something for this: he would have to sell Merck to the option holder at 160. Suppose this was done. The option seller would then have $1,050 for the option, $270 in dividends, and a capital gain of $450 ($16,000 minus $15,550) for a total of $1,770, this being $2,124 annualized, for a return of 13.7 percent. And remember, if the stock fell by less than 10½ points, the owner would still have a profit.

The catch comes if the stock moved much higher than 160. Note that during the past year Merck had moved almost 60 points. If it did so again in the next seven months, the purchaser of the option would have multiplied his original investment several times.

By now you can see that involving oneself with selling calls can provide a good return on investment, safeguard against declines, but at the same time means foregoing large profits during major moves to the upside. Those willing to make the swap should consider this simple device.

Now for a somewhat more complicated strategy, the one the widow and orphan with AT&T might employ. Look at the Merck 150, 155, and 160 options and you will see that the seller of the July 150s might buy it back for $825 and simultaneously sell the

[6]The tax situation would be a wash—a capital gain of $1050, an unrealized capital loss of the same amount.

October 150s for $1250 and receive $425, this a payment for what amounts to extending the time period by three months. The key to understanding options is that time is money here, which is to say the longer the option has to go to expiration, the larger the time premium. Now observe that the individual who months back had sold the July 150 option might buy it back for $825 and sell the January 160s for $1050, receiving $225 and "moving up" 10 points on the ladder. This is so because he has extended his period by six months, and the market rewards him accordingly. It can be done indefinitely; in fact, there is no reason why sellers ever have to be "called out" of their stocks, but rather can rack up nice returns years in, year out.

You may have observed that in an environment where the stock's price is advancing, the owner will amass capital losses (because he will have to repurchase the options at higher prices than had been paid for them) and unrealized capital gains (due to the higher stock price), while the cash return on investments could be lower than they would have been if he had simply purchased the stock and remained away from options. The rule here is the faster the unrealized capital gains are racked up, the smaller the cash return. The opposite holds true as well. Options sellers who see the options expire will have substantial capital gains but could suffer unrealized capital losses.

As noted, the simultaneous purchase of a stock and the sale of the call option is a form of hedging, one of the simplest in which small investors can engage. If the stock moves up, the price of the option will as well. The owner is cheered by the stock's advance, but sobered when realizing that one day he may have to repurchase the option at a higher price. And should the stock's price decline he is saddened, but compensated in part by knowing that the option will cost less to repurchase, or even expire unexercised.

Some individuals aren't equipped psychologically for this kind of investment strategy, since they are confused as to whether to hope for a rise or a fall. The answer is that one does best with advancing stocks, though it may not be apparent at first blush. Let the stock rise and the shareowner may find himself chasing it up the options ladder for months, even years, all the while accumulating capital losses and unrealized capital gains. On occasion the repurchase and sale may require him to lay out some additional money, which may give him pause. This would happen if the stock moved up very sharply. The result in such a situation would be large losses and large unrealized gains. For example, in early 1986 the turnover on IBM options cost the owner two points to advance 10 over a six-month period. The shareholder might have considered that in effect, the two points was insurance premium paid just in case the stock had fallen. With the options strategy, he moved up 8 points; without it, the move would have been 10.

This options strategy really doesn't require much monitoring, since it works automatically. One simply has to remember that it is employed with blue chip stocks, the kind which even if they fall usually recover, that the owner has to be alert around options expiration date but not so much of the rest of the time, and that he is trading away the opportunity to receive great profits for a higher return on capital over the long run as well as diminished risk.

Those investors willing to monitor the options market on a more or less daily basis may come across special situations that could be rewarding. This isn't an everyday thing, and it can only be done with "hot" stocks that have become speculative favorites, and requires fast movement.

Begin with the fact that when certain stocks become glamorous they attract speculators, who more often than not prefer to buy call options rather than the security itself, so as to obtain the maximum leverage. This results in a higher than usual price for the option, which is where you might want to come in.

Take the case of Reebok, the manufacturer of those funny-looking shoes, whose stock had been red hot in 1986, having quadrupled in price in less than a year. In late August Reebok common sold for 23¾, the January 25 option, 3⅜.

Suppose you had purchased the stock and sold the option. This would give you a round lot of Reebok for $2375, and $337 for the option, which would require you to sell to the holder for $2500 on or before January 16, 1987.

This option price in this case was higher than ordinarily would be the case—in fact, almost twice as high—because many speculators seem convinced that by January Reebok would be selling for way over 28⅜ (the strike price of 25 plus the option price of 3⅜).

Assume the buyers are right, that by January Reebok is selling for 35. If so, the stock would be called at 25, and for the five months the seller would have a capital gain of $125 (25 − 23¾) plus $337 for the option, for a total of $462 on a layout of $2375, which comes to an annualized yield of 47 percent.

Suppose Reebok closed at the same price as it was purchased. The annualized return, due to the options sale, would be 34 percent.

Finally, should Reebok fall to 20⅜, the investor would be even, since the 3⅜ point decline would be matched by the 3⅜ received for the option.

The risks assumed by the options seller in this case are fairly clear. Should Reebok fall under 20⅜ he would have a loss; should it rise above 28⅜, he would have foregone a larger gain. But if Reebok closed anywhere between these two prices, he would be ahead, and as can be seen, by a sizable amount.

Note that the spread between Reebok's price and the call price is 1¼, and the option went for 3⅜. Compare this with Coors— not a speculative favorite at the time—whose stock was selling for 28, the price for the January call at 30, 1⅝. This is more normal. The options seller benefits, then, from catering to the dreams of the option buyer.

The best way to play this strategy is to watch the news to discover which stock is the subject of favorable rumors. You can be pretty sure speculators would have gotten to the options already if you read about it in the daily press.

PUTS

Now for a few words regarding the use of puts by investors, and not necessarily by those who want to "play" the market. One technique already has been mentioned, namely the use of puts rather than short sales to limit downside risk. Also, puts may be used to protect investors against declines. The stockholder who fears his holding may fall could purchase a put at a slightly lower than market price as insurance against a fall. Puts may be seen as mirror images of calls, to be purchased when a decline is anticipated and sold to realize additional revenues when the stockholder is reasonably convinced there will be no significant decline in the price of the stock.

One method by which a prudent investor might use puts profitably would be in place of limit orders, these being orders placed with brokers to purchase a stock if and when it falls to a specified price. Suppose a stock you admire is selling currently for 120, and you would want to buy it on a pullback to 110. You could place an order at that price, good till canceled, with the broker. Or you might want to sell a put option on the stock at that price, and receive the premium. For example, on March 13, 1986, after a major advance, IBM was selling for 150¼, and rumor had it that the company was having difficulties in meeting some orders, while management warned the first quarter's results might not be too pleasing. Stocks were soaring but IBM was in the midst of a slight decline from its high of 161.

Would the stock go lower? Investors might have concluded IBM would be a buy at 140, and placed a good till canceled order at that price. Alternately, they could have sold an April 140 put and received 1 point, or a July 140 for 3⅛. At the time it seemed that IBM would not fall that low, in which case the investor who used the market order would have nothing, while the put seller would have some profit, since the option would expire unexercised. As it turned out, IBM went under 140 in July, so the option for that month was exercised.

Of course, these are just the barebones of stock options, an attempt to survey the territory as it were.

INDEX OPTIONS

Now for a consideration of index options. These are employed by arbitrageurs who, as noted in Chapter 1, monitor the spread between the option and the underlying stocks, and are willing to buy one simultaneously and sell the other to realize a comparatively small percentage profit—which can add up when dealing in millions of dollars. For small investors, however, index options play a quite different role.

Suppose an investor feels strongly that the market is due for a sharp rise or fall. With this in mind, he makes purchases or sales of what he deems to be representative stocks. But this time out they zig when the rest of the market zags. The investor might have been correct about the market's direction, but the stocks he had purchased didn't do him much good.

The existence of index options changed all of this. Now the investor who thinks the market will rise can purchase the index— any of several, as has been noted. So if the NYSE Composite was at 143.96 on June 30, 1986, that investor might have bought the 150 July option at $5/16$, the August at $1\frac{1}{8}$, and the September at $2^{11}/_{16}$. This meant that if the September call were purchased and the NYSE Composite close before the close was at, say, 155.23, the holder would close out the position for a 5.23 point gain, which minus the cost of $2^{11}/_{16}$, which comes to 2.54 points. And of course were it at 148.99, he would have lost all. But what if the Composite was at or within a small fraction of 150 either way? The impulse for major players to push and shove the underlying stocks would be irresistible.

During the trading on that triple witching hour day discussed in Chapter 1 the NYSE Composite traded between 134.80 and 136.50. Imagine the churning as bulls tried to push it above 135 while bears attempted to keep it under that level. Simultaneously they—and others—were playing the arbitrage game, watching the spread between the price of the index and the underlying stocks. When it moved a fraction they would rush in and either buy or sell the underlying stocks or the options. The rise or decline from $\frac{1}{8}$ of a point to $\frac{1}{16}$ is a halving, and sizable amounts can be involved for individuals with thousands of contracts.

As it turned out the bears won this time around; the option expired worthless.

Finally, let's turn to the matter of commissions. Stated simply, posted rates are often so high as to make the game unattractive to many. Those buying or selling a single option from a house where the minimum commission is $35 can find commissions accounting for half the $70 involved in a deal. If you do go for options, it would be wise to use the services of a discount broker. Also, most of those who utilize options do so in multiples, which is to say they deal in units of 10 or more options. This translates into a suggestion that prudent investors do not sell options to enhance income unless they can do so in sufficient volume to mitigate the commissions situation.

10 THE MUTUAL FUNDS PATH

Now for a suggested means to resolve the investment dilemma. It isn't perfect, but reflect that you don't get the key to the universe for $24.95 (or whatever you paid for this book).

Recall if you will the scene in the first pages of Mario Puzo's *Godfather*. Amerigo Bonasera, the bewildered and deeply wronged undertaker, goes to Don Corleone to ask for justice, believing the system is rigged against people like him, who lack knowledge and influence. The Don provides it, the moral being that powerless individuals like Bonasera need the help of one who not only knows how the system works, but can get things done.

If *this* book has a message, it is that investors now find themselves in a financial jungle, populated by new life forms they cannot fully comprehend and aren't prepared to contest. It's one thing to enter the wilderness knowing that you might be attacked by a lion, but what will you do in the improbable situation of a tiger shark leaping at you from the branches of a nearby tree? Especially if you didn't know fish from fowl?

Such is the situation of today's investor, attempting to function equipped with the knowledge of how things used to be a decade or so ago. The small investor, accustomed to seeking safety in blue chips, finds them the playground of arbitrageurs, while the OTC market is frequented by individuals far more knowledgeable than he can ever hope to be.

The proper response is that found by Bonasera, which is to say, seek a godfather, and the best most investors can hope for is the managers of mutual funds.[1]

SOME MORE HISTORY

To understand just why mutual funds are so attractive today one must first gain the kind of insights that can be obtained only through a historical survey. What follows in the next few paragraphs, then, is a short history of mutual funds, concentrating on the way new instruments and approaches appeared to meet changes in the market. In other words, know the market and you'll realize how and why the funds were created, flourished, declined, and were reborn. Moreover, you'll gain perspective on how they may be employed, and what might be anticipated in the future.

Something akin to investment trusts, a union of like minded individuals seeking to share risks and rewards, existed in the Mediterranean region during the Age of Pericles, when Greek merchants banded together in ventures that had a limited life. These continued through the Roman Empire, the Middle Ages, and afterwards. Permanent funds based on securities originated in Scotland in the early nineteenth century, and similar vehicles soon made their appearance in England, France, and elsewhere in Europe.

---

[1]The Investment Company Institute, which represents the industry, offers this definition: "A mutual fund is a financial service organization that receives money from its shareholders, invests it, attempts to make it grow, and agrees to pay the shareholders cash on demand for the current value of his investment."

Instruments that might be described as private mutual trusts originated in Boston and New York in the late nineteenth century. A group of investors would pool portions of their resources which would be placed with a trustee, charged with investing and making distributions. These were for families and friends, usually the kind who had sufficient funds to invest, but not enough to warrant the full-time services of a trustee. Such trusts were not offered publicly, and their shares were not available on any exchange or market.

The situation changed dramatically in the late 1920s, when hundreds of thousands of speculators were drawn to Wall Street and the dream merchants were in their heyday. This was a golden age for the $2 better, the person always on the prowl for the hot tip.

That stocks were being manipulated and rigged was no secret; note has been taken of the fact that in those pre-SEC years pirates like Jesse Livermore, Arthur Cutten, the Fisher brothers, Joe Kennedy, and others organized bull and bear pools to push hot stocks up or down. On occasion rivals would line up against each other, with the lesser fry on the sidelines, placing wagers on one or the other. "Mr. Cutten may be said to be the leader of the largest and most influential group operating in the market today," wrote *The New York Times* in early September 1928, adding that he was allied temporarily with the Fishers and opposed to Livermore and his crowd.

The fortunate few—those who knew some of the players and had money—might join a blind pool, putting up a fixed sum which the manipulator would use in one or another of his forays, after which profits were distributed or losses absorbed. The small investors fairly yearned to be in on such groups, but of course they were on the outside, and in any case lacked capital for such ventures.

It was for the likes of them that investment trusts appeared. These were highly leveraged pools that could be purchased on high margin, which is to say a large amount of their capital was raised through the sale of bonds and preferred stock paying fixed interest and dividends, leaving much of the profits to owners of the more speculative common shares, which investors could buy at the market with 10 percent cash, the rest borrowed from the broker. The underwriter received a juicy commission and a management fee for running the portfolio.

Several of these (Goldman Sachs Trading, Lehman, Tri-Continental, United, United Founders were the best known) were stars on the markets. Tri-Continental was selling for over 350 percent of its book value, Goldman Sachs not far behind at 295 percent, which worked out to a P/E multiple of well over 100 for each.

The investment trusts grew rapidly, their assets coming to over $1.5 billion in early 1929. At the time of the Crash numerous additional trusts were in the hands of underwriters; 24 offerings were made in October, even as the market collapsed late that month.

Most of the trusts went under, and by 1931 those few that remained sold at a substantial discount from their book value. During the moribund markets of the 1930s the small investors who had been burned in the Crash and its aftermath remained away from the Street, as did the generality of investors, while speculators concentrated on low-priced shares traded over the counter or at the Curb Exchange.

As can be seen, these were *not* mutual funds, and today are known as "closed end funds," in that shares are not offered on a regular basis. Several of the old ones remain in business to this day, but none are particularly interesting. In recent years the closed end business has revived in the form of specialty funds designed to invest in shares of foreign countries or in special segments of the market.

Several barely noted mutuals worked their way through the bull market of the 1920s. The first of these, Massachusetts Investment Trust, was founded in 1924, and its small band of representatives made a handful of sales in the Boston area. The main difference between the mutuals and the investment trust was that the manager stood prepared to redeem shares at net asset value and sell them for that price, plus a commission. So there would be no premiums such as those realized by Goldman Sachs.

These funds were managed by professionals, not underwriters, and so could not claim to possess inside information. Mutuals were conservative vehicles, which may have been one of their strengths, but also proved a drawback. The kinds of people to whom they were offered generally preferred life insurance, while others wanted the speculative kicker offered by the trusts. The result was that mutuals were a small dot on a generally bleak scene during the Great Depression and World War II.

The situation started to change in the late 1940s, when a new generation, scarred by bad times and war, started to nibble at the markets. No wild speculators these, but middle-aged, middle class people eager to preserve capital and perhaps obtain better returns than then available from savings accounts.

At that time there was little interest in stocks. Annual volume at the NYSE in 1946 came to 253 million shares, about a quarter of what it had been in 1929. The busiest session that year saw 2.2 million shares traded, while on a hot, lazy day in late August the grand total of 476,000 shares changed hands. But the economy was strong; that there would be no long-feared post-war depression was now taken for granted, and there was some faint stirring on Wall Street.

THE REBIRTH OF MUTUALS

Throughout America newly recruited cadres of mutual fund salespeople were beating the bushes, seeking accounts. It was said at the time that mutual funds weren't bought, they were sold, and such indeed was the case.

Some no-loads were around. These were funds offered without commissions, usually through newspaper and magazine ads, and did not employ salespeople. Their existence was known to experienced investors, but not to novices. Many studies have shown that as a group no-load funds perform as well as the loads. In any case there were few of these in the 1940s and early 1950s, and none matched the popularity of the load operations which, as indicated, were geared to the kind of individuals who didn't know a stock from a bond, and who often had to be "educated" by the mutual fund representatives.

The majority of the funds that year were of the "balanced" variety, which is to say they divided their portfolios between stocks and bonds. There was straight bond funds as well, and for the venturesome, 100 percent common stock operations, concentrating on blue chip issues.

Fortunately for those who purchased shares in the funds, Wall Street was about to witness the most sustained bull market in American history, and those who had become mutual fund shareowners then did well for themselves. The industry boomed too. By 1950 there were almost 100 funds with a total of 939,000 accounts and assets of over $2.5 billion; five years later there were 125 of them with over 2 million accounts and assets of $7.8 billion. The number of funds had swollen to 161 in 1960, accounts to 4.9 million, and assets to over $17 billion.

In the 1950s and 1960s these funds continued to be considered proper vehicles for individuals new to the investment scene, the way to go while they learned the ins and outs of the market, after which they switched to direct investment. The generation of investors that grew up in these years thought funds were fairly stodgy, certainly not the place to be for those seeking "action."

Then came a change that met the needs of speculators who wanted and were eager to accept more volatility. The bull market started to sizzle in the late 1960s, when Wall Street took on the appearance of a playground for hot shots, "gunslingers" in the parlance of the time, young men who spoke airily of achieving profits of 50 to 70 percent with a great degree of regularity. There was Fred Alger and the Alger Fund, Dave Meid who energized the Winfield Fund, Fred Carr and the Enterprise Fund, and a number of others. Some were downright speculations, engaging in daring hedge operations; these included Lawrence Blum and Harold Newman's Hawthorne Associates and Charles Hurwitz's Hedge Fund of America.

A hundred or so of these funds came to market in 1968–1969,

and a third of them were permitted by their charters to borrow money, while several were geared to purchase restricted securities, sell short, use options, and engage in related activities. To some it seems a replay of the late 1920s, but there was a difference: the SEC was there, and if not exactly an activist agency, its presence limited the activities of the wild men. But they did attract individuals whose parents had been dazzled by Livermore and Cutten in that earlier period—namely gamblers and speculators willing to take risks and eager to pay a fee so as to obtain the best thinking of these glamorous stock-pickers.

The Great Barbecue came to a crashing end in 1969. By 1972 when the hedge funds were out of business and their go-go managers had fled the district, the industry posted more redemptions than sales. There had been 10.9 million fundholders in 1971; 10 years later there were fewer than 7.2 million, and the business seemed destined to slowly decay. At the same time, however, no-loads grew in popularity, appealing to more sophisticated investors seeking to diversify their risks by utilizing professional managements in a period of uncertain market conditions.

MONEY MARKET FUNDS

Then something new appeared: money market funds, almost all sold without a load, investing in short-term instruments (so the net asset value per share remained constant) offering a better rate than insured bank deposits. These resulted from the same forces that later would make Ginnie Maes so popular. At the time money instruments, such as Treasury bills, paid much more than time deposits at banks and savings and loan associations, causing larger accounts to "disintermediate," meaning they would remove their deposits and buy the Treasury bills directly, and not permit the savings institutions to reap those huge rewards by paying 5¼ percent on deposits and taking the money and purchasing a safe piece of paper paying 11 percent or so.

The money market funds were geared to the needs of small investors, who couldn't purchase a $10,000 Treasury bill, and effectively did so by pooling resources in the fund. Thus they appealed to a different kind of person than did the mutuals; their customers wanted high yields, and not investments in stocks or bonds. The mutual fund owner wanted to participate in markets; his money fund counterpart wanted a more attractive form of a savings or checking account.

There was only one money market fund in existence in 1971 (Reserve Fund), with assets of less than $100 million. Then, as interest rates rose, the funds became more popular. By 1985 there were over 300 of them, with assets topping $215 billion. Today they account for more than half the total assets of all mutual funds.

Generally speaking, the higher the yield from money funds the more popular they become. In 1977 yields averaged 5 percent, and the funds had assets of $3.5 billion; in 1981 when yields of 16 percent were common, the figure soared to $170 billion. Then, as yields declined, assets leveled off. In 1984 the money funds had $215 billion in net assets, which was deemed a good indicator of the state of investor confidence: the higher the amount the greater the fears of inflation.

The popularity of money market funds stirred the creative juices within the industry. These instruments met a felt need in the investment community, just as had the trusts of the 1920s, the conservative balanced funds of the 1940s and early 1950s, and the go-go operations of late 1960s. What were the requirements of the 1970s and beyond? High yields—and tax-free income.

The country was prosperous in a period of sharp inflation, pushing many individuals into higher tax brackets and making tax-exempt securities appear much more attractive and to more people than before. Hence the appearance of funds specializing in tax exempts. The beginning came with tax exempt unit trusts, somewhat redolent of the closed end trusts of the 1920s, but these were quickly followed by mutual fund-type operations. Approximately 10 percent of today's money market funds these are devoted to short-term municipal instruments, aimed at individuals in the higher tax brackets who seek the benefits of stable unit prices plus tax free income. The first of these, the Kemper Municipal Bond Fund, appeared in 1976, but the going was slow; in 1979 these funds had assets of $300 million; by 1985, the figure was over the $25 billion mark.

THE PROLIFERATION OF MUTUALS

These were followed by funds specializing in international investments, funds geared to deal in options, short-, intermediate-, and long-term bond funds, Ginnie Mae funds, "sector" funds (concentrating on individual industries), funds specializing in the OTC market, investments in sunbelt companies, and so on. There were real estate investment trusts, sold as units, and then attempts to develop a mutual fund variant.[2]

Out of this have come the concept of families of funds. Even during the 1950s several fund organizations saw the wisdom of offering a variety of mutuals to customers. This derived more from necessity than anything else. Salespeople trying to peddle balanced funds late in the decade found that some potential clients were more interested in growth, and their reports prompted to creation of funds with that in mind. Large mutual fund operations might have offerings in the bond, balanced, growth, and income areas, the hope being not only that additional customers would be attracted, but that older ones might consider purchasing more than one.

It hardly was a new idea; GM, Ford, and Chrysler have offered a variety of automobiles for different buyers for decades. It cost little to get into a new field—a couple of additional managers, a

---

[2]Not surprising, the more specialized the fund, the more likely it will be to rank among the best or worst performers. If all your money is in a computer sector fund and the industry performs well, you'll be delighted, but a sharp decline in the industry could cause substantial losses. Generally speaking, the more speculative your inclinations, the more likely you will be attracted to sector funds.

few secretaries, an enhanced relationship with the registrar, and not much more. Indeed, there were economies of scale to be realized, as research could be shared by several managers. Moreover, this extra service justified fees. The sophisticated investor preferred no-loads, since he knew, despite propaganda from the load segment, that well-managed commission-free operations did as well as their load counterparts; the message was trumpeted loudly by *Forbes* and *Barron's*, both of which run regular surveys of performance widely quoted in the general press. But these same individuals would pay a load if by so doing they got into a family of funds. Little wonder, then, that the load funds enjoyed a renaissance in the late 1970s, and that in the same period fund families proliferated.

FAMILY FUNDS: THE WAY TO GO

Led by the fund families, the numbers expanded. In 1981 there were 486 funds with 7.2 million accounts and $55.2 billion in assets, with net sales that year of $2.2 billion. For 1984 net sales came to $25.5 billion, total assets to $137 billion, for the 820 funds in existence and their 14.7 million accounts.

Why were they so popular? The growing complexity of markets and instruments was a major factor: just as sophisticated speculators in the late 1920s and late 1960s purchased trust and fund shares to go with apparently astute managers, so knowledgeable investors in the late 1970s and beyond wanted help from experts in the complicated markets of our times. Then too, mutual funds were fine instruments for individual retirement accounts and Keogh plans, especially the former for they permitted individuals to dollar-cost average. By 1985 10 percent of all IRA accounts and 27 percent of Keoghs were in mutual funds.

There was yet another reason, reflected in a crucial statistic: the redemption rate. From 1952 through 1971 the rate never went into the double digits; most shareholders appeared to be in for the long haul. Redemptions picked up during the market decline of the early 1970s, which was to have been expected. In every year from 1972 through 1979 there were more redemptions than sales, and in the latter year the rate came to 17.9 percent, this an all-time record.

Something strange happened in the years that followed. Sales soared, but the redemption rate remained high—15.4 percent in 1983, 16 percent in 1984. The reason was clear to all within the industry: mutual fund owners were engaging in a gigantic game of switch. Just as big time traders at Salomon Brothers, Goldman Sachs, and Morgan Stanley were whipping in and out of bonds denominated in dollars, marks, yen, and sterling, so the small players were switching in and out of sector, Ginnie Mae, index, and money market accounts as sudden breezes stirred the investment landscape.

As noted throughout this book, prudent investors have to be aware of a wide variety of instruments nowadays, and be prepared to go from one to another as conditions dictate. For some investors this means selling GM common and with the proceeds purchasing stock in Hitachi, or Siemens bonds, or Ginnie Maes, or long-term municipals, or simply park the money in a money fund. It may mean switching out of Exxon because of declining oil prices or into drug stocks because that group is doing well. And at each switch, the investors are obliged to accumulate information, engage in a spot of research, and of course, pay commissions.

There could be an easier way. Early in 1974 the Franklin Group permitted clients to switch from one of its funds to another, first by written request, and soon after by telephone. A load fund family, Franklin considered this a means of attracting new accounts, which seemed to justify the expense. There was no added sales charge for the service, but rather a nominal fee of $5 per switch.

This created a problem. Franklin did attract new clients, but many switched on a monthly, even weekly or daily basis, leading to the kind of volatility that made it difficult to maintain an orderly investment stance. Soon after Franklin limited the amount of transfers.

Problems remained to be ironed out, but clearly family funds with the switching feature became the way to go. Fundpack, a no-load operation, thought as much; within a year it too offered switching—but with a 1½ percent load. Next came the giant Fidelity group, with its switching option in effect in 1975. Pennsylvania followed, and then others came aboard—First Multifund, T. Rowe Price, and Financial Group. Nowadays it is difficult to find families of funds that do not offer switching.

Then the big wire houses got into the act. On the prowl for new products for their brokers to offer, they developed families of funds, most sold with a load, almost all of which permit switching. So there are two ways to go: with the old line mutual fund specialists or the newer entry, families organized by brokerages. And this is the situation today.[3]

Right now it appears there are more growth-oriented funds than any other (always excepting the money market varieties), followed in order of popularity by fixed income, growth and income, capital appreciation, equity income, international, and small company growth. It isn't difficult to see how this could change rapidly. For example, if the price of gold starts to rise due to increased inflationary prospects, investors could switch from these to the gold funds, of which there are around 15 right now, and more would be organized. A roaring bull market could lead to increased popularity for the options funds (fewer than 10 are operating now), or funds specializing in natural resources (around the same number exist). The international funds enjoyed a great vogue in 1986, and a rush of switches into them tested the adroitness of the managers, who by then had become accustomed to the volatility.

Some of the larger of these families, in alphabetical order, that have 800 telephone numbers, are: American (421-9900), Colonial

---

[3]For example, Vanguard permits six switches a year, Fidelity four (with exceptions) and Price three. Prudential Bache has unlimited switches, and charges a 5 percent commission on sales (none on purchases) with the understanding the figure declines a percentage point a year, so that funds liquidated after five years are free of fees. Rates and terms are constantly changing, so it pays to ask and compare before making commitments.

(225-2365), Dean Witter (221-2685), Dreyfus (645-6561), Eaton Vance (225-6265), Federated (245-5000), Fidelity (544-6666), First Investors (223-6300), Franklin (632-2180), Kemper (225-2618), Keystone (225-2618), Massachusetts Financial (343-2829), National Securities (223-7757), Oppenheimer (221-9839), T. Rowe Price (638-5660), Prudential Bache (872-7787), Putnam (225-1581), Scudder (225-2470), Stein Roe (621-0320, Value Line (223-0818), and Vanguard (662-7447).[4] A call will bring prospectuses, and you can check these, and records, to see which are suitable. There is a simpler way to check on the portfolios of many funds. The *Mutual Fund Sourcebook* (Mutual Fund Sourcebook Inc., 53 West Jackson Boulevard, Chicago, IL 60604, 1-800-228-2028) is a quarterly survey containing complete portfolios along with articles of interest.

Fidelity and Vanguard often have several funds on the best performer lists, and they offer two of the widest selections as well. Both have Ginnie Mae, income, growth, bond, overseas, tax exempt, and the like. Fidelity has individual sector funds for those who like one special segment of the market at a particular time: Computer, Software, Technology, Brokerage/Management, Electronics, Chemicals, Safety, Leisure, Utility, Telecommunications, Food/Agriculture, Gold, Metals, and so forth, and Vanguard covers most of these as well. The others are coming up rapidly, however, and a good record one year is no guarantee it will be repeated the next.

Carefully consider the benefits of investing through families of funds. Though obvious, one of the less important of these are the lowered charges; while you will be paying management fees and in some cases a commission, these will be considerably less than the commissions you might have to pay for individual transactions, even at a discount broker. Far more important is the lower price individual investors pay for professional advice by utilizing this approach.

[4]Among those big funds without 800 numbers are: American Capital (713-993-0500), Hutton (212-742-5432), Investors Diversified Services (612-372-3733), Merrill Lynch (609-282-2800), Shearson (212-577-5794), and Twentieth Century (816-283-4000).

Think about the decision one might make to move part of a stock portfolio into Ginnie Maes, long-term bonds, foreign securities, or a money market fund. Which stocks should be sold, and which bonds and Ginnie Maes should be purchased? How would you evaluate those foreign securities? Are you interested in junk bonds? Which carry the least risk while offering the most rewards?

For a small management fee a staff of full time pros at Vanguard, Price, or Fidelity will help you make the selection. Are you interested in small high tech stocks? Or genetic engineering issues? Or OTC issues? You could go through the tens of thousands of issues available, devote time and money for computer screens and other esoteric methods of picking stocks. Or pay a fee, less than one percent of the value of the investments per year, and possibly that commission, for the expertise.[5]

This doesn't mean you can check your brains with the experts. Even if they will try to do their best in their sector of specialized fund, you will still have to decide which to buy and when to do so—and to sell or switch, or go to the sidelines in a money market fund.

There even is a way to beat the odds on this one. In mid-1986 there were a dozen or so market letters devoted to mutual funds and more on the way. The *Mutual Fund Forecaster* (3471 N. Federal Highway, Fort Lauderdale, FL 33306) is the largest of these with 40,000 subscribers. The publication ranks the funds and offers general advice and news of the industry. The *Telephone Switch Newsletter* (P.O. box 2538, Huntington Beach, CA 92647) goes further, offering in addition to ranking timing advice, telling sub-

---

[5]Which isn't to suggest it is all that simple. In the mid-1970s veteran market analyst Heinz Biel noted that a major West Virginia bank with a $200 million trust portfolio advertised for an analyst to be in charge of $70 million or so of it. The candidate "may also manage common trust funds," in a post where he would have "minimum supervision and decision-making freedom." According to the advertisement, the candidate should have "2–3 years of trust experience." Biel noted, "When a bank promises minimum supervision to a man with minimum experience, it is best to go elsewhere." Sad to say, the situation at some mutual fund families has not improved.

scribers when and where to switch, and boasts of being able to rack of 20 percent gains, year in and year out. *The Fund Exchange Report* (1200 Westlake Ave. North, Seattle, WA 98109), does the same kind of work. *NoLoad Fund X* (235 Montgomery St., San Francisco, CA 94104) offers information on track records and relative rankings, as does *United Mutual Fund Selector* (212 Newbury St., Boston, MA 02116). There are others, of course, but these are some of the better known.

For those seeking to simplify their lives—for a fee—Charles Schwab & Co., one of the leading discount brokers, handles orders for over 200 no loads and low loads, and can make switches for you and arrange for margin purchases. This is handy for individuals wanting to go, say, from Fidelity Electronics to Value Line Special Situations or from Bull & Bear Equity Income to T. Rowe Price Growth & Income. Do it on your own and you will have to mail or wire in the sale, wait for the money to arrive by mail or get into your account, and then make the purchase. With Schwab you can call in the sell and the next day make the buy, with a commission charged on the sale alone. The convenience would be worth the commission for those intending to switch between funds, but not necessary for individuals remaining within one fund family. For additional and current information, call the Schwab 800 number, which is 526-8600.

By the mid-1980s switch mutuals had become the hottest game in town for individual investors, some of the most astute of whom had become aware of the many forces at play in the market outlined in the first chapter. "Mutual funds represent a sea change in the way people invest," said Michael Lipper of Lipper Analytical Associates, which covers the industry. "American investors are no longer doing their own betting on the market," added Albert E. Sindlinger of Sindlinger Research, noting in late 1985 that one of his studies indicated that a record 11.2 million individuals who did not own stocks had shares in mutuals. In contrast, a year earlier only 5.2 million fundholders owned no stocks. That there had been a massive shift to funds, especially switch operations, is manifest.

As is the fact that the mutual fund organizations have become original in their marketing approaches. Fidelity, one of the leaders in this department, announced in the late summer 1986 that henceforth it would price its sector funds on an hourly basis, permitting plan holders (some 300,000 of them at the time) to switch in or out during the trading day, rather than having the pricing done after the markets closed.

What this means is that an investor who shortly after 1:00 P.M. sees a move beginning in, say, the broadcasting stocks, could switch into that sector fund from one of the others, and have the pricing set at whatever it would be at 2:00 P.M. There is a switch fee involved, but this is modest compared even to discount broker commissions. "We're providing a proxy for the stock market," claimed Ellen G. Hoffman, who is marketing manager for Select Portfolios. So it is.

Of course, the investor who might like one particular stock would have to buy the bundle in the fund's portfolio; this clearly isn't for everyone. Nonetheless, it is an intriguing ploy, and one other funds doubtless will imitate before long.

The message is clear enough. Many small investors have abandoned the central markets, knowing they are dangerous places for all but the truly sophisticated. IBM, GE, GM, and the others may be fine for institutions, they seem to be saying, but not for us. They will buy them instead through mutual funds specializing on the large capitalization issues. Last year approximately 80 percent of all action on the NYSE was accounted for by institutions. The Amex, traditionally the home of small speculators, reports that around 40 percent of its volume comes from institutions. So it would appear that small investors are best off with mutuals, and small speculators with options or the off-track betting parlors and lottery tickets.

It remains to be said that there is a danger in all of this. Suppose some untoward, unexpected political or economic event takes place, prompting hundreds of thousands of mutual fund investors to pick up their phones and make switches, say, from bond funds to stock funds. This could cause the bond funds to dump paper on the market so as to obtain needed cash to transfer to the stock operations, resulting in a collapse of bond prices. Similarly, if switches went from stocks to bonds, mutual fund selling could lead to panic at the NYSE, or if not that, at least a better than hundred point decline in the Dow. Or it could happen in a different fashion. Programmed selling by institutions could cause the Dow to decline sharply, and *this* could trigger mutual funds switches.

The problem of expertise remains. No matter how far you travel down the road of running with the crowd, in the end the decision will be yours. There is just so much hedging that can take place before you'll have to pick up the phone and give an order. Remember too that you are not alone in this; millions of small investors are doing the same—while hundreds of money managers are playing against them.

Think about all of this the next time some character sidles up to you to whisper the latest rumor regarding takeovers, mergers, and institutional sales. At one time—as recently as the 1960s—you might have given some credence to such talk. By the time you hear about it today, several hotshots at computer consoles in New York, Tokyo, and London, and all points in between, have made their moves. So listen politely and move on, and consider W. S. Gilbert's thought regarding sharpies, put in the mouth of the Mikado as he contemplates how he would "make the punishment fit the crime."

The billard sharp whom anyone catches
His doom extremely hard—
He's made to dwell—
In a dungeon cell
On a spot that's always barred
And there he plays extravagant matches
In fitten finger-stalls
On a cloth untrue,
With a twisted cue
And elliptical billiard balls!

SELECTED BIBLIOGRAPHY

Ansbacher, Max. *The New Stock Index Market*. New York: Walker, 1983.

Amling, Frederick. *Investments*, 4th ed. Englewood Cliffs, NJ: Prentice-Hall, 1978.

Bernstein, Peter L. *The Theory and Practice of Bond Portfolio Analysis*, 2 vols. New York: Institutional Investor, 1979, 1980.

Boesky, Ivan. *Merger Mania*. New York: Holt, Rinehart & Winston, 1985.

Bullock, Hugh. *The Story of Investment Companies*. New York: Columbia University Press, 1959.

Cohen, Jerome, Edward Zinbarg, and Arthur Zeikel. *Investment Analysis and Portfolio Management*, 4th ed. Homewood, IL: Irwin, 1982.

Crane, Burton, *The Sophisticated Investor: A Guide to Stock Market Profits*. New York: Simon & Schuster, 1964.

Darst, David. *The Complete Bond Book*. New York: McGraw-Hill, 1975.

Dreman, David. *The New Contrarian Investment Strategy*. New York: Random House, 1982.

Edwards, Robert D., and John Magee. *Technical Analysis of Stock Trends*. Springfield, MA: John Magee, 1967.

Fong, H. Gifford. *Bond Portfolio Analysis*. Charlottesville, VA: Financial Analysts Research Foundation, 1980.

Fosback, Norman. *Stock Market Logic*. Fort Lauderdale, FL: Institute for Econometric Research, 1977.

Francis, Jack. *Investments: Analysis and Management*. New York: McGraw-Hill, 1976.

Friedman, Benjamin, ed. *Corporate Capital Structures in the United States*. Chicago: University of Chicago Press, 1985.

Gart, Alan. *The Insider's Guide to Financial Services*. New York: McGraw-Hill, 1854.

Gastineau, Gary. *The Stock Options Manual*. New York: McGraw-Hill, 1977.

Graham, Benjamin. *The Intelligent Investor*. New York: Harper & Row, 4th ed. 1973.

Graham, Benjamin, and David L. Dodd. *Security Analysis: Principles and Techniques*. New York: McGraw-Hill, 1934 and subsequent years.

Hagin, Robert, with Chris Mader. *The New Science of Investing*. Homewood, IL: Dow Jones-Irwin, 1973.

Hamilton, William P. *The Stock Market Barometer*. New York: Harper, 1922.

Hirt, Geoffrey A., and Stanley B. Block. *Foundation of Investment Management*, 2nd ed. Homewood, IL: Irwin, 1986.

Hoffman, Paul. *The Dealmakers*. New York: Doubleday, 1984.

Homer, Sidney, and Martin Liebowitz. *Inside the Yield Book: New Tools for Bond Market Strategy*. Englewood Cliffs, NJ: Prentice-Hall, 1972.

Levine, Sumner N., ed. *Investment Manager's Handbook*. Homewood, IL: Dow Jones-Irwin, 1980.

Light, J. O., and White, William L. *The Financial System*. Homewood, IL: Irwin, 1979.

Livermore, Jesse. *How to Trade in Stocks: The Livermore Formula for Combining Time Element and Price*. Palisades Park, NJ: Investor's Press, 1966.

Loeb, Gerald M. *The Battle for Investment Survival*. New York: Simon & Schuster, 1965.

Loeb, Gerald M. *The Battle for Stock Market Profits*. New York: Simon & Schuster, 1971.

Lorie, James H., Peter Dodd, and Mary Hamilton Kimpton. *The Stock Market: Theories and Evidence*. Homewood, IL: Irwin, 1985.

Magee, John. *The General Semantics of Wall Street*. Springfield, MA: Author, 1958.

Mather, Ike. *Personal Finance*. Cincinnati, OH: South Western, 1984.

Mehr, Robert. *Fundamentals of Insurance* Homewood, IL: Irwin, 1983.

Neill, Humphrey B. *The Art of Contrary Thinking*. Caldwell, ID: Caxton, 1954.

Neill, Humphrey B. *Tape Reading and Market Tactics: The Three Successful Steps to Successful Stock Trading*. Burlington, VT: Fraser, 1970.

Reilly, Jim. *Bonds as Investments in the Eighties*. New York: Van Nostrand Reinhold, 1982.

Rhea, Robert. *The Dow Theory: An Explanation of Its Development and an Attempt to Define Its Usefulness as an Aid to Speculation*. Colorado Springs, CO: Author, 1932.

Roll, Richard. *The Behavior of Interest Rates*. New York: Basic Books, 1970.

Russell, Richard. *The Dow Theory Today*. New York: Author, 1960.

Siegel, Joel. *How to Analyse Businesses, Financial Statements and the Quality of Earnings*. Englewood Cliffs, NJ: Prentice-Hall, 1982.

Sobel, Robert. *Inside Wall Street*. New York: Norton, 1977.

Sobel, Robert. *Salomon Brothers: 1910–1985*. New York: Salomon Brothers, 1986.

Sweeny, Allen, and Robert Rachlin, eds. *Handbook of International Financial Management*. New York: McGraw-Hill, 1984.

Stevenson, Richard A., and Edward H. Jennings. *Fundamentals of Investments*. New York: West, 1984.

Train, John. *Dance of the Money Bees*. New York: Harper & Row, 1974.

Train, John. *The Money Masters*. New York: Harper & Row, 1980.

Tuccille, Jerome. *The Optimist's Guide to Making Money in the 1980's*. New York: Morrow, 1978.

Tracy, John. *Fundmentals of Financial Accounting*. New York: Wiley, 1973.

Weiner, Neil. *Stock Index Futures*. New York: Wiley, 1984.

INDEX

HG 4921 .S6156 1987
Sobel, Robert, 1931 Feb. 19-

The new game on Wall Street

HG 4921 .S6156 1987
Sobel, Robert, 1931 Feb. 19-

The new game on Wall Street

DATE DUE	BORROWER'S NAME	ROOM NUMBER
APR 5 '89	NATN EFFENDI	
MAY 1 '89	ANGELA BROWN	